AF607957

The Immanence of the Infinite

Elizabeth Brient

The Immanence of the Infinite

Hans Blumenberg and the Threshold to Modernity

The Catholic University of America Press
Washington, D.C.

The paper used in this publication meets the minimum requirements of American National Standards for Information Science—Permanence of Paper for Printed Library Materials, ANSI Z39.48-1984.

LIBRARY OF CONGRESS CATALOGING-IN-PUBLICATION DATE
Brient, Elizabeth, 1964–
The immanence of the infinite : Hans Blumenberg and the threshold to modernity / Elizabeth Brient.
p. cm.
Includes bibliographical references and index.
ISBN 0-8132-1089-5 (alk. Paper)
1. Immanence of God—History of doctrines. 2. Blumenberg, Hans. Legitimität der Neuzeit. 3. Nicholas, of Cusa, Cardinal, 1401–1464. 4. Eckhart, Meister, d. 1327. I. Title.
BT124.B83 2001
901—dc21 2001017238

To my parents,

John and Mary Beth Brient

&

In memory of my grandmother,

Ethel Nadine Grigg

Contents

Acknowledgments

This book has grown out of my dissertation work with Karsten Harries at Yale University. The extent to which it is indebted to the spirit and substance of his thought is inestimable and can be felt throughout the book. I am deeply grateful for having had the opportunity to study with him, and for his generosity of spirit as both a teacher and a scholar. I would also like to thank John E. Smith and Louis Dupré, who have both had a tremendous influence on the course of my studies, the development of my thought, and the direction of this book.

Donald Duclow read the original manuscript and provided me with invaluable comments for which I am extremely appreciative. I would also like to thank Michael Halberstam (formerly at The University of South Carolina), Hagi Kenaan (at Tel Aviv University), Steven Brown (at the Institute of Medieval Philosophy and Theology at Boston College), and my colleagues at the Department of Philosophy at The University of Georgia for their invitations to present early versions of parts of this book. Their feedback and support in numerous ways has been extremely important at various stages in the development of this project. For their helpful comments, conversations, and support I would also like to thank Leora Bilski, Bettina Blumenberg, Laurence Bond, Peter Casarella, Ellen Chris Fanizzi, Michael Holquist, Vered Kenaan, Clyde Lee Miller, Dermot Moran, Willemien Otten, Ingrid Scheibler, and Robert Wallace.

I would also like to express my appreciation to David J. McGonagle, Director of Catholic University of America Press, for the gracious way in which he has supported this project. I am deeply indebted to Susan Needham, my editor at CUA Press for the great care and sensitivity that she brought to bear in the final editing of the manuscript, and for her unflagging encouragement. Aaron Price and Beth Benevides at CUA Press also deserve thanks for their care and attention. I am grateful to John O'Connor for his invaluable help in preparing the original version of the manuscript, to Sarah Calder Traut for her help with the page proofs, and to Sonam Kachru and Heather McEachern for their assistance with the index. Others contributed to this book in fundamentally spirit-sustaining ways, and to them I am also profoundly grateful: Shirley Bassler, Sean Brient, Ellen Blumenthal, Sima Misra, and Vanessa Rumble.

And finally I would like to thank O. Bradley Bassler, for all the many ways, only he knows, in which he helped this project at last see the light of day. Certainly without him this book would not have been written.

Portions of the first part of this book have appeared in two articles entitled "Hans Blumenberg and Hannah Arendt on the 'Unworldly Worldliness' of the Modern Age," in *Journal of the History of Ideas* 61 (2000): 513–30; and "From *Vita Contemplativa* to *Vita Activa:* Modern Instrumentalization of Theory and the Problem of Measure," in *International Journal of Philosophical Studies* 9 (2001): 19–40. Portions of the third part of this book have appeared in an article entitled "Transitions to a Modern Cosmology: Meister Eckhart and Nicholas of Cusa on the Intensive Infinite," in *Journal of the History of Philosophy* 37 (1999): 575–600.

Abbreviations

DI *De Docta Ignorantia*

DW *Meister Eckhart: Die deutschen und lateinischen Werke: Herausgegeben im Auftrage der Deutschen Forschungsgemeinschaft. Die deutschen Werke.* Stuttgart: W. Kohlhammer, 1958– .

EE *Meister Eckhart: The Essential Sermons, Commentaries, Treatises, and Defense.* Translated by Edmund Colledge, O.S.A., and Bernard McGinn. New York: Paulist Press, 1981.

LW *Meister Eckhart: Die deutschen und lateinischen Werke: Herausgegeben im Auftrage der Deutschen Forschungsgemeinschaft. Die lateinischen Werke.* Stuttgart: W. Kohlhammer, 1936– .

TP *Meister Eckhart: Teacher and Preacher.* Translated by Bernard McGinn, Frank Tobin, and Elvira Borgstädt. New York: Paulist Press, 1986.

W *Meister Eckhart: Sermons and Treatises.* 3 vols. Translated by M. O'C. Walshe. Shaftesbury, Dorset: Element Books, 1979 and 1987.

The Immanence of the Infinite

Introduction

This book aims at a reconsideration of the character of the epochal threshold between the Middle Ages and modernity, with a view toward illuminating contemporary efforts at self- and world-understanding. It takes as its point of departure a critical assessment of Hans Blumenberg's extraordinarily rich and provocative reading of this transition in *The Legitimacy of the Modern Age.* In light of contemporary debates concerning the status of modernity, which all too often assume a facile and caricatured reading of the emergence of the modern age, Blumenberg's work provides a welcome and much needed perspective.

While I disagree with much of what Blumenberg has to say about the epochal threshold, and much of this book is devoted to a critique of particular aspects of his own reading, I am in agreement with his fundamental approach to the problem: if we are seriously to evaluate the status of the "legitimacy" of the modern world view, then we must seek to understand the emergence of that world view in its historical context. It is not possible to evaluate the legitimacy of any given system of self- and world-interpretation in isolation, apart from its particular context, as though at any point in time humanity is in a position to take its pick from countless available *Weltanschauungen.* Rather, the way in which we are able to make sense of the world and of ourselves is essentially contextual and has to do with the way in which we find ourselves already imbedded in the intricate web of interpretations woven and re-woven over time. The very questions we feel compelled to ask about the world and about our place in it are motivated in one way or another by the history of interpretations which we have inherited, and to which we feel compelled to respond in order to tell *our* story about ourselves and our world. Hence, in seeking existential orientation in the present, we always, already find ourselves in a responsive dialogue with the interpretive systems of the past.

~

Since this book takes Blumenberg's reading of the transition to modernity as its point of departure, I would like to begin by giving a brief account of the man and his work. Blumenberg is best known through his major works as an interpreter of the modern age *(The Legitimacy of the Modern Age)*, a historian of cosmology *(The Genesis of the Copernican World)*, a theoretician of myth, metaphor, and non-conceptuality (*Work on Myth, Shipwreck with Spectator, Die Lesbarkeit der Welt* [The legibility of the world], *Höhlenaugänge* [Cave exitings]), and of the human experience of time (*Lebenszeit und Weltzeit* [Life-time and world-time]). Blumenberg's corpus as a whole includes 18 books, more than 160 essays and scholarly articles, numerous encyclopedia entries, and editions of the works of Nicholas of Cusa and Galileo.[1] He has written extensively on Husserl, Augustine, Copernicus, Galileo, Plato, Nicholas of Cusa, Giordano Bruno, Epicurus, Marcion, Kant, Freud, Goethe, Nietzsche, and Bach, among many, many others. This extraordinarily wide-ranging body of work has made Blumenberg the leading European interpreter in his generation of the history of western thought.

No less astonishing than the breadth of his scholarship is the detailed richness of his analyses, which are always anchored in the texture of concrete historical examples. Indeed, for Blumenberg, the important lessons are often to be found in the details—for example, in a letter written by Goethe to Merck in August 1778 describing his ascent to the summit of the Brocken, or in the fact that Husserl, in his old age, used the back of the official notice that informed him of his expulsion from the university as scratch paper for philosophical notes.[2] Blumenberg weaves the fabric

1. See the comprehensive bibliography compiled by Peter Behrenberg and David Adams in *Die Kunst des Überlebens: Nachdenken über Hans Blumenberg*, ed. Franz Josef Wetz and Hermann Timm (Frankfurt: Suhrkamp, 1999), 426–70.

2. Hans Blumenberg, *The Legitimacy of the Modern Age*, trans. Robert M. Wallace (Cambridge: The MIT Press, 1983), 342 and 236. This and all subsequent references to the

of his accounts with the richness provided by just this sort of historical detail, and it is precisely the careful threading of these examples which brings patterns of historical development into sharp and often provocative focus.

Blumenberg's historical analyses, however, for all their concrete richness, are not simply works in the history of ideas. Rather, they are works in (or works on) a philosophical anthropology that is fundamentally dynamic, dialogical, and functional in orientation. That is to say, Blumenberg consistently insists that one cannot separate systematic philosophy from its dialogical function within a broader history of self- and world-interpretation. Theoretical concepts, just as much as cultural metaphors, develop and transform in response to historically specific interpretive needs. The histories of these transformations tell the story of shifting modes of existential orientation, of changing expectations for and of meaning, and of the ever-transforming ways human beings have of viewing the world and themselves.

Franz Josef Wetz, who wrote the volume on Hans Blumenberg for the Junius "Introduction to" series on major philosophers, began with the observation that although we have learned a great deal from Blumenberg, we actually know very little about him. He almost never sought out publicity, and in his later years he became so reclusive, that, Wetz (writing his *Introduction* in 1993) could begin by remarking, tongue in cheek, that one would have to doubt that Blumenberg actually existed at all, were it not for the attestations of his own teacher, Odo Marquard, who had in fact, himself, seen Blumenberg many times. For all his elusiveness, however, Wetz pointedly remarks, "Blumenberg is no phantom. He is as alive as his books are real."[3] To encounter Blumenberg, one has only to read him. Providing a biographical sketch of Blumenberg, however, is a task that is

Legitimacy are from Wallace's translation of the revised German edition, *Die Legitimität der Neuzeit (erweiterte und überarbeitete Neuausgabe)* (Frankfurt: Suhrkamp Verlag, 1973, 1974, and 1976).

3. "Wir wissen viel von Hans Blumenberg, zugegeben, aber nur wenig über ihn. Denn der Verfasser ebenso zahlreicher wie umfang-, einfalls- und geistreicher Bücher liebt es, sich zu verstecken und zu bedecken. Blumenberg ist zwar lesbar, nicht aber sichtbar. Er hält sich im

limited by the paucity of facts concerning his life. The brief synopsis which follows collects most of those facts which are, to my knowledge, publicly available. And indeed, much of this information was first made available after his death in 1996.

Hans Blumenberg was born in Lübeck on July 13, 1920 and attended the same famous *Gymnasium* (secondary school) as Thomas Mann, the Lübeck *Katharineums*. By all accounts he was a brilliant student, and he graduated first in his class in 1939. Because he was a *"Halbjude"* (a "half Jew" in the language of National Socialism), however, the director of the school refused to shake Blumenberg's hand at graduation and would not allow him to give the valedictorian's speech. After graduation, he was barred from attending a German university, and so the "Catholic" Blumenberg ended up studying at philosophical-theological academies in Paderborn and Frankfurt. Eventually this, too, was forbidden him, and he returned to his hometown, where he worked in the Lübeck *Dräger-Werk* and so was protected for a time. In 1944, however, he was arrested and taken to a labor camp. Luckily, he was able to escape and found refuge with the family of his future wife in Lübeck, where he survived through the end of the war.

When the war ended, Blumenberg left his hiding place and finally brought his study of philosophy, German literature, and classical philology to completion at the University of Hamburg. He was awarded the title of Doctor of Philosophy in 1947, and in 1950 he was promoted to university lecturer at the university in Kiel.[4] He taught philosophy successively at the universities in Kiel, Hamburg, Gießen, Bochum, and finally Mün-

Verborgene. . . . Er entzieht sich dem Wissenschaftstourismus und somit der Kamera der Fotografen ebenso wie der Fernsehens. Fast hat es den Anschein, als müßte man zweifeln, ob Blumenberg überhaupt existiert, wenn mir nicht z.B. mein Lehrer Odo Marquard versichert hätte, ihn bereits mehrmals gesehen zu haben. . . . Dennoch ist Blumenberg kein Phantom. Er ist so lebendig wie seine Bücher wirklich sind, aber zu Gesicht bekommt man ihn deshalb noch lange nicht. Treffend bemerkt Michael Krüger: 'Wer ihn sehen will [. . .], muß ihn lesen.'" Franz Josef Wetz, *Hans Blumenberg zur Einführung* (Hamburg: Junius, 1993), 7.

4. Hans Blumenberg, "Beiträge zum Problem der Ursprünglichkeit der mittelalterlich-scholastischen Ontologie" (Ph.D. diss., Kiel, 1947); and "Die ontologische Distanz. Eine Untersuchung über die Krisis der Phänomenologie Husserls" (*Habilitationsschrift*, Kiel, 1950).

ster, where he taught from 1970 until his retirement in 1985.[5] Blumenberg was active, early on, in the academic community, and was the recipient of numerous honors and awards.[6] From 1966 to 1970 he was general editor, together with Jürgen Habermas, Dieter Henrich, and Jacob Taubes, of the *Suhrkamp Theorie 1* series. He was a co-founder, with Clemens Heselhaus, Wolfgang Iser, and Hans Robert Jauß, of the research group *Poetik und Hermeneutik,* which held a series of colloquia that began in 1963 in Gießen. The papers presented have been published in successive volumes, along with transcriptions of the discussions of the participants. These meetings quickly became a dynamic and focal arena for the interdisciplinary exchange of ideas between scholars working in philosophy, literature, and the humanities in Germany. Jauß was accounted the pacesetter of the group, but Blumenberg was the dominating philosopher and his formative influence continued to be felt well past the seventh colloquium in 1974, after which Blumenberg left the group.[7]

Indeed, by the end of the sixties Blumenberg had begun to withdraw in general from the public—in his last years he withdrew entirely—in order to devote himself to his writing. Odo Marquard has attributed this

5. For the details of Blumenberg's biography here and in what follows, see Franz Josef Wetz and Hermann Timm's preface to *Die Kunst des Überlebens,* 9–13; Odo Marquard, "Entlastung vom Absoluten," in *Die Kunst der Überlebens,* 17–27; David Adams and Peter Behrenberg, "Bibliographie Hans Blumenberg zum 70. Geburtstag," *Zeitschrift für philosophische Forschung* 44 (1990): 647–49; and Robert Wallace, "Blumenberg: An Overview," *Annals of Scholarship* 5 (1987): 1–2. I am indebted, as well, for some of these details to the biographical sketch provided by Bettina Blumenberg, when she spoke about her father and read from his unpublished work in New York, on April 23, 1998, at a public conference organized by Anselm Haverkamp and sponsored by The Poetics Institute with the Graduate Student Theory Group of the New York University English Department, entitled, "Curiously Invisible: Work on Blumenberg," April 23–25, 1998.

6. In 1960 Blumenberg became a member of the Academy of Science and Literature in Mainz. After the death of Erich Rothacker in 1965, he became the director of the Commission for Philosophy, a position he held until the end of 1973. In 1974 the University of Heidelberg gave him its Kuno Fischer Prize for his work in the history of philosophy. In 1980 the German Academy of Language and Literature, in Darmstadt, gave him its Sigmund Freud Prize for scholarly writing. In 1982 he was conferred with an honorary doctorate at the University of Gießen.

7. See Marquard, "Entlastung von Absoluten," 18–19. According to Marquard, Blumenberg would have liked to have seen it change into a society which corresponded through letters.

reclusiveness to Blumenberg's personal experience of the shortness of his own life, intensified by his awareness of the years stolen from him during the Nazi period.[8] Marquard reports a telling conversation he had with Blumenberg on the occasion of the conferral of the Freud Prize in Darmstadt on October 16, 1980, in which Blumenberg remarked, "You haven't lost any time in your life. I've lost eight years, for which I have to make up." In an effort to win back this lost time, Marquard reports, Blumenberg had early in his life begun to sleep only six times a week, in order to gain an extra day per week. His subsequent withdrawal from public life, in order to devote himself single-mindedly to his writing, must also be understood against the backdrop of this ongoing struggle to make up for the lost eight years.[9] Blumenberg's daughter, Bettina Blumenberg, recounted that at the end of his life, the mayor of Lübeck sent an official letter of apology to Blumenberg for the injustices he had suffered during the Nazi time and an invitation to an awards ceremony conferring on him honorary citizenship. He was at once bitter and moved, she reported, and while he accepted the invitation it was unclear that he actually intended to guarantee its realization. Blumenberg died on March 28, 1996, a few days before the date set for the conferral of the award.[10]

It has been remarked that Blumenberg was a philosopher who kept himself hidden and withdrawn not only in life, but in his books as well.[11] Indeed, anyone who has tried to read one of his texts is immediately confronted with extraordinarily dense and complex prose, in which the author's voice is often difficult to hear in the rush of wave after wave of specific and meticulously analyzed historical examples. Blumenberg's own theoretical orientation is not always clearly presented, and the un-

8. For a philosophical analysis of the gap between the necessarily limited time alloted to individual human lives and the endless time of a world indifferent to our desires, see Blumenberg's *Lebenszeit und Weltzeit* (Frankfurt: Suhrkamp, 1989).

9. Though his scholarly activity continued unabated, he did not publish his last works. He has left behind a formidable *Nachlaß*, and volumes of his works continue to be published posthumously. See Marquard, "Entlastung von Absoluten," 27.

10. Bettina Blumenberg, New York, April 23, 1998.

11. Wetz, *Hans Blumenberg zur Einfuhrung*, 8.

derlying arguments and basic theses of his often Byzantine analyses are seldom transparently understandable on a first reading. However, the patient reader who rises to the challenge posed by his demanding texts is more than amply rewarded for the investment of time and effort. It becomes clear that Blumenberg's genius is revealed precisely in the careful choice of his examples, which act as beacons illuminating specific historical patterns and connections which had previously remained obscure and therefore unexplained. Blumenberg's powerful attentiveness to the significance of such focal examples allows for an incisive reflection on the motivating questions, attitudes, and expectations driving the development of the history of western thought and culture.

But for all the attentive and minute care he gives to his analyses, and for all the light this throws on the historical development under consideration, just as striking are his omissions, his lack of attention to other historical figures, to other patterns of development, and to other orienting questions. His choice of foci is, in this sense, deliberately provocative. And these omissions are themselves potentially very suggestive. Indeed, Blumenberg's texts invite the reader to re-examine the account he gives and to consider, instead, alternative foci and the patterns of historical movement, motivations, expectations, and questions which they may in turn bring to light. Hence, not only are Blumenberg's texts powerfully original and illuminating in their own right, but they also serve to provoke the reader into rethinking the development of western thought and culture in new ways.

This book was born out of just this sort of fruitful grappling with Blumenberg's analysis of the transition from the late medieval to the early modern world in *The Legitimacy of the Modern Age.* My aim in this book is both to present Blumenberg's reading of this transition and to provide a critique of that reading through a shift in focus. Where Blumenberg highlights the role played by late medieval nominalism's interpretation of divine transcendence, for example, I will underscore the role played by late medieval Neoplatonic interpretations of divine immanence. And where Blumenberg interprets the process of the infinitization of the medieval cosmos by focusing on the pair, Cusanus-Bruno, I will shift attention to the pair, Eckhart-Cusanus. In the spirit of Blumenberg's own work, my alternative analysis of these two thinkers will be grounded in an in-depth reading of the transformations in function, meaning, and application of a particular metaphor—that of the infinite sphere. The changes Eckhart and Cusanus make in their respective appropriations of this metaphor signal deep transformations in self- and world-interpretation in the transition to the modern age, and help bring to light characteristically modern interpretive needs—needs which continue to be felt as pressing—for existential orientation in an infinite world.

Let me proceed, therefore, to offer a brief synopsis of the project I undertake in this book. In Part One, I present Blumenberg's account of the origin of the modern existential attitude of "self-assertion," an account which grounds his argument for the "legitimacy" of modernity. Blumenberg's defense of the legitimacy of the modern age is based on his contention that the leading concepts and attitudes of modernity are, on the one hand, new and original (i.e. *not* illegitimately usurped from an earlier period, not simply the secularizations of "properly" theological ideas and values), and on the other hand, existential responses necessitated by the theological crisis provoked by the theological absolutism of late medieval nominalism. Blumenberg's argument for the legitimacy of the modern age is further bolstered by his claim that modernity had been successful in overcoming the anti-cosmic world-view of ancient Gnosticism, a feat which medieval theology, for all its attempts, had been unable to accomplish.

Blumenberg's defense thus depends first of all on a critique of the thesis that central modern ideas are merely secularized versions of properly theological concepts, and secondly on the positing of an alternative model of historical transition which would account for the worldliness of the modern age without positing a substantial historical content which is preserved in the transition. Hence Blumenberg posits a dialogical model of historical change, in which continuity between ages is marked far more by interpretive function than by transformation in substantive content. I welcome his critique of the secularization thesis and the static form of historical substantialism which lies at its root, while nevertheless wanting to allow for more continuity of content between the medieval and the modern age than Blumenberg is willing to admit. I will also challenge his claim that the medieval period as a whole derives its epochal unity from the task of "subduing its Gnostic opponent." This understanding of the Middle Ages is far too reductionistic and leads to a misreading of the role and significance of the Neoplatonic tradition, in particular, both in shaping the character of the Middle Ages itself and in the epochal transition to modernity.

I conclude Part One by using Hannah Arendt's reading of the world-*less*ness of the modern age to challenge Blumenberg's claims for the legitimacy of the modern, "worldly" project of self-assertion. In order to provide a defense of this modern attitude, more needs to be said than that it was a historically necessitated response to a late medieval crisis. Indeed, even if self-assertion presents itself as a solution to that particular historical crisis, it nevertheless raises new and peculiarly modern problems. In the infinitized, mechanistic, homogeneous universe of the new science, what will provide the measure for mankind's self-assertive activity? Here I use Blumenberg's dialogical reading of epochal change to underscore the emergence of a new modern problem, that of the need for measure (both ethical and epistemological) in the newly "infinitized" universe. This is indeed a characteristically modern problem, and one which is addressed in the transition to the early modern age with the resources developed in the tradition of Neoplatonism.

Hence, I agree with Blumenberg that the epochal threshold between the medieval and the modern world is fundamentally marked by the process of the infinitization of the cosmos. But Blumenberg views the transference of the attribute of infinity from God to the cosmos as little more than a characteristic of the modern rejection of the medieval tendency to locate the measure of self- and world-understanding in a transcendent deity. The worldliness of the modern age, he holds, must be understood as a reaction to the extreme intensification of divine transcendence in late medieval nominalism. In the face of an absconded God, modern self-assertion aims at the immanent realization of this-worldly possibilities through the mastery and alteration of reality. I agree with Blumenberg that the primary expression of this self-assertion has been seen in the progress of modern science. The possibility of that progress, however, is grounded in an understanding of nature as a law-like and yet inexhaustible field of investigation directing thought toward an objectivity that is never entirely realized. And the origin of such a regulative ideal is to be found in late medieval Neoplatonic speculation on the nature of God's omnipresence in the world, in particular in the notion of the immanence of the infinite in the finite.

Hence, in Part Two, I set up the main historical argument (provided in Part Three) by criticizing Blumenberg's reading of the epochal threshold as inadequate. At issue, ultimately, is how to interpret the late medieval / early modern process of the infinitization of the cosmos. If anything deserves to be called a process of secularization, Blumenberg says, it is the way in which the universe takes on the theological attribute of infinity at the end of the Middle Ages. He interprets this process, however, as one of reoccupation rather than of secularization. Blumenberg situates the "epochal threshold" between Nicholas of Cusa (on the late medieval side) and Giordano Bruno (on the early modern side), and interprets the epochal transition in terms of the systematic reoccupation of worldly for theological "positions" in their respective systems. I will show, however, that Cusanus' system of self- and world-understanding addresses a fundamental "assertion need" of the modern age—the need for measure in the newly infinite universe, which Bruno's system ignores.

Blumenberg's analysis of the role played by theological and cosmological conceptions of infinity in the transition to the modern age, and indeed in the prehistory leading up to that transition, is simply not nuanced enough. Hence, in addition to a presentation of Blumenberg's original and insightful reading of the historical preconditions for the emergence of the new astronomy and cosmology (specifically, the destructive effect of nominalist theological speculations on the traditional, Aristotelian world-picture), I offer a supplemental and corrective reading of this prehistory, one which attends to the complex dynamics involved in the metaphysics of divine infinity. By drawing on the resources of the Neoplatonic tradition, particularly as they are transformed in the speculative mysticism of Meister Eckhart, Cusanus develops a proto-modern conception of nature as infinitely rich, and so as conceptually inexponable. In doing so, he transforms the traditional measure for truth as adequacy to "what is" into a *regulative* ideal guiding potentially endless progress in knowledge.

Part Three is thus devoted to a consideration of the theological origins, not only of the extensive infinitization of the cosmos, but of its intensive infinitization as well. In order to attend to this phenomenon I focus my reading on the way in which the immanence of the divine infinite in the world is conceived and transformed by Eckhart and then again by Cusanus in their respective appropriations of the pseudo-hermetic metaphor of the infinite sphere: "God is an infinite sphere whose center is everywhere and whose circumference is nowhere." Cusanus' transferal of the infinite sphere metaphor from God to the universe is, of course, of particular epochal significance. Equally important is the way in which he uses the notion of the world-immanent, intensive infinite in order to respond to the need for a principle of ontological determinacy, which can function as a regulative ideal for human knowledge.

PART ONE

The Question of the "Legitimacy" of the Modern Age

BLUMENBERG has chosen a deliberately provocative title for his study of the epochal transition from the late medieval to the early modern age. It suggests not only that modernity's claim to legitimacy has been disputed but that it can and will be defended. Blumenberg begins his study with a critique of those theorists who view modernity and its characteristic forms of consciousness as the end result of a bankrupt tradition, or who insist in one form or another that somewhere along the way in the long development of western culture, something has gone wrong, something fundamental has been forgotten. This general point of view is a recurrent feature of the central theses of a striking number of the major thinkers of the late nineteenth and early twentieth centuries.

Heidegger tells the story of the "forgetfulness of Being" (the impoverishment of thought since the pre-Socratics), Freud that of "repression" (both on an individual and on a historical/cultural level); Husserl traces the "crisis of European humanity" back to an inadequate formulation of the "theoretical attitude" at the beginning of the European tradition, and Max Weber locates the historical origin of capitalism in Puritanism. All these theories, Blumenberg underscores, suggest that a more or less distant event in the past is somehow responsible for what is wrong in the present.[1] Marxist social theory may certainly be added to this list, for although Marx himself maintains a fundamentally future-oriented and optimistic view of progress in history, Marxist social theorists of this century regularly tie the vagaries of the capitalist system to the pitfalls of just the sort of Enlightenment rationality Marx presupposed. Think in this context for example of Lukács' *History and Class Consciousness,* or *The Dialectic of Enlightenment* by Horkheimer and Adorno.

The thesis that modern consciousness is marked by "forgetfulness," "denial," and "repression," indeed, that it represents a "false consciousness," is followed by a corresponding call for a "working through" of past circumstances, for a recognition of hidden assumptions, for the unmasking of ideology in all its forms. In line with the sort of "archeological" work that would unearth a forgotten but eerily efficacious past, is a growing body of work in the history of philosophy and of ideas which aims at uncovering the "true" origins of modern thought itself. Such an approach clearly serves to call into question modernity's own self-interpretation: that the modern age constitutes a new historical beginning grounded solely in reason and indifferent to the historical context in which it finds itself. The suspicion that the "age *of* reason" may not in fact be grounded *by* reason raises to the fore the question of its legitimacy. How can modernity's claim to have radically broken with tradition and to have founded a truly new and modern age *(eine Neuzeit)* be justified in the face of the reality of history, which knows no wholly new beginnings? As Blumenberg explains:

1. Hans Blumenberg, *The Legitimacy of the Modern Age,* trans. Robert M. Wallace (Cambridge: The MIT Press, 1983), 116–18. All references are from Wallace's translation of the revised German edition, *Die Legitimität der Neuzeit (erweiterte und überarbeitete neuausgabe),* (Frankfurt: Suhrkamp Verlag, 1973, 1974, and 1976).

> Like all political and historical problems of legitimacy, that of the modern age arises from a discontinuity, and it does not matter whether the discontinuity is real or pretended. The modern age itself laid claim to this discontinuity vis-à-vis the Middle Ages. Consequently the continuous self-confirmation of its autonomy and authenticity by science and technology is brought into question by the thesis that "the modern world owes its uncanny success to a great extent to its Christian background." The extent of the success determines the extent of the injustice committed by forgetting, denying, or not wanting to recognize its true preconditions.[2]

The idea that an unrecognized cultural debt underlies the very foundation of the modern age gives lie to its assertions of epochal self-grounding through conformity to an autonomous reason. It is a fairly easy step to move from this recognition (that modernity did not create itself *ex nihilo*) to the idea that the modern age has surreptitiously "borrowed" and recast many (or all) of its best ideas from the very tradition it claims to have left far behind.

That the modern age may be viewed in large as a "secularization" of the Christian Middle Ages is by now a familiar thesis. The modern notion of progress is said to be a secularization of eschatology, communism a secularized version of the biblical paradise, the transcendental subject a secularization of the all-knowing God, the concept of the political equality of all citizens before the law a secularization of the prior notion of equality of all human beings before God, and so on. Such formulas are meant to render intelligible a hidden dimension of meaning, obscured by the newness of the form in which the older, more familiar ideas appear. If we view *Robinson Crusoe*, for example, as a secularized retelling of the spiritual journey undertaken by the Puritan, that is, as a modern-day *Pilgrim's Progress*, then we unmask, as it were, the worldly guise of our hero and recognize in him and his story a depth and a significance of which we had previously been unaware. Latent in the rhetoric of secularization, Blumenberg claims, is the implication that the "worldliness" of the modern age is perhaps no more than a superficial veil thrown over and concealing an alienated and more originary meaning.[3] Such an interpretation

2. Blumenberg, *Legitimacy,* 116. Blumenberg cites here from C. F. von Weizsäcker, *The Relevance of Science* (New York and Evanston: Harper and Row, 1964), 178.

3. Blumenberg, *Legitimacy,* 17.

would expose the illegitimacy of the modern age in its claim to be, in fact, modern, to be original and authentic in its own right. And depending on one's attitude, it would reveal modernity either as a spiritually impoverished shadow of a richer and more meaningful world-view, or as the unfortunate continuation of an already bankrupt tradition.

Karl Löwith, for example, had argued in *Meaning in History* (1949) that the modern philosophies of history of the eighteenth and nineteenth centuries, which operated on the central assumption of progress in history, must be understood as the products of the secularization of Christian eschatology, of the Christian teleological orientation toward the future as the domain of the "last things." In doing so, he aimed to show the fundamentally false consciousness of modern thought, which purports to be an expression of authentic human rationality. Löwith's thesis, while widely known and elaborated upon, was not criticized until 1962 when Blumenberg read a paper at the Seventh German Philosophy Congress entitled "Secularization: Critique of a Category of Historical Illegitimacy." In it Blumenberg provided a thoroughgoing critique of secularization theories like Löwith's. This paper was revised and expanded to include his own alternative account of the origin of the modern notion of progress, and eventually reappeared as Part I of *The Legitimacy of the Modern Age*.[4]

Blumenberg begins his critique of the secularization thesis by distinguishing between descriptive and explanatory uses of the term "secularization." He has no quarrel with those who use the term descriptively to point out a progressive decline in the power and influence of religious institutions or even to describe changes within the social forms of religion (e.g. the church as a social-cultural institution, sponsoring youth sports teams, support groups, or daycare). "Whether as an observation, a reproach, or an endorsement," writes Blumenberg, "everyone is familiar

4. The original paper was revised and expanded and reappeared as Part One of *Die Legitimität der Neuzeit* in 1966. It was further revised in order to respond to criticism of the first edition, including that of Löwith, in the second edition of Part One which appeared in 1973. See Löwith's review of the 1966 edition in *Philosophische Rundschau* 15 (1968): 195–201. See also Robert Wallace's discussion of their debate in "Progress, Secularization and Modernity: The Löwith-Blumenberg Debate," *New German Critique* 22 (Winter 1981): 63–79; and his "Translator's Introduction" to the English edition of the *Legitimacy*, xi–xxi.

with this designation [secularization] for a long-term process by which a disappearance of religious ties, attitudes to transcendence, expectations of an afterlife, ritual performances, and firmly established turns of speech is driven onward in both private and daily public life."[5] Secularization, understood in this way, designates that process by which the realm of the sacred increasingly gives way to the realm of the profane. That the modern age is more worldly in orientation than the Middle Ages, Blumenberg takes as a fairly straightforward and unproblematic comparative statement.

The difficulty comes when one attempts to account for this state of affairs, by invoking the secularization thesis as a tool of historical *explanation*.[6] Here theorists employ propositions of the form "B is the secularized A" (e.g. "The modern work ethic is secularized monastic asceticism" or "The president of the Federal Republic [of Germany] is a secularized monarch").[7] Assertions of this form are meant to serve the hermeneutic function of revealing a hidden dimension of meaning (e.g. to uncover certain attitudes or structures in the work ethic or the office of President that help to powerfully define the modern forms but can be explained only as transformed variations of pre-modern attitudes and assumptions).[8] Such

5. Blumenberg, *Legitimacy*, 3.

6. Ibid., 9.

7. These are two examples Blumenberg gives on p. 4.

8. See Hans-Georg Gadamer's review of Blumenberg's first (1966) edition of *Die Legitimität der Neuzeit*, in *Philosophische Rundschau* 15 (1968): 201–9. Despite Blumenberg's original critique, Gadamer insists that the concept of secularization "performs a legitimate hermeneutic function," indeed, that it "contributes a whole dimension of hidden meaning to the self-comprehension of what has come to be and presently exists, and shows in this way that what presently exists is and means far more than it knows of itself" (as quoted by Blumenberg, *Legitimacy*, 16, 17). This is true also and precisely, he says, for the modern age. Nevertheless, Gadamer goes on to remark that the historical and philosophical achievement of Blumenberg's book remains independent of his introductory polemics against the secularization hypothesis. While Gadamer may be correct that Blumenberg's original and provocative reading of the emergence of modernity does not depend directly on his critique of the secularization thesis, it is nevertheless an alternative account at odds with the secularization hypothesis. Indeed, the historical methodology which Blumenberg employs in his reading was developed as an alternative to the substantialistic interpretive scheme presupposed by the secularization theorists. And, it is Blumenberg's functional and dialogical approach to the problem of historical transition that grounds the originality and richness of his reading, a reading which Gadamer is at pains to praise.

formulations move beyond the mere description of a new state of affairs (e.g. the constitutional separation of Church and State), beyond merely underscoring the simple absence of what was once present (e.g. a sacramental view of nature). They are meant to explain the present as a particular sort of transformation of something past, intelligible only in relation to that past. Here a certain specific "secular" content (idea, attitude, institution) is explained as a form alienated from its original and properly sacred meaning and function.

But why does the secularization thesis imply alienation? Couldn't the new secular form be viewed, rather, as the product of a natural evolution, and thus as a higher and more developed form of the original? Hegel, for example, would certainly argue that the process of secularization which ushers in the modern age should properly be viewed as the emergence of a higher stage in the unfolding of Reason, the coming of age of previously obscure content, which has at last reached a higher and more authentic manifestation. Recognizing this possible reading, Blumenberg underscores that "everything turns on the question whether the worldly form of what was secularized is not a pseudomorph—in other words: an inauthentic manifestation—of its original reality."[9] What does he have in mind?

In the first instance,[10] Blumenberg is concerned with the manner in which the concept of secularization is used as a term, the way in which it is applied as a category of historical understanding. Formulas of the form "B is a secularized A" generally imply with a sort of rhetorical wink that B is "at bottom" nothing other than A, that B is "really" or "simply" a secularized A; the implication being that the outward, "worldly" form of B is superficial, a veil or disguise which hides and even distorts its true identity and content. The content is preserved, but in a deficient mode, and depends for its meaningfulness on a substantial, concealed core. The rhetorical success of this use of the notion of secularization comes from its apparent power to unmask the imposter, to expose the "pseudo-

9. Blumenberg, *Legitimacy*, 17.

10. As we shall see in what follows, Blumenberg would take issue in any case with this sort of Hegelian interpretation because it relies on a substantialistic conception of historical change.

morph," and trace the alienated form back to a violation of the original form.

That the concept of secularization carries connotations of such a violation, Blumenberg believes, can be seen if we attend to the term's "latent metaphoric content," which derives from its legal use in canon law. Blumenberg argues that the early use of the term to refer to the political expropriation of church property served to color the way in which the concept later developed and gave it a certain rhetorical flavor. That is, the idea of expropriation came to be metaphorically associated with the term as it developed into a more general concept.[11] Blumenberg cites the following definition of secularization as an example of a late stage in the process of the "terminologization" of the concept: "'Secularization, that is to say, the detachment of spiritual or ecclesiastical ideas and thoughts, and equally the detachment of spiritual (consecrated) things and people, from their connection to God.'"[12] Thoughts, ideas, people, and things are understood, here, as different types of transferable "property" belonging originally and properly to the Church and through it to God. By attending to the "background metaphorics" of the term, Blumenberg claims, three salient features of secularization as expropriation may be brought to the fore: the identifiability of the expropriated property, the legitimacy of its initial ownership, and the unilateral nature of its removal.[13] It is the connotation of *blame*, the underlying assumption of illegitimate usurpation, in the concept of secularization that provides the rhetorical edge in its use as an historical category of explanation. Indeed, it is precisely this connotation which makes Blumenberg balk at the claim that the epochal

11. Blumenberg is *not* arguing that this legal use of the term was its original use; in fact he underscores that this is probably not the case. He argues only that "this historical association impelled the development of increased precision in the term's use in a particular direction." Thus "it is not the usage that is metaphorical but the orientation of the process of concept formation" (Blumenberg, *Legitimacy*, 18, 22). For a detailed discussion of Blumenberg's notion of "background metaphorics," see his "Paradigmen zu einer Metaphorologie," *Archiv für Begriffsgeschichte* 6 (1960): 69–83.

12. Blumenberg, *Legitimacy*, 23. Blumenberg cites an article by S. Reicke, "Säkularisierung," in *Die Religion in Geschichte und Gegenwart*, 3d ed., vol. 5 (Tübingen: J. C. B. Mohr, 1961), col. 1280.

13. Blumenberg, *Legitimacy*, 23–24.

originality of the modern age may be understood as the result of the secularization of the Christian Middle Ages.[14]

Again, what is at issue for Blumenberg is not *that* the modern age is characterized as worldly—indeed for Blumenberg worldliness is the fundamental characteristic of the modern epoch—but rather the insinuation that this worldliness is merely the result of a process of secularization. "In the application of the category of secularization, it is admitted, and has to be admitted consistently, that the modern age is an epoch of original character; it is only denied that this is on its own account, by virtue of the rational authenticity it claims for itself."[15] Blumenberg's project in the *Legitimacy*, then, is to show that the worldliness of the modern age is indeed characterized by an authentically modern content, a genuinely modern form of self- and world-interpretation. In order to do so he must first show that the secularization thesis is fundamentally mistaken and then provide an alternate account of the worldliness of the modern age, which does justice to both historical continuity and novelty.

14. The motto of the first edition of the *Legitimacy*, taken from André Gide's novel *Les Faux-Monnayeurs*, reads: "C'est curieux comme le point de vue diffère, suivant qu'on est le fruit du crime ou de la légitimité."

15. Blumenberg, *Legitimacy*, 125.

[1]

Blumenberg's Attack on the Secularization Thesis

Blumenberg finds the secularization thesis fundamentally unacceptable as a tool of historical explanation for two reasons: (1) it presupposes a substantialistic ontology of history, and (2) it introduces a theological element into our understanding of historical process not transparent to theory itself. As we shall see, the second is closely related to the first.

First, the thesis that fundamental concepts, institutions and attitudes of the modern age are really just secularized versions of medieval correlates presupposes the identity of an originally sacred content or substance that is preserved (though transformed) in the transition to the modern world. It thus depends on an understanding of history dominated by the category of substance, so that this history becomes the story of repetitions, transformations, superimpositions, and conversions of this originally sacred content to new functions.[16] The task of the historical theorist would then become that of identifying the core content, to unmask layers of "hidden meaning," or a series of "alienated forms." The transfer in "ownership" of ideas, institutions, etc. from ecclesiastical to secular hands at the end of the Middle Ages is thus understood as a falling away from the original context in which they most properly belong.

16. Ibid., 9, 16.

Blumenberg claims that a residue of Platonism attends the secularization thesis and its imputation of blame. Why? Because the secularized idea is able to demonstrate the legitimacy of its possession of a share of the truth only by recalling the debt it owes to the original source which determines it and from which it springs. Within the Platonic framework, an idea is true by virtue of being an image or copy of an original and absolute Truth. This original came to be identified in a Platonized Christian theology with God or the Word of God. For the early Christian thinker, to assert the truth of an idea meant recognizing its ontological status as an image constituted by and derived from the divine source of all truth. Thus the blame implied by secularization has to do with the way an image may become detached from its original source, so that its status as image is forgotten; it then no longer stands *for* the true, but rather *instead* of the true, making remembrance seem superfluous. "The work of the historian or philosopher of history in uncovering secularizations," says Blumenberg, "reestablishes anamnesis and leads to a kind of restitution through the recognition of the relation of debt."[17] The secularized idea is then understood in a deeper way or rather, truly understood for the first time, once its essential connection to its theological origin is made explicit. But this hermeneutic process of uncovering operates on the assumption that all truth is essentially bound in a relationship of indebtedness to a transcendent, divine source.

The concept of secularization (as expropriation) is committed to the notion of an original property in ideas, which can be legitimately transferred only by an act of free bestowal originating in the transcendent realm of the divine. It is precisely this notion which, Blumenberg claims, makes the secularization thesis anachronistic in the modern age.[18] This is because the connection between the concept of truth and the idea of ownership fundamentally changed in the transition to the modern era. Rather than claiming that an idea is true because it derives from an absolute truth of which it is a copy, the modern age, says Blumenberg, "pro-

17. Ibid., 72.
18. Ibid., Part I, Chapter 6.

duced the axiom that the legitimate ownership of ideas can be derived only from their authentic production. This is important if only because it renders the idea of a legitimate secularization paradoxical, while at the same time it gives the criterion of genuine ownership its specific importance for the first time."[19]

For the modern thinker, Blumenberg insists, the truths of reason are marked by their internal necessity, and knowledge is generated through a rational method potentially available to anyone.[20] This model of knowledge acquisition through immanent self-production is fundamentally inconsistent with the secularization thesis, which presupposes the notion of an original (and divine) property in ideas. "When historical understanding makes use of this category," says Blumenberg, "it enters into religion's self-interpretation as a privileged access to truth. It takes over the assumption, which is necessarily bound up with the claim to have received a revelation, of a beginning that is not historically explicable, that has no immanent preconditions."[21] It is not the religious nature of the assumption *per se* that bothers Blumenberg, but the notion of a beginning which has no *immanent* preconditions, of a beginning which has its source in something which transcends the immanent unfolding of historical conditions. Much like Kant's positing of the transcendental ego which breaks into the causal chain of natural phenomena, it introduces into the theory of history (specifically here the history of ideas or knowledge) a transcendent element not available to theory itself. It "implants in the unaltered historical process a mystery that the theoretical onlooker cannot penetrate."[22]

The secularization thesis adopts the (in this case religious) premise that at a certain point in the stream of history, something broke into the historical process from a unique and unsurpassable source. It adopts the

19. Ibid., 72.

20. It should be noted, however, that this potential availability of knowledge to all human beings is not in conflict with a theory of knowledge which depends on the ideal of a transcendent truth, so long as the knowledge anyone can construct for him or herself is understood to be conjectural. That this is an important qualification will, I hope, become clear in Part Three.

21. Blumenberg, *Legitimacy*, 74.

22. Ibid., 24. See also 38.

presupposition that the secularized, "worldly" content derives from an absolute and transcendent origin. As such, Blumenberg claims, the secularization thesis becomes entangled in paradox. For how can it be possible to arrive at a notion of secularization that is transparent to the theoretician who uses it? To delineate a use which is immanent to theory *("einen wissenschaftsimmanenten Gebrauch")?* Does not the very concept exclude itself from the whole process of secularization, of making worldly, of making immanent? Blumenberg cites C. H. Ratschow's definition of Enlightenment *(Aufklärung)* as "acute secularization" when he restates the problem as the impossibility of using the concept of secularization in a transparent *(aufgeklärt)* way. Because an "unavoidably theological element" unavailable to the worldly understanding of reality is implicit in the term's meaning, "clarification" *(Aufklärung)* cannot proceed to the secularization of the concept of secularization itself. In other words, the sort of philosophy of history that makes use of secularization as an explanation of history involves itself in the contradiction that it excludes its own tool (the secularization thesis) from the rational criticism that it assigns to itself as the characteristic of its historical standpoint.[23]

Whether or not Blumenberg is correct in asserting that it is anachronistic in the modern age to adhere to a theory of knowledge which depends on the ideal of a transcendent truth—and I will have reason to question this assumption in what follows[24]—he is quite right to underscore the extent to which the secularization thesis is committed to a substantialistic conception of historical transition. Indeed, Blumenberg views the secularization theorem as a special case of historical substantialism in general, akin to contemporary "*topos* research" *(Toposforschung)*. In both cases, theoretical success is spelled out in terms of the identification of substantial constants *(topoi)* in history. It is here that Blumen-

23. See Blumenberg, *Legitimacy,* 10–11, 18, 49.

24. Gadamer, too, is critical of Blumenberg's turning of the specific methodology of modern science against the (teleological) idea of truth, by insisting on the disassociation of the idea of truth from theoretical effectiveness (Gadamer, review of *Die Legitimität der Neuzeit,* 208). Indeed, Gadamer questions whether Blumenberg has adequately grasped the nature of curiosity because he does not recognize the teleological orientation of all human theorizing (ibid., 206).

berg raises his deepest and most compelling objection to the secularization thesis. Any such substantialistic approach is problematic insofar as it limits the aims and expectations of critical inquiry by simply assuming from the outset that results will, and must, be articulated in terms of such fixed constants. The theorist knows in advance what to look for. This not only severely limits the scope and range of what he or she will be capable of recognizing as historically relevant phenomena, it also predetermines the pattern of interpretation given to whatever is discovered in this way.[25]

Indeed, if one operates solely with a substantialistic conception of historical transition, then the emergence of new ideas, institutions, forms of consciousness, etc. will always appear to be the result of a development, or a transformation, of some earlier element or elements. The explanation of the new form will, in turn, inevitably involve a search for the relevant "precursors" or "forerunners." Gadamer has remarked on the fruitfulness of Blumenberg's method, which refuses to limit its interpretive scope in this way. Instead, Blumenberg greatly extends the interpretive range of his reading of historical transition by attending to the ways in which given historical elements may indeed prepare the way for the emergence of something new without themselves being "precursors" or "anticipations" of it.[26]

Take for example Blumenberg's analysis of the emergence of the new cosmology in *The Genesis of the Copernican World.*[27] Here Blumenberg is particularly concerned to distinguish the series of *preconditions,* which prepared the way for the revolution in cosmology, from the *history of effects (Wirkungsgeschichten)* through which that revolution took place. In this case, nominalism loosened the authority of Aristotelian science and

25. Blumenberg does not rule out the possibility that there are some substantial constants in history. But he insists that this is not something that the theorist should make an assumption of inquiry. "No a priori statement whether there are substantial constants in history can be made; all we can say is that the historian's epistemological situation cannot be optimized by the determination of such stable elementary historical quanta" (Blumenberg, *Legitimacy,* 29).

26. Gadamer, review of *Die Legitimität der Neuzeit,* 203.

27. Hans Blumenberg, *The Genesis of the Copernican World,* trans. Robert M. Wallace (Cambridge: MIT Press, 1987); originally published as *Die Genesis der kopernikanischen Welt* (Frankfurt: Suhrkamp, 1975).

so served as a precondition for the emergence of the new cosmology by opening up the conceptual space in which Copernicus could challenge the ancient system. Nominalist theorists were not "precursors" of Copernicus, and yet they provided the necessary preconditions for the shift which he then initiated. As we shall see, this same approach underlies a good deal of Blumenberg's analysis of the significance of the role played by nominalism in the emergence of the modern age in the *Legitimacy* as well.

Blumenberg's approach has the further advantage of being able to do justice to both the continuity of historical transition and, at the same time, the genuine novelty of new conceptual forms. The new forms do not appear on the historical scene *ex nihilo* as unconditioned and inexplicable events, nor are they simply reduced to "that which was already there all along."[28]

28. Elías José Palti ("In Memoriam: Hans Blumenberg [1920–1996], An Unended Quest," *Journal of the History of Ideas* 58 [July 1997]: 503–24) provides a helpful analysis of Blumenberg's alternative approach to historical transition in the *Genesis*. I disagree, however, with his claim that this is a new development, not already to be found in the *Legitimacy*. What Palti has to say about Blumenberg's approach to the history (of science) in the *Genesis* can equally well be said, more generally, of the *Legitimacy:* "Recent epistemologies [e.g. Kuhnian] depart from evidence of the actual occurrence of historical ruptures in the sciences; but they are unable to explain how it is possible that a consecutive stage, resulting necessarily . . . from preexisting conditions, could, however, be something other than the mere unfolding of what was already prefigured embryonically in them. Blumenberg tried instead to think how something radically new could emerge necessarily from preexisting conditions (something that new epistemologies tend to obliterate) but not as a mere prolongation of them (as the evolutionary concept of historical change postulates)" (Palti, "In Memoriam," 513).

[11]

Blumenberg's Dialogical Functionalism

Part II of the *Legitimacy* aims at providing an account of the "worldliness" of the modern age, an account which does not make recourse to the secularization thesis and indeed utilizes an entirely different historical methodology. In lieu of the historical substantialism which underlies the secularization thesis (and indeed most speculative and all perennialist philosophies of history), Blumenberg proposes what has been termed a "phenomenological" approach to history,[29] an approach squarely grounded in the immanent unfolding of the historical context itself. Consequently, he focuses less on the content and more on the contextual function of the ideas, values, and attitudes of a given historical period. He views these ideas and attitudes as constituting a sometimes more, sometimes less coherent framework of self- and world-interpretation.

In a period of epochal change, a new set of ideas, values, and attitudes may come to replace an older configuration. Such a shift occurs when the older configuration, for one reason or another (and it is always a very his-

29. See Robert Pippin's description of Blumenberg's project: "In this sense, reading Hegel's account of his own denial of the possibility of a priori, or 'external,' formal epistemologies and critiques, one could call Blumenberg's narrative an internal narrative or phenomenology of 'epochal' change" ("Blumenberg and the Modernity Problem," *Review of Metaphysics* 40, no. 3 [March 1987]: 542).

torically specific set of circumstances), is no longer able to provide individuals with adequate orientation in the world. Insofar as new responses are offered to old problems which had been solved differently in a previous historical period, they may be said to "reoccupy" the position of the old ideas and attitudes. That is, they serve the same function, they answer the same "carry-over" questions, but the answers they give in responding to the inherited problems are not the same. The ideas and attitudes are new and provide original solutions that are appropriate in the context of the new epoch.

If there were a fixed set of perennial questions or problems that were answered ever anew by each succeeding epoch, then Blumenberg's "reoccupation" thesis would simply offer another form of historical substantialism: form (questions) would take the place of content (answers) as the fixed element in historical transition.[30] This is a position, however, which Blumenberg rejects. "We are going to have to free ourselves from the idea that there is a firm canon of 'the great questions' that throughout history and with an unchanging urgency have occupied human curiosity and motivated the pretension to world and self-interpretation."[31] Indeed, the questions that are felt to be existentially pressing are *not* always constant from one epoch to the next. It is only what Blumenberg terms "carry over questions," problems that continue to be felt as pressing in the transition from one epoch to another, that make for the *identity* in historical process which has so often erroneously been interpreted as a continuity of content.

Take, for example, the question of the overall meaning of human histo-

30. Elías Palti seems to interpret Blumenberg's reoccupation thesis in the *Legitimacy* as "essentialist" in this sense. He reads Blumenberg, here, as revealing strong structuralist tendencies in an apparent commitment to "the idea of fixed structures" (Palti, "In Memoriam," 509). Palti views Blumenberg's subsequent work (in particular in *The Genesis of the Copernican World* [1975]) as more historicist in character and a departure from the "rigidity" of this earlier "functionalist model" (521). Palti is too quick, however, in his assessment of Blumenberg's use of the notion of reoccupation in the *Legitimacy* as structuralist and essentialist, and too quick to see in Blumenberg's early work a tension between "historicist" and "structuralist" tendencies. On the contrary, Blumenberg's reoccupation thesis in the *Legitimacy* is thought in the context of a "dialogical" and not a static structuralist model of epochal change, as I show in what follows.

31. Blumenberg, *Legitimacy*, 65.

ry.[32] Does human history, taken as a whole, have some redeeming point to it? Now this is not a perennial question. The ancient Greeks did not ask it. The meaning of history as a whole did not appear to them as a problem to be solved. It simply was not an issue. In the wake of Christian theology with its salvation history, however, questions about the meaning and pattern of human history arose quite naturally in the modern age. Theology had thus created new "positions" in the framework of the statements about the world and about human existence which demanded a response. Blumenberg describes this sense of *debt,* this sense of *having* to find answers to these inherited questions, as *Bedürfnisreste* ("residual needs"): an inherited sense of what we *need* to know about our world and ourselves.

What mainly occurred in the process that is interpreted as secularization, at least (so far) in all but a few recognizable and specific instances, should be described not as the *transposition* of authentically theological contents into secularized alienation from their origin but rather as the *reoccupation* of answer positions that had become vacant and whose corresponding questions could not be eliminated.[33]

To return to our example, Blumenberg thus views the modern philosophies of history of the eighteenth and nineteenth centuries as attempts to answer the inherited question about the overall meaning of human history by using the modern concept of progress. But the concept of progress

32. This was, we recall (see p. 16), the theme of Karl Löwith's *Meaning in History: The Theological Presuppositions of the Philosophy of History* (Chicago: University of Chicago Press, 1949). He had argued that the modern conception of progress in history is a secularization of Christian eschatology. Blumenberg criticized Löwith's thesis in the first edition of the *Legitimacy* by pointing out that the secularized content in the two cases is not structurally analogous. Eschatology assumes a transcendent intervention into history from outside of history. Progress assumes a process at work within history itself. Löwith had responded that this is, after all, precisely what is meant by secularization: the making worldly (immanent) of something which was originally transcendent. What remains the same for both, he claimed, was that both think of history as moving toward a goal to be fulfilled in the future, and both live in hope for the futural goal (Löwith, *Meaning in History,* 198–99). In the revised edition of the *Legitimacy,* Blumenberg countered by showing that although eschatological expectations may have begun in antiquity as an aggregate of hopes, this positive expectation radically shifted its valence in the course of the Middle Ages to one of terror and dread of the final judgment and destruction of the world (Blumenberg, *Legitimacy,* 31). Indeed, Blumenberg's detailed exposition of the history of eschatological expectations in Part I, Chapter 4 of the *Legitimacy* provides a decisive refutation of Löwith's thesis.

33. Blumenberg, *Legitimacy,* 64–65.

had itself emerged piecemeal in quite different contexts: that of the advances made by astronomy in the sixteenth and seventeenth centuries and that of the artistic *querelle des anciens et des modernes* in the late seventeenth century.

The astronomical advances made by Copernicus, Galileo, and Kepler were possible only on the basis of observations made over great spans of time and thus depended on a sustained theoretical effort which spanned generations. Hence the idea of "progress" understood here as a continuous movement which builds upon and surpasses whatever has already been achieved arose quite naturally in this sphere. A somewhat different sense of "progress" emerged later in the seventeenth century in the context of literary and aesthetic debates concerning the status that should be accorded to the literature and art of antiquity. The Renaissance had viewed ancient works of art as unsurpassable models, which should function as permanent prototypes and obligatory ideals for any future artistic production. The "moderns" rejected this view and advanced the notion instead, that the arts should strive to express the creative spirit of their particular age, and emphasis was placed on the demiurgic power of the creative subject. Indeed it is in this context that we begin to see the emergence of the notion that human beings create their own reality.

The full-blown idea of "progress in general," in all fields of human endeavor, spanning the centuries, Blumenberg claims, arose gradually from the synthesizing of the partial experiences in these local fields. Indeed, he insists that it was only after a long development over the course of two centuries that this emergent notion of progress formed into an idea comparable in scope to that of Christian eschatology.[34] And it was only at this point that it could be utilized in order to answer the carry-over question concerning the meaning of history as a whole. Thus the modern concept of progress is not a "secularization" of the content of Christian eschatology at all, but rather it developed independently of questions concerning

34. See Blumenberg, *Legitimacy*, 30–34, and Blumenberg's article, "On a Lineage of the Idea of Progress," *Social Research* 41 (1974): 5–27. See also Robert M. Wallace, "Progress, Secularization and Modernity: The Löwith-Blumenberg Debate," *New German Critique* 22 (Winter 1981): 70–71.

the meaning of history and was only subsequently adopted and utilized in order to satisfy the residual need for such answers.[35]

Further, it was only in the wake of Christian theology that the question "What is the meaning of history?" became explicit as such. From within the context of Christian theology itself, there was no need to pose the question, because salvation history already provided an answer. In this sense then, the (medieval) answer preceded the (modern) question. Blumenberg notes that this is not at all unusual in the "dialogical" relationship between one age and the next. "Questions do not always precede their answers."[36] The need to shift to a new system of self- and world-interpretation has everything to do with the way in which traditional answers become untenable or problematic, in such a way that their corresponding questions become visible *as* questions for the first time, as pressing questions that demand new answers.[37]

When the credibility and general acceptance of such [old] answers dwindle away, perhaps because inconsistencies appear in the system, they leave behind them the corresponding questions, to which then new answers become due. Unless, perhaps, it

35. Löwith, in his review of the *Legitimacy,* does not seem to see why Blumenberg makes such an effort to show that there are structural disanalogies between the content of Christian eschatology and the content of the modern notion of progress. Löwith, after all, is not trying to show that they are alike in all ways. Indeed, he insists that his thesis says no more and no less than that Old Testament prophetics and Christian eschatology created a horizon of question positions and an intellectual climate, which made the emergence of the modern concept of history with its belief in worldly progress possible in the first place (p. 198). He even goes on to agree with Blumenberg's assessment that the modern concept of progress was used in order to answer the old (theological) question of the overall meaning of history. He denies, however, that the concept of progress taken in itself has an origin independent of eschatology precisely because, he says, the sense of the totality of history belongs so necessarily to the post-Christian philosophies of history (p. 200). Löwith is simply unable, here, to make the differentiation between the content and the function of a concept. If the Christian function (giving meaning to the totality of history) lives on in the modern age, it can only do so, he assumes, through a transformation of the Christian content (eschatology). See Robert Wallace's ("Löwith-Blumenberg Debate," 77) helpful discussion of their exchange.

36. Blumenberg, *Legitimacy,* 66.

37. "In a cartoon by Jean Effel in *L'Express,* de Gaulle was pictured opening a press conference with the remark, 'Gentlemen! Now will you please give me the questions to my answers!' Something along those lines would serve to describe the procedure that would have to be employed in interpreting the logic of a historical epoch in relation to the one preceding it" (Blumenberg, *Legitimacy,* 379).

turns out to be possible to destroy the question itself critically and to undertake amputations on the system of world explanation.[38]

Returning to our example, Blumenberg explains that in the transition to the modern age, the intensification of theological absolutism led to just such inconsistencies in the medieval system—we shall have more to say about that in the next chapter—leaving behind the question of the overall meaning of history. This was a question which the modern age was originally ill-equipped to answer and yet felt obligated to address because of Christianity's influence on people's expectations of what any world-view ought to be able to explain. As a result the early modern idea of progress, which was originally limited in scope to the possibility of progress in a limited field, was enlisted in order to respond to this great carry-over question. In the process, however, the originally more modest notion of progress was "overextended" by the eighteenth- and nineteenth-century philosophies of history, which proclaimed faith in an inevitable and necessary progress in human history overall.[39] That, in the end, these philosophies failed to convince, says Blumenberg, is not surprising when one recognizes that the concept of progress was being made to satisfy a need for which it was never rationally equipped.

At this point Blumenberg breaks with the sort of Enlightenment assumption which one might expect—that is, the assumption that once the question of the meaning of history is recognized as a carry-over question, inherited from an earlier age and stemming from assumptions at odds with those presently embraced, we might at last be in a position to understand why our attempts to answer the question have foundered and to finally stop asking the question. That is, we may be able to "destroy the question itself critically," to show why it is no longer, or need no longer be, a question *for us.* While Blumenberg clearly believes that our own epochal self-understanding is optimized by our ability to understand why it is that we feel compelled to ask the sorts of questions we do, and while he admits that it may in fact be possible to undertake such "amputations on the system of world explanation"—after all we are dealing here not with an eternal question, but with a question that has a specific, historical

38. Ibid., 66.

39. Ibid., 48–49.

origin—he is not at all sanguine about the ease with which such an amputation might be attempted. Indeed, Blumenberg notes rather emphatically that history has shown repeatedly that this elimination of carry-over questions is not, and cannot in fact be, a purely rational operation.[40] Precisely for this reason, Blumenberg speaks of "needs" here, and not, for example, of "prejudices" to be overcome by critical analysis.

It is important to emphasize that the problematic of carry-over questions is not a new phenomenon peculiar to the modern age. Christian theology itself experienced "a comparable 'problem pressure' in its confrontation with questions that were originally foreign to it."[41] For example, in the patristic period there was considerable pressure to come up with something on the basis of the biblical story of creation that would be comparable to the great cosmological speculations of Greek philosophy. And Greek philosophy, in its turn, experienced similar demands vis-à-vis Greek mythology, which "'prescribed' to the nascent philosophy what questions it had to assume responsibility for and what systematic scope it had to possess."[42]

> In history the price we pay for our great critical freedom in regard to the answers is the nonnegotiability of the questions. This does not exclude the possibility that these questions derive from a human interest that lies deeper than the mere persistence of the epochal carry-over; but it does make clearer how much more difficult it is to demonstrate the universality of a human interest than simply to point to the fact that it has been able to survive a few centuries.[43]

Blumenberg's allusion here to the possibility of a human interest that lies deeper than the mere persistence of the epochal carry-over, however, remains suggestive, as does his remark that the elimination of carry-over questions cannot be a purely rational operation. He does not develop either theme at length in the *Legitimacy,* although he hints that the theoretical attitude is haunted by its failure to measure up to the standard of achievement originally set for it by myth. "Far beyond its initial phase,

40. Ibid., 66.

41. Ibid., 65. It is in this sense that Blumenberg speaks of the early "secularization" of Christianity as a system of world explanation at the end of antiquity. See also *Legitimacy,* Part I, Chapter 4.

42. Ibid., 66–67.

43. Ibid., 69.

philosophy, as the embodiment of the early theoretical attitude, continues to bear the imprint of the effort to measure up to this supposed standard of its achievement and to postpone or to gloss over the disappointments that could not fail to appear."[44] Here we recognize at once a central theme of Blumenberg's subsequent work, that of the continuing power and relevance of myth and other forms of non-conceptuality in making sense of, and indeed making possible, human life.[45]

In the *Legitimacy* Blumenberg only alludes to the possibility of a human interest that might lie deeper than whatever problems may carry over from one age to the next. The idea that there is, indeed, a fundamental and lasting problem to which human culture responds ever anew is a central thesis of Blumenberg's later *Work on Myth* (1979). When our primitive ancestors adopted upright, bipedal posture and left the forests for the open savanna, Blumenberg theorizes, human beings became a species without a clearly defined biological niche and had to cope with our lack of naturally adapted instincts in order to survive. Confronted with the problem of the "absolutism of reality," human beings responded with the creation of culture. The solution to the problem was to *become,* as it were, the *animal symbolicum.*[46] Myth—along with reason—was developed as a

44. Ibid., 67.

45. See especially *Work on Myth,* trans. Robert M. Wallace (Cambridge: MIT Press, 1985); originally published as *Arbeit am Mythos* (Frankfurt: Suhrkamp, 1979). See also "An Anthropological Approach to the Contemporary Significance of Rhetoric," trans. Robert M. Wallace, in *After Philosophy,* ed. Kenneth Baynes, James Bohnan, and Thomas McCarthy (Cambridge: M.I.T. Press, 1987), 427–58; original German: "Anthropologische Annäherung an die Aktualität der Rhetorik," in *Wirklichkeiten in denen wir leben* (Stuttgart: Reclam, 1981), 104–36. See also "Prospect for a Theory of Nonconceptuality," in *Shipwreck with Spectator: Paradigm of a Metaphor for Existence,* trans. Steven Rendall (Cambridge: M.I.T. Press, 1997), 96; originally published as *Schiffbruch mit Zuschauer: Paradigma einer Daseinsmetapher* (Frankfurt am Main: Suhrkamp Verlag, 1979). See also his early essay, "Paradigmen zu einer Metaphorologie," *Archiv für Begriffsgeschichte* 6 (1960): 7–142.

46. Blumenberg criticizes Ernst Cassirer (Ernst Cassirer, *The Philosophy of Symbolic Forms* [New Haven, Conn.: Yale University Press, 1953–1957]) for assuming that symbolic forms are simply expressions of human nature, the free creations of the *animal symbolicum,* as it were, and so for failing to explain why such forms arose. See Blumenberg's "An Anthropological Approach," 438; and *Work on Myth,* 160–61, 167–68, 641, 648. See also Blumenberg's "Ernst Cassirers gedenkend," *Revue Internationale de Philosophie* 28 (1974): 456–63; and D. Adams, "Metaphors for Mankind: The Development of Hans Blumenberg's Anthropological Metaphorology," *Journal of the History of Ideas* 52 (1991): 152–66.

tool for coping with our maladaption to our environment and for responding to the *Angst* its life-threatening aspect engendered.

Myth functions, according to Blumenberg, to calm this general *Angst* by giving separate names to the powers of nature, which can then be addressed and dealt with through storytelling. This relieves pressure and creates a space in which to go about the practical business of survival, including developing rational tools for the comprehension and technical control of our surroundings. To the extent that we are still not definitely free from our biological origins, myth continues to play this crucial function for us. As Robert Wallace explains in his lucid introduction to *Work on Myth,* "[Rational] comprehension and control cannot take the place of—cannot perform the function of—the old stories. Knowledge is always only partial; the absolutism of reality was (or is, or would be) total, and requires something other than knowledge alone to overcome it, to put it behind us."[47] Blumenberg's analysis of the significance and function of myth (along with his continuing interest in metaphor and other forms of nonconceptuality) in his later work, then, represents a sophisticated working out of his initial insight in the *Legitimacy,* that the theoretical attitude is haunted by its failure to measure up to the standard of achievement originally set for it by myth. It also helps to explain why it is that the elimination of "carry-over questions" from one age to the next cannot be a purely rational operation.

Blumenberg is drawing for his analysis of the origins of human "symbolic forms" on the work of the European philosophical anthropology movement, which flourished from the 1920s to the 1940s. He credits Paul Alsberg with a first attempt at a philosophical anthropology that interpreted what had previously been considered "natural" human cultural forms as "artificial" responses designed to further human survival.[48] Blumenberg is also clearly indebted to the work of Arnold Gehlen, who had claimed that human beings are distinct from other animals in that they

47. Wallace, introduction to *Work on Myth,* xi.

48. Paul Alsberg, *Das Menschheitsrätsel: Versuch einer prinzipiellen Lösung* (Dresden: Sibyllen Verlag, 1922). See Blumenberg's "Anthroplogische Annäherung," 114–15. See also Alsberg's updated *In Quest of Man: A Biological Approach to the Problem of Man's Place in Nature* (Oxford and New York: Pergamon Press, 1970).

lack adaptive instincts and so develop culture as a means of orienting themselves within their environment.[49] There is also evidence Blumenberg read and was influenced by the work of Helmuth Plessner. Plessner had insisted that the "open questions" of the human sciences do not reflect so much a characteristic in the object under study—an elusive human nature that somehow defies conceptuality—but are, rather, reflections of the open question which the human being is as such.[50]

What Blumenberg finds so appealing in these thinkers is the idea that the cultural forms produced by human beings—the myths, symbols, metaphors, and conceptual schemes that we use to make sense of ourselves and our world—are not somehow natural cultural forms that arise out of the depths of an essential human nature. (Blumenberg's suspicion of essential "content" is once again evident.) These symbolic forms are, rather, inventions. They are artifacts produced as tools for survival in response to the need for orientation in the environment in which we find ourselves. Such an understanding of the origin and function of human cultural forms allows for just the sort of dynamic, dialogical or responsive, functionalism that is characteristic of Blumenberg's general interpretive strategy.[51]

49. Arnold Gehlen, *Der Mensch: Seine Natur and seine Stellung in der Welt* (Berlin: Duncker & Dünnhaupt, 1941). Blumenberg also draws (critically) on Gehlen's theory of "institutions" as elaborated in *Sozialpsychologische Probleme in der industriellen Gesellschaft* (Tübingen: Mohr, 1949), translated by Patricia Lipscomb as *Man in the Age of Technology* (New York: Columbia University Press, 1980), and later reissued as *Die Seele im technischen Zeitalter* (Hamburg: Rowohlt, 1957). See also Gehlen's *Urmensch und Spätkultur* (Bonn: Athenäum, 1956). The term "institutions" signifies inherited, habitual, and unquestioned forms of behavior or patterns of thought that allow one to act without having to analyze every situation as it comes along.

50. Helmuth Plessner, *Zwischen Philosophie und Gesellschaft* (Berne: Francke, 1953). Charles Turner ("Liberalism and the Limits of Science: Weber and Blumenberg," *History of the Human Sciences* 6, no. 4 [1993]: 68–69) sees a connection here with Blumenberg's account of absolute metaphor, and Wayne Hudson ("After Blumenberg: Historicism and Philosophical Anthropology," *History of the Human Sciences* 6, no. 4 [1993]: 110) suggests an echo of Plessner in Blumenberg's identification of "self-assertion" as the principle of the modern age. Hudson also notes the influence of the work of Erich Rothacker (Erich Rothacker, *Zur Genealogie des menschlichen Bewusstseins* [Bonn: Bouvier, 1966]; also *Philosophische Anthropologies* [Bonn: Bouvier, 1982]), who emphasized the "questions" which dominate the thought of a given culture and developed a theory of "significance" to which Blumenberg responded in *Work on Myth.* See also Robert Wallace's discussion of Blumenberg's indebtedness to the philosophical anthropologists in his introduction to *Work on Myth,* xiv–xxix.

51. Palti views Blumenberg's three works, *The Legitimacy of the Modern Age* (1966), *The*

This raises the question of how to situate the account that Blumenberg gives of the transition from medieval to modern forms of self- and world-understanding in the *Legitimacy* within the framework of the philosophical anthropology that he develops in *Work on Myth*. From the perspective of his later *Work on Myth*, the account in the *Legitimacy* would have to be viewed as a local analysis to be subsumed within his broader anthropological interpretation of the persistent human need for orientation in the world. It would be one chapter in the continuing story of human attempts to respond to the overarching "question" or challenge posed by the absolutism of reality. The local achievements arrived at in the emergence of modernity (and indeed in any age) would in turn have to be seen in the overall context of the "functional system of the elementary human accomplishment called 'life.'"[52] Hence, it is my view that, far from discrediting or undermining the value of the functional and dialogical approach to epochal change which Blumenberg takes in the *Legitimacy*, these later developments serve to elaborate on and deepen intuitions already present in his early work.

~

Let us return now to the "local" analysis Blumenberg provides of the emergence of modern "worldliness" in the *Legitimacy*. If the fundamen-

---

Genesis of the Copernican World (1975), and *Work on Myth* (1979) as exhibiting methodologies which are in tension. He sees the *Legitimacy* as oscillating between "historicist" and "structuralist" positions. He views *Genesis* as moving in the historicist direction, and *Work on Myth* reverting to a more structuralist position. As I have already noted, I believe that this is a misleading dichotomy. Blumenberg operates in the *Legitimacy* with a dynamic, dialogical functionalism and it is this functionalist approach which is operative in his corpus as a whole. This is a feature of Blumenberg's work that Wallace has remarked on (Introduction to *Work on Myth*, xvi–xix), although he does agree with Palti that the application of *function* to the problem of myth yields a distinctly new perspective: "The functional explanation of all of man's 'symbolic forms'" decisively "subsumes the earlier model of the structure of 'positions'" (xix). Joseph Leo Koerner ("Ideas about the Thing, Not the Thing Itself: Hans Blumenberg's Style," *History of the Human Sciences* 6, no. 4 [1993]: 2) has also underscored this fundamentally functionalist and dynamic aspect of Blumenberg's thought and style.

52. Blumenberg, "An Anthropological Approach," 439. In this same essay, Blumenberg remarks that the modern philosophies of history and their proposition that man "makes" history, "can only be understood if one perceives the 'reoccupation' that is accomplished by means of it. I introduced and explained this concept in my *Legitimacy of the Modern Age* (1966), but I did not yet see that it implies a rhetorical transaction" (451). Hence, Palti is correct when he remarks that the phenomena of *reoccupations* as described in the *Legitimacy* are, given the new perspective of

tal concepts and attitudes of the modern age are *not* to be explained simply as "secularizations" of medieval forms of self- and world-understanding, then how *are* we to account for the worldliness of the modern age? What is needed, according to Blumenberg's dialogical model of historical transition, is a story about the way in which the credibility and general acceptance of traditional medieval answers to carry-over questions inherited from antiquity was undermined, generating a demand for new answers, a new system of self- and world-interpretation. That is precisely the sort of reading Blumenberg offers in the *Legitimacy*. Thanks to the perspicuity provided by his historical methodology and his extraordinary command of the intellectual tradition, Blumenberg is able to offer a marvelously supple, original and at least partially compelling account of the origins of the worldliness of the modern age. It is to this account that we will now turn in the next two sections of Part One.

That analysis will be followed in turn by the concluding section of Part One, in which I will offer a re-evaluation of Blumenberg's characterization of the modern age as fundamentally "worldly" in orientation, by considering Hannah Arendt's diagnosis of the peculiarly "worldless" character of modernity. While granting that the modern age is characterized by a profoundly new, active, indeed constructive, approach to the world, Arendt calls attention to the *Unheimlichkeit* of modern reality, to the paradox that modern worldliness is attended by an uneasy sense of world alienation. The oddly world*less* character of the modern age cannot be explained simply in terms of the problem pressure of carry-over questions alone, but must be understood in terms of new dilemmas that were actually generated by the very solutions the moderns posited to the carry-over questions they had inherited. The "worldless" character of the modern age may then be recognized as a new, *modern* problem, generated by the new (modern) system of self- and world-interpretation.

---

his later work, to be "subsumed under the category of *significance (Bedeutsamkeit)*, a term [Blumenberg] takes from Dilthey. This concept explains how a given cultural artifact emerges, in a particular context, from a vague background of probabilities to be invested with meaning or value that confers on it what Blumenberg calls *pregnance, geprägte Form*, as opposed to indifference. This is for Blumenberg, the most general mechanism of transmission, selectivity, and transformation of cultural systems" (Palti, "In Memoriam," 520).

[III]

The Emergence of Worldliness and Otherworldliness as Loci of Existential Orientation

Blumenberg devotes Part II of the *Legitimacy* to his own account of the emergence of modern worldliness, that is, to the emergence of what he terms "human self-assertion" as the fundamental existential attitude of the modern age. What he has in mind here is a radically active, indeed re-constructive, orientation to the world, in which the world appears now as something to be "mastered" and reality something to be constructed or re-constructed according to a human order. According to Blumenberg this shift in self- and world-understanding had as its precondition the theological absolutism of late medieval nominalism. By taking the thesis of divine omnipotence to its logical conclusion, Blumenberg argues, nominalist theology rejected any claim for the necessity of a rational and providentially ordered cosmos on the grounds that it would limit God's power. This led to an *Ordnungsschwund* which so radically transformed the aspect of the world confronting mankind that it prepared the way for a radically new stance within that world—i.e. the creative, world-transforming activity of modern self-assertion.

In order to explain why this shift occurred, Blumenberg points to a fundamental failure of the medieval system of self- and world-understanding to respond successfully to a carry-over question which it had inherited from antiquity: the question of the origin of evil. In order to avoid the Gnostic solution to this problem (which posited an evil demiurge responsible for creating the world, wholly distinct from the redeeming God of salvation), Augustine had insisted on the unity of the God of creation and salvation and so shifted responsibility for evil in the world to the human will. His doctrine of original sin, however, combined with that of predestination, created tensions within the medieval system of self- and world-understanding, which intensified and came to a head in late medieval nominalist theology. Hence, Blumenberg introduces his analysis of the origin of modern worldliness with the (original and unexpected) thesis that, "The modern age is the second overcoming of Gnosticism."[53] Its success in overcoming the problem of Gnostic dualism—where the Middle Ages had failed—is, as we shall see, a key factor in Blumenberg's assessment of the "legitimacy" of the modern age.[54]

"WORLDLINESS" AS A DUAL TERM

Blumenberg begins his account of the modern turn to "worldliness" by pointing out that worldliness is itself a dual term and draws its meaning from an opposite: otherworldliness. When we speak of something or someone as worldly, we presuppose this opposition. We intend to highlight an engagement in *this* world that stands in contrast to the possibility of an *other*worldly orientation. This concept-pair, says Blumenberg, has its origin in an unexpected situation in the development of early Christianity: the dogged persistence and durability of the world over time despite eschatological expectations of its impending destruction. Initially,

53. Blumenberg, *Legitimacy,* 126.

54. Blumenberg introduces Part II of the *Legitimacy* noting that there are those who impugn the originality and integrity of the modern age with the claim that it represents a relapse into Gnosticism. He cites Eric Voegelin ["Philosophie der Politik in Oxford," in *Philosophische Rundschau* 1 (1953/4): 43], for example, who had remarked that the modern age "would be better entitled the Gnostic age." See also Hans Jonas, "Epilogue: Gnosticism, Nihilism and Existentialism," in *The Gnostic Religion: The Message of the Alien God and the Beginnings of Christianity,* 2d ed., enl. (Boston: Beacon Press, 1963), 320–40. Blumenberg agrees that there is an important relationship between modernity and Gnosticism, but interprets it in an unexpected and novel way (Blumenberg, *Legitimacy,* 126).

Blumenberg remarks, Christianity was not otherworldly in orientation, but rather wholly unworldly. That is to say, the world itself was removed from the arena of human interests and concerns by the belief in its imminent destruction within the believer's own lifetime. In this *initial* Christian situation, "an interest in the world [i.e. worldliness] is not just put in question by the presence of an alternative [e.g. otherworldliness]; rather it is robbed of all meaning because no time remains for the world."[55] Hence there was no such thing as "worldliness" before there was the opposite of "unworldliness." This opposition, which first presented an alternative, an either/or, was not possible until the world proved more durable and reliable than initially expected, until it became clear that even the downfall of the Roman Empire did not herald the world's end.[56] Given the world's persistence, the simple fact of its durability, eschatological expectations were pushed into the indefinite future beyond the present generation. In this situation, "the things of this world" demanded real attention, and the initial form of Christian "unworldliness" disappeared. Its function in the believer's interpretive system was gradually reoccupied by an entirely new form, which emphasized the "otherworldly" concerns of the soul *as opposed to* the "worldly" concerns of "this" life.

As Blumenberg describes the transition, the position left vacant by the

55. Blumenberg, *Legitimacy,* 42.

56. See Hannah Arendt's discussion in *The Human Condition* (Chicago: The University of Chicago Press, 1958), 74. Here Arendt acknowledges the validity of the traditional explanation of the origin of Christian "otherworldliness" as a consequence of thwarted eschatological expectations. In an interesting contrast to Blumenberg, however, she points to another root of Christian otherworldliness, "perhaps even more intimately related to the teachings of Jesus of Nazareth, and at any rate so independent of the belief in the perishability of the world that one is tempted to see in it the true inner reason why Christian alienation from the world could so easily survive the obvious non-fulfillment of its eschatological hopes.

The one activity taught by Jesus in word and deed is the activity of goodness, and goodness obviously harbors a tendency to hide from being seen or heard. . . . For it is manifest that the moment a good work becomes known and public [most importantly, even to the doer of the deed himself], it loses its specific character of goodness, of being done for nothing but goodness' sake. . . . Good works, because they must be forgotten instantly, can never become part of the world; they come and go, leaving no trace. They truly are not of this world.

It is this worldlessness inherent in good works that makes goodness, like wisdom in antiquity, an essentially non-human, superhuman quality" (74–76).

original form of unworldliness came to be reoccupied by "the Platonic-Neoplatonic concept of transcendence." Blumenberg makes no distinction between Platonism and Neoplatonism here and equates the Platonic conception of the transcendence of the Ideal realm of Forms with the Neoplatonic notion of the transcendence of the One.[57] What Blumenberg has in mind is the emergence of a dualism of realms, each making its demands on the life of the believer. This is crucial for Blumenberg, who holds that this Platonic/ Neoplatonic schematism of transcendence delineates an extra-worldly realm and "presupposes a dualism of decision between simultaneously existing possibilities, intentions, directions."[58] The Christian now had to choose between the concerns of "this world" and those of "the next," as between two very real options each of which had something to offer.

GNOSTICISM AND THE PROBLEM OF THE ORIGIN OF EVIL

In order to understand how it came about that at the beginning of the modern age the claims of "this" world, the realm of immanence and of history, won out over those of the transcendent realm of the divine, Blumenberg says, we must look again at the early foundations of the "Christian Middle Ages." For it is here, he claims, that the seeds of a theological absolutism are sown, which placed an unbearable strain on this dualism of competing realms and so eventually lead to the collapse of the medieval world system.

Blumenberg interprets this collapse as the eventual consequence of dogmatic positions taken by the early Church Fathers at the beginning of the period to refute the heresy of Gnosticism. Indeed, Blumenberg advances the thesis that the entire Christian Middle Ages, as a meaningful and coherent structure spanning centuries from Augustine to the height

57. This is, however, as I hope to show in what follows, a serious misreading of Neoplatonism, for which the transcendence of the One is always also understood in terms of its immanence in the many. *This* form of transcendence is not thinkable as convertible with a dualism of separate "realms," as in traditional Platonism.

58. Blumenberg, *Legitimacy,* 41–42.

of Scholasticism, can be understood only as a (failed) attempt to overcome late-antique and early-Christian Gnosticism. The modern age, characterized by the move to self-assertion in the world, would then be interpreted as a second, this time successful, overcoming of the "Gnostic opponent."[59] On Blumenberg's reading, the failure of the first attempt necessitated and motivated the second.

~

The name "Gnosticism" is used by historians as a collective heading designating a group of sectarian doctrines, which appeared in and around Christianity during its first two to three centuries. Of the various Gnostic sects only a few actually referred to themselves as "Gnostics." Most took their names from their founders, localities, or doctrines. The term "Gnosticism" is derived from the Greek word for "knowledge," *gnosis.* It was already used by the early Church Fathers in their attacks on this religious movement because of the common emphasis placed on a supernatural kind of *knowledge* as the necessary means for attaining salvation. Gnosticism, in the many varieties in which it flourished during the first three centuries of the Christian era, may be generally described as a dualistic, anti-cosmic religion of transcendent salvation.[60] The various Gnostic sects shared a rejection of the material world, which they believed was created and governed by an evil (or at least inferior and ignorant) deity, hostile to the human spirit. The human soul, according to the Gnostics, is enslaved in this world by the creator god and imprisoned in a body. It is into this "foreign" world that the transcendent God sends the divine messenger, who imparts a saving knowledge of the homeland "beyond."[61] The Gnostics pushed the traditional Greek dualism of soul and matter to such an extreme that the material world came to be understood as evil by definition, having its ontological foundation in a fundamentally evil creative and governing principle.

The ground was laid for this move, according to Blumenberg, in the Platonic tradition, which viewed the world as "the great failure to equal

59. Ibid., 126.
60. See Jonas, *The Gnostic Religion,* 32.
61. See ibid., 45.

its ideal model."[62] The difference between the idea and its material substratum, Blumenberg claims, was further increased in the Neoplatonic tradition in which "the *theologizing* of the Idea" corresponds to "the *demonizing* of matter."[63] Hence, Blumenberg interprets Gnostic dualism as the result of a systematic reoccupation of the "dualistic" positions prepared in the thought of Plotinus: to the "theologized" Idea now corresponds the transcendent God of salvation, and to "demonized" matter, the demiurge as the principle of badness.[64]

The appeal of Gnosticism for the early Christians, claims Blumenberg, lay in the power and coherence of its answer to the carry-over question concerning the origin of what is evil in the world. Clearly the early Christians could not follow the ancient Greek tradition in viewing a preexistent or eternally existent material principle as the cause of what is bad in the world.[65] The Christian God is not simply a benevolent demiurge, who does the best he can to give order to a recalcitrant material substrate. He is, rather, an omnipotent creator. He is responsible not only for the order of the world, but for the existence of the world itself, including its matter. Hence, the doctrine of *creatio ex nihilo* deprives matter of its dualistic pre-givenness by including matter itself in a creation from nothing. Further, the text of Genesis clearly asserts the excellence of the nascent world: "And God saw *everything* that he had made, and behold, it was very good."[66] If the creation, as such, is good, how then are we to account for the evils in the world? The problem is further complicated by the eschatological pathos of the New Testament, which ties the salvation of mankind to the destruction of the created cosmos.

The Gnostics found in their separation of the creator god from the

62. Blumenberg, *Legitimacy,* 128.

63. Ibid.

64. I will have reason to criticize this interpretation in what follows.

65. Even the Neoplatonic doctrine of necessary emanation is, in its pagan form, at odds with the Christian notion of a *willed* creation *ex nihilo.* See for example the discussion in Steven Gersh's *From Iamblichus to Eriugena* (Leiden: E. J. Brill, 1978). It should be emphasized, however, that later Christian Neoplatonists were able to work out a more or less orthodox interpretation of the "eternity of creation," in response to this difficulty. Both Eckhart and Cusanus, for example, following Augustine's lead, held such a doctrine.

66. Gn 1.31, New Revised Standard Version. My emphasis.

god of salvation an easy solution to this Christian dilemma. And the particular explanation that was offered by Marcion of Sinope in Pontus (c. 140) was undoubtedly the most historically consequential. As Hans Jonas explains, Marcion "was the most resolutely and undilutedly 'Christian' of the Gnostics," and at the same time, he propounded perhaps the most extreme form of anti-cosmic dualism. As a result, he presented Christian orthodoxy with its greatest challenge. His, more than any other "heresy," Jonas emphasizes, shaped the direction and form of the orthodox creed itself. "It was in answer to Marcion's attempt to thrust his canon and with it his whole interpretation of the Christian message upon the Church that the latter proceeded to establish the orthodox canon and the orthodox dogma"[67] Hence Blumenberg focuses his consideration of Gnosticism, and of its significance for the medieval system of self- and world-interpretation, on a reading of Marcion in particular.

According to Marcion, the creator God of the Old Testament is himself an evil tyrant, who laid down a law impossible to fulfill, created a natural order hostile and oppressive to the human spirit, and plunged the soul into a body subject to suffering, sickness, and death. Thus the creator God himself would become the principle and source of all evil in the world. The God of the New Testament, on the other hand, is a "foreign god," the transcendent God of salvation, whose purpose is no longer the redemption *of* the world but rather redemption *from* the world, as from all that is evil. "Gnosticism," writes Blumenberg, "has no need of theodicy since the good God has never had anything to do with the world. Even the bringer of salvation, sent by the good God to deliver the lost *pneuma* [spirit] through knowledge [*gnosis*], can only appear to assume a human body in order to deceive the demiurge's watchmen. The downfall of the world becomes the critical process of final salvation, the dissolution of the demiurge's illegitimate creation."[68]

The price Marcion had to pay for this resolution of the dilemma that confronted early Christianity was of course the dignity of the ancient cosmos itself and man's harmonious place within it. The Greek word *kosmos*

67. Jonas, *Gnostic Religion,* 137 and 146.
68. Blumenberg, *Legitimacy,* 128–29.

literally means order, and it was used generally as a term of praise and even admiration. The universe was considered in the classical tradition to be the perfect exemplar of divine order and the source of all order in its particular parts. Thus, for the ancients, the "cosmos" was considered to be both beautiful and rational in the highest degree (beauty embodying the sensible aspect of order and reason its intelligible aspect).[69] It was venerated as a perfect whole, ensouled (life giving), intelligent (mind governed) and wise (perfectly ordered).

Man himself was seen as an integral part of that whole, with his own peculiar status in it. "Born to contemplate the cosmos and to imitate it," Cicero wrote, "he is far from being perfect, but he is a little part of the perfect."[70] In this sense cosmic piety dictates that man submit himself to the requirements of the whole. On the other hand, mankind does not share in the perfection of the universe by simply being a part in the greater whole. Man has the capacity to perfect himself, to transcend his position as a mere part, by contemplating and imitating the perfection of the cosmos through the exercise of his reason and in the practice of his conduct. This latter is possible only insofar as man himself is in possession of a mind and so recognizes within himself an identity with the ruling principle of the cosmos.[71] The Greek notion of cosmos, here, gives voice to a profound sense of belonging to the world.

The Gnostic revaluation of the classical cosmos, on the other hand, is motivated by an equally profound sense of human alienation from the world. The Gnostics retained the notion of cosmos as "order," but with a vengeance. The attribute of order and lawfulness, which in the classical tradition had secured the attunement of human reason and action to the cosmological order, was now viewed as radically opposed to the inner essence and aspirations of mankind. The cosmic order was no longer understood to be in harmony with human reason, but was experienced now as an alien force acting only to thwart human freedom. All meaning and goodness were located outside of this order, outside of this world.

69. Jonas, *Gnostic Religion,* 241–42.
70. Cicero, *De Natura Deorum* 2.11–14, cited by Jonas in *Gnostic Religion,* 245.
71. See Jonas, *Gnostic Religion,* 246.

Of course this negative valuation of the cosmos was in turn counterbalanced by a positive conception of a strictly "other-worldly" deity. The true God is an alien God, totally Other, not merely supra-mundane, but fundamentally contra-mundane. With this, as Hans Jonas writes, "the sublime unity of cosmos and God is broken up, the two are torn apart, and a gulf never completely to be closed again is opened: God and world, God and nature, spirit and nature, become divorced, alien to each other, even contraries."[72] But if these two are alien to each other, then the Gnostic position forces recognition that man and world, man and nature, man and body, too, are alien to each other. Thus the Gnostic solution to the problem of the origin of what is bad or evil in this world was bought at the price of an irreducible alienation from the world and from ourselves as worldly, embodied beings.

Still the persuasive power of Gnosticism for early Christianity lay in the eschatological pathos of the time. Why concern oneself with questions about the creation of the world and the history of mankind, when all this was soon to be made null and void? Belief in the world's imminent end rendered such questions meaningless. Salvation was near at hand, and Gnosticism explained why the world deserved destruction. The unexpected persistence of the world, however, raised the old questions regarding its origins and dependability, and demanded that one take a stance toward it one way or the other. The eventual decision against Gnosticism, claims Blumenberg, had less to do with the superiority of the dogmatic system worked out by the Church Fathers, and far more to do with "the intolerability of the consciousness that this world is supposed to be the prison of the evil god and is nevertheless not destroyed by the power of the god who, according to his revelation, is determined to deliver mankind."[73]

Despite the blow this non-event (the simple persistence of the world) dealt to the Gnostic system, the Church Fathers were still left with the overwhelming problem of the justification of God. If God is omnipotent and if his creation (including matter) is indeed good, where does all that

72. Ibid., 251.
73. Blumenberg, *Legitimacy*, 131.

is evil in the world come from? The Christian response would seem to be as radical as the difficulty it is confronted with: Evil simply does not exist. Whatever exists is good, since all being derives from God. Evil, therefore, is pure nothingness, *privatio,* or lack of what ought to be. Here the Christian position resembles the ancient understanding of evil as a principle of privation resulting in the lack of attunement to an ideal order. However, for the Christian theologian—and here we find common ground with pagan Neoplatonism—this principle of privation can have no *ontological* foundation. The failure of "what ought to be" to *be* in fact realized, is not due to the recalcitrance of an irrational, unformed reality, but must be explained for the Christian thinker in terms of a recalcitrant human will.[74]

The Christian tradition has consistently maintained a distinction between *malum culpae,* moral evil, and *malum poenae,* suffering. To commit evil acts (in the failure to "love one's neighbor") by forcing one's will upon another out of anger, jealousy, resentment, or any number of selfish motives, is understood as moral evil. Suffering at the hands of others or from natural and unavoidable causes is not. How then to explain this second form of evil, evil as suffering?

Again, the Christian answer is based on the premise that all evil (including suffering inflicted by nature) is due to privation, to the distance between what is and what ought to be. For the Christian this amounts to the distance between the world and its perfection, which is God. And again, this separation is not grounded ontologically (in the created world as *factum,* distinct from God) but morally, in man's willful turning away from God. Human suffering may then be understood as *malum poenae,* God's just punishment for man's disobedience.[75] This is the answer Au-

74. "[I]n Christian terms the act of creation is good by definition and produces nothing but good. Evil is nothingness, *privatio,* lack of what ought to be; whatever is, is good as far as it is *(esse et bonum convertuntur)* since *esse* is entirely from God. Having no ontological foundation, evil is a matter of evil will (and the purely human, i.e., self-centered, will is rebellious and by definition evil)" (Leszek Kolakowski, *Religion* [New York: Oxford University Press, 1982], 43).

75. As Blumenberg remarks, "The guide to his solution of the problem of the origin of the bad *(unde malum?)* had already been given to Augustine by the linguistic fact that ancient philosophy had not distinguished in its language between the wickedness that man perpetrates and the bad things that he encounters. That these bad things are the world's reflex to his own

gustine gives to the dilemma of reconciling God's omnipotence with his goodness, and so preserving belief in a just God.[76]

"With a gesture just as stirring as it was fateful," writes Blumenberg, "[Augustine] took for man and upon man the responsibility for the burden oppressing the world."[77] The concept of human freedom together with the doctrine of original sin steps in to bear the burden of all that is evil in the world. The deficiencies of the world, injustice, suffering, and death are interpreted as the just punishment God inflicts on humanity for the evil use of his free will. Augustine finds in Paul's Letter to the Romans the theological grounds for his doctrine of the original and universal guilt of mankind and the free gift of grace which alone can absolve humanity from this guilt. "There he also found the doctrine of absolute predestination, which restricted this grace to the small number of the chosen and thus left the continuing guilt of the all too many to explain the lasting corruption of the world."[78] The doctrine of absolute predestination may account for why the consequences of sin continue to plague the world, but does it not push responsibility for the sinful soul back onto God?

With the doctrine of original sin and of absolute predestination, the dignity of the cosmos itself had been saved from Gnostic dualism but, Blumenberg claims, the "heresy" lived on in a new form: as the absolute separation of the elect from the rejected. Ironically, the unified and ab-

---

wickedness was thus already implicit in the formulation of the question" (Blumenberg, *Legitimacy*, 133).

76. See Kolakowski's discussion in *Religion*, 43f.

77. Blumenberg, *Legitimacy*, 133.

78. Ibid., 135. See also C. H. Dodd's discussion in *The Epistle of Paul to the Romans* (New York and London: Harper and Brothers Publishers, 1932), 148–60. In order to argue that God's choice or election is not limited to the Jewish people alone—indeed, that a new way of salvation has been revealed which rules out in principle any special privilege for Israel or any other historical 'people'—Paul must establish God's absolute sovereignty and His complete freedom to choose whomever He wants at any given time to be the recipients of His favor and the instruments of His divine plan. It is neither through natural descent nor through the merit of good works that one is reckoned a child of God, but rather by divine mercy alone. But Paul does not stop here, in declaring the mercy of God to be a freely given and unearned gift. He goes on to assert that God is *also* responsible for creating the stubborn disposition which would reject God's gift of grace. Not only does he have "mercy upon whomever he wills," but he also "hardens the heart of whomever he wills" (Rom 9.10–21, New Revised Standard Version).

solute God, for whose sake humanity was to take on the burden of original sin, once again became indirectly responsible for the corruption of the world through the introduction of the idea of predestination. "Gnosticism," asserts Blumenberg, "had not been overcome but only transposed [and] returns in the form of the 'hidden God' and His inconceivable absolute sovereignty."[79] It was with this that the self-assertion of reason had to deal at the end of the Middle Ages, when the theological absolutism of nominalism finally pushed the tension in this situation to the breaking point.

GNOSTICISM "TRANSPOSED" AND NEOPLATONISM

Before turning to Blumenberg's reading of the epochal transition to the modern age I would like to raise two critical points regarding his treatment of the role of Gnosticism here. The first concerns his interpretation of Gnosticism as a "lasting opponent," which is not overcome by the emergent orthodoxy of the Church Fathers, but only "transposed" into a new form. The second has to do with his interpretation of Gnostic dualism as a systematic reoccupation of "dualistic" positions supposedly prepared in the thought of Plotinus.

Gnosticism "Transposed"

What are we to make of Blumenberg's claim that Gnosticism was not overcome by Augustine's solution to the origin of evil but "only transposed," indeed, that it "returns in the form of the 'hidden God' [of nominalism] and His inconceivable absolute sovereignty"?[80] In his account of the transposition and return of Gnosticism, Blumenberg is clearly making use of just the sort of historical substantialism he had been at such pains to criticize in the proponents of the secularization thesis. Only in his reading, it is not the modern age which reiterates in a new form the contents of the Middle Ages, but rather the Middle Ages which carry over the Gnostic content of late antiquity. While he may hope to claim that his reading of the epochal transition from the Middle Ages to the modern age

79. Blumenberg, *Legitimacy*, 135.
80. Ibid.

is free of any appeal to the sort of historical substantialism inherent in secularization theories, his analysis of the shift from the ancient to the medieval world clearly is not. Insofar as Blumenberg understands the emergence of modernity as a *response* to the Gnostic opponent lurking in the theology of late medieval nominalism, it would seem he only shifts an appeal to historical substantialism into the earlier transition.

A possible reply to this criticism would be to claim that the "translation" of the problem of Gnosticism into the problem of theological absolutism at the beginning of the Middle Ages is not to be understood as a transformation of a substantial historical "content," but rather as the *reoccupation* of a given framework of self- and world-understanding by another which structurally corresponds to the first in terms of function. Such a reading has its merits but is difficult to square with Blumenberg's own rhetoric in numerous passages, which seems to indicate that he is indeed thinking in terms of a far more substantial continuity.

At the beginning of the Middle Ages, Blumenberg insists, Gnosticism was not "overcome" but only transposed and indirectly reintroduced through the idea of predestination. "The Gnostic dualism had been eliminated as far as the metaphysical world principle was concerned," he writes, "but it lived on in the bosom of mankind and its history as the absolute separation of the elect from the rejected." Or again: The medieval belief in "the senselessness of self-assertion was the heritage of the Gnosticism which was not overcome but only 'translated.'" Further, the end of the Middle Ages was characterized, according to Blumenberg, by a marked resurgence and heightening of these retained Gnostic elements in the speculative philosophy of nominalism. "[Nominalist] philosophy won its autonomy precisely on account of the renewal of the 'Gnostic' assumption that the omnipotent God and the God of salvation . . . are no longer conceivable by reason as identical." And again, Blumenberg writes that nominalist speculation served "to reintroduce Gnostic dualism in fact if not in the original formulation." Finally, the epochal transition into the modern age itself represents for Blumenberg, the "final overcoming of the Gnostic inheritance."[81]

81. Blumenberg, *Legitimacy*, 135, 136, 172, 174 (see also 133–36, 154, 176).

As we shall see, there are indeed striking similarities between the world-view adopted by the ancient Gnostics and that presented by late medieval nominalists. Both assume a radical disjunction between human reason and worldly needs on the one hand and the world-order produced by the creator God on the other. Both reject the (ancient and Scholastic) conception of a beautiful and intelligible cosmos, hierarchically and teleologically ordered, in which human nature finds its natural place. Both reject the (ancient and Scholastic) view of mankind as contemplator of the universe, in harmony with the ruling principle of the cosmos through the highest part of the soul, the intellect. For both, human good and meaning ultimately lie outside this world-order altogether, dependent on the transcendent God of salvation. Blumenberg's assertion that late medieval nominalism exhibits the resurgence of certain elements of ancient Gnosticism is thus not without some warrant, at least superficially.[82]

His thesis, however, that "the medieval period, as a meaningful structure spanning centuries, had its beginning in the conflict with late-antique and early-Christian Gnosticism and that the unity of its systematic intention can be understood as deriving from the task of subduing its Gnostic opponent"[83] is far too simplistic and reductionistic a generalization to bear careful historical scrutiny. One of the real weaknesses of Blumenberg's analysis in the *Legitimacy*—for all his anti-substantialistic rhetoric, and despite the sophistication with which he approaches epochal transition—is his tendency to read historical epochs, themselves, as characterized by one overarching theme. In the case of the Middle Ages it is that of theological absolutism and the subduing of the Gnostic opponent. In the case of the modern age, it is that of human self-assertion and worldly self-realization. But historical epochs do not speak in only one voice, with one overarching project. Their unity is far more nuanced and multi-valenced, with multiple themes and projects co-existing in competitive and often

82. For a critique of Blumenberg's reading of late medieval nominalism as a resurgence of Gnosticism, see Wolfgang Hübener, "Das 'gnostische Rezidiv' oder wie Hans Blumenberg der spätmittelalterlichen Theologie den Puls fühlt," in *Religionstheorie und politische Theologie*, vol. 2, *Gnosis und Politik*, ed. J. Taubes (Munich/Paderborn: Fink/Schöningh, 1984), 37–52.

83. Blumenberg, *Legitimacy*, 126.

fruitful interaction. Blumenberg has indeed isolated central themes in each case, but the unity of each epoch cannot be reduced to them.

For instance, Blumenberg fails to explain why it took several centuries (the whole of the "Christian Middle Ages") for the tensions in Augustinian theology to emerge again with such destructive power in the "theological absolutism" of late medieval nominalism. One answer would surely be that the doctrine of the creation of mankind in the image of God, the sacramental view of nature, and the theology of the Incarnation all served to bridge the distance between the human and the divine, between God and creation. Indeed, throughout the Christian tradition emphasis on divine transcendence was at the same time balanced with a corresponding emphasis on divine immanence. And, as we shall see, it was a systematically central concern of the Neoplatonic tradition—both in antiquity and throughout the Middle Ages—to provide a theoretical framework for the understanding of the simultaneous transcendence and immanence of the divine in the world.

Blumenberg's Consistent Misreading of Neoplatonism

Blumenberg consistently either misreads or ignores the significance of this aspect of the Neoplatonic tradition in his historical analysis in the *Legitimacy*. A case in point is his interpretation of Gnostic dualism as a systematic reoccupation of dualistic positions supposedly prepared in the thought of Plotinus. In his cursory treatment of the problem of evil in ancient thought, we recall (pp. 41–44 above), Blumenberg conflated the Platonic and the Neoplatonic ontological framework. He views Neoplatonism as a simple intensification of the Platonic dualism of Form and matter, and Gnosticism as a straightforward reoccupation of Neoplatonic "demonized" matter with Gnosticism's creator god, and Neoplatonic "theologized" Form with Gnosticism's god of salvation. This reading, however, not only distorts the fundamental character and spirit of Plotinus' thought, it also ignores fundamental structural differences in the three systems (Platonic, Neoplatonic, and Gnostic), which would make the idea of such a "reoccupation" untenable.[84]

84. See in this context Armstrong's discussion of the notion of the *tolma* in Plotinus and in

It is, of course, misleading to speak of "matter" in Plato himself. Aristotle seems to have been the first philosopher to use the term in a technical philosophical sense, borrowing a Greek word *(hyle)* that originally meant "wood" or "timber." Nevertheless, it may certainly be argued that Plato operates with a concept of something analogous to matter (or a material substrate or a material principle) which is co-eternal with the Forms and necessary in order to account for the image-world of becoming.[85] In Plato's account of creation in the *Timaeus,* for example, he distinguishes three "natures" or "kinds of being": the eternal intelligible patterns (Forms), the generated imitation of the pattern (the image-world), and the receptacle, the eternal space or natural recipient of the likenesses *in* which the generation takes place.[86] Plato felt compelled to introduce this "third thing" in order to account for the imperfections evident in the world of appearances, that is, in order to account for the image's failure to attain the perfection and completeness of its archetype. The image-world (the world of the senses, of becoming, change, individuation, and plurality) falls short of the imaged reality, which is characterized by eternal and unchanging Unity. Hence, Plato introduced a principle of negation and difference that is responsible for the separation of the image-world from its archetype, for its existence in a state of otherness and multiplicity. Indeed, without such a principle the images would be unable to exist at all, for they themselves are only the shadows of reality and have no inherent power of subsistence. They must derive their existence, even as mere "image-beings," from the receptacle which receives them.[87]

Within the receptacle, image-beings are defined and set off from one another in a matrix of relationships. The receptacle itself is underived, an

---

Gnostic thought, A. H. Armstrong, "Plotinus," Part 3 of *The Cambridge History of Later Greek and Early Medieval Philosophy,* ed. A. H. Armstrong (Cambridge: The Cambridge University Press, 1967), 242–45. See also Plotinus' own passionate refutation of Gnosticism in his treatise *Against the Gnostics, Enneads* 2.9.

85. Aristotle, for instance, did not hesitate to speak of matter and Form, in this sense, in Plato. See, for example, *Metaphysics* 1.6.988A8–13. See Leonard J. Eslick, "The Material Substrate in Plato," in *The Concept of Matter in Greek and Medieval Philosophy,* ed. Ernan McMullin (Notre Dame, Indiana: University of Notre Dame Press, 1965), 39–54.

86. See Plato *Timaeus* 48e–49b, 50c–d, 52a–b.

87. Plato *Timaeus* 52c.

eternal source of negativity, so that multiplicity has its source not in Unity, but in this principle of difference.[88] Thus an *ontological* dualism of principles grounds Plato's understanding of the generation of the world of appearances. Insofar as the world of sense falls short of the perfection and intelligibility of the Forms, it represents a falling away from Unity and Goodness; and it is the principle of negation and difference—which comes to be identified later in the tradition with matter—that is responsible.

For Plotinus, in contrast, the material universe is the last and "lowest" production or "emanation" of the divine One. The production of the One is entirely spontaneous, the outflowing of its superabundant and inexhaustible life, and the immediate consequence of its unbounded perfection. The One produces eternally the Divine Intelligence *(Nous),* the One-Being, which in some sense corresponds to the Platonic world of Forms or Ideas. The Forms are the eternal archetypes of all else that to any degree exists. Soul proceeds from Intelligence in much the same way Intelligence proceeds from the One. Plotinus distinguishes between a lower phase of Soul, which is "nature," the immanent principle of life which gives form to all material beings, and a higher "World-Soul," which orders and governs the universe.

The material universe generated and governed by Soul is the best possible reflection of its intelligible archetype. It is, however, immeasurably inferior to the archetype, both because the forms that appear in it are the weakest reflections of the Forms in Intellect, and because the matter which underlies it is pure negativity and so further weakens them and makes them less real and good than they might otherwise be. As A. H. Armstrong points out, "Plotinus is so concerned to stress the absolute unreality of matter that he makes it very clear that everything observable in the material universe, including its spatiality and corporeality—everything, that is, except its necessary imperfection—is form, not matter, and

88. The indeterminate "receptacle" of the *Timaeus* has often been linked with the unlimited of the *Philebus.* "And the people of old . . . have bequeathed us this tale, that whatever is said to be consists of one and many, having in its nature limit and unlimitedness" (Plato, *Philebus* 16C–D).

all activity in it is the activity of soul; and form and soul as such are good."[89]

It is for this reason that Plotinus (in contrast to Plato) does not consider embodiment to be an evil *as such,* but only insofar as it implies limitation and separation. Thus, for example, Plotinus considers celestial bodies to be divine. Incorruptible and eternal, the heavenly bodies are wholly governed by soul and, unlike earthly beings, completely unhindered by their embodied state.[90] Thus, it is not insofar as the heavens are embodied that they lack the perfection of the One, but because they exist on a lower spiritual level of separation. It is also for this reason that Plotinus does not disparage but rather praises the value and beauty of works of art. A great artist, for Plotinus, is not to be understood as a mere copyist of the image world, whose products are mere imitations of imitations and so twice removed from true reality, as in Plato.[91] The true artist, for Plotinus, himself looks to the forms of the intelligible world and directly produces an image from them. The great work of art is thus an incarnation of the divine, and may even surpass the beauty of nature.[92]

The stages in the descent from the One and the Good are characterized by a progressive decrease in perfection, a steady diminishing of unity, goodness, and reality. The matter of the world of sense experience lies at the inevitable end of this descent from the One as an absolute metaphysical limit, the point of absolute otherness from unity, goodness, and reality. This matter is absolute privation. By virtue of its absolute unreali-

89. Armstrong, "Plotinus," 231.

90. Armstrong notes that, "There is a good deal of resemblance between the contrast of earthly with heavenly bodies made by the Neoplatonists and the contrast of 'natural' with 'spiritual', post-resurrection, bodies made by Christians, as Augustine remarks [*City of God* X 29; XXII 26]" (Armstrong, "Plotinus," 232).

91. Plato *Republic* Book 10, 597e.

92. "But if anyone despises the arts because they produce their works by imitating nature, we must tell him, first, that natural things are imitations too. Then he must know that the arts do not simply imitate what they see, but they run back up to the forming principles from which nature derives; then also that they do a great deal by themselves, and, since they possess beauty, they make up what is defective in things. For Pheidias too did not make his Zeus from any model perceived by the senses, but understood what Zeus would look like if he wanted to make himself visible" (Plotinus, *Enneads,* 7 vols., trans. A. H. Armstrong. Loeb Classical Library [Cambridge: Harvard University Press, 1966–88], 5.8.1.34–40).

ty and negativity, its otherness from the One and the Good, Plotinus designates the matter of the sense world as absolute evil. It is important to stress, however, that Plotinus is *not* a metaphysical dualist. Matter for him is not to be equated with the "blind necessity" of Plato, co-eternal with and independent of the world of Forms. Matter and Form are not metaphysical co-principles for Plotinus, for even the lowest matter is produced by the principles which come before it, and so derives ultimately from the One itself.[93] Thus Plotinus is not the dualist that Plato is, but rather a passionate monist, and in fact far closer here to the theology of orthodox Christianity than to the radical dualism of Gnosticism, as Blumenberg would have it.

Here, as indeed throughout his analysis in the *Legitimacy,* Blumenberg ignores the crucial cosmological and ontological role played by the notion of divine immanence. This omission leads to a distorted reading not only of the character of the Middle Ages as a whole, but also of the epochal threshold to modernity. Indeed, it is precisely because of his persistent tendency to read Neoplatonism in any form as profoundly dualistic that he fails to recognize the epochal significance of the shift in the Neoplatonic tradition which occurs at the end of the Middle Ages, when the immanence of the One in the many is reinterpreted as the immanence of the infinite in the finite.

Hence, in my own reading of the transition to the modern age I will highlight the contributions of the Neoplatonic tradition as both a correction and an essential supplement to the reading Blumenberg provides in the *Legitimacy.* Where Blumenberg focuses on the continuity and transformation of Gnostic elements in the speculative theology of late medieval nominalism, for instance, I will draw attention to the continuity and transformation of Neoplatonic themes in the speculative theology of Meister Eckhart and Nicholas of Cusa.

Dialogical Functionalism and Continuity of Content

To what extent do these reflections on Blumenberg's treatment of Gnosticism and Neoplatonism serve to undermine the viability of his

93. See Armstrong, "Plotinus," 256.

overall historical methodology? The answer, I think, is: not nearly as much as one might at first believe, although they do imply that his interpretation of the epochal threshold will have to be fundamentally reevaluated. At first glance, it might seem that Blumenberg's methodology commits him to a model of historical transition which understands continuity exclusively in terms of functional reoccupation, and that by admitting any continuity of content from one age to the next, Blumenberg would violate his own stricture against historical substantialism. This is simply not the case, however. In his reading of the transition from late antiquity to the early Middle Ages Blumenberg frequently refers to the medieval appropriation of, continuation of, or transformation of ancient ideas and assumptions. For example, Blumenberg emphasizes that the medievals appropriated and developed the ancient association of contemplation and human fulfillment, as well as the "Platonic" belief in the (divine) ownership of ideas, and the understanding of truth as adequacy to a transcendent ideal. Crucial in Part III of the *Legitimacy* is his reading of Augustine's continuation of the Socratic prioritization of the concerns of the soul over curiosity about nature.

Indeed, even in his reading of the epochal transition to modernity Blumenberg admits that there are "a few recognizable and specific instances" of secularization, which should in fact be described as "the *transposition* of authentically theological contents into secularized alienation from their origin."[94] His critique of the secularization hypothesis in Part I of the *Legitimacy,* therefore, is not intended to rule out the possibility of a continuity of content from one age to the next. Rather, it is aimed at showing that a great many of the modern ideas and attitudes that have been taken to be secularized versions of medieval forms actually are not. The reason why the secularization hypothesis seems so plausible, and has been so widespread in historical analysis, is that most theorists tend to assume that historical continuity *must* be explained in terms of a continuity of content. They assume that the only possible way to account for the emergence of a new idea or attitude in history is to explain it in terms of the appropriation or transformation of some pre-existing form or forms.

94. Blumenberg, *Legitimacy,* 65. Unless otherwise specified emphasis is in the original.

This assumption, however, severely limits the interpretive scope of the theoretician attempting to give an account of a particular historical constellation, because the explanation will inevitably confine itself to the identification of relevant "precursors" or "forerunners." Blumenberg's dialogical functionalism, on the other hand, refuses this interpretive limitation. It expands its range to include a consideration of the way in which certain ideas and attitudes may *prepare* for the emergence of a new conceptual form without themselves being precursors or anticipations of it. They may do so, for example, by undermining theoretical assumptions that stand in the way of the adoption of the new form. Blumenberg's method also gives careful attention to the role of *functional* continuity (reoccupation) in historical transition. That is, it attends to the way in which new forms of self- and world-interpretation may be used in order to provide new answers to the carry-over questions of an earlier age, once the traditional answers are no longer workable.

It is certainly possible, however, for a carry-over question to be answered in a new way, but by transforming the content of a traditional concept or conceptual scheme and applying it in this new and unexpected context. This is precisely what Blumenberg thinks happened in the transition from late antiquity to the Middle Ages. Here, he argues, the carry-over question of the origin of evil was answered by Augustine in a new way that "translated" Gnostic dualism into the separation of the elect from the rejected in the doctrine of predestination.

In his zeal to refute the secularization theorists and to defend the originality of modern concepts like progress in knowledge and the autonomy of reason, however, Blumenberg fails to recognize the extent to which, in the transition to modernity, traditional medieval concepts are transformed and utilized in order to answer inherited carry-over questions to which new answers have become due. In what follows I will show that transformations in late medieval ontology led to the demand for a new answer to the question: what is the measure for human knowledge? This carry-over question was then answered by utilizing conceptual tools developed in the Neoplatonic tradition. Hence, I will argue for more continuity of "content" between the medieval and the modern age than Blumenberg is willing to admit. However, I view this continuity—from within the context of his own dialogical reading of epochal transition—as the innovative transformation of a traditional conceptual scheme in order to answer a "carry-over question" in a *new* way.

Let us turn first, then, to a consideration of Blumenberg's reading of the emergence of modern worldliness, which, indeed, offers rich and original insights into the nature of the epochal threshold.

[IV]

Worldliness as the "Signature of the Modern Age"

On Blumenberg's reading, it took several centuries—the long working through of the Middle Ages—for the contradictions which were already inherent in Augustinian theology to come to a head. The sublimated, or "transposed," Gnosticism was responsible for humanity's long resignation in the face of a hostile and painful reality for which mankind had only itself to blame.[95] Any attempt to fundamentally transform the world, to use our knowledge of nature in order to radically "re-make" it in a human image, could only appear as a hubristic act. That human reason was ever put to work to control and radically transform the natural order has its prerequisite, Blumenberg insists, in a new understanding of the nature of reality itself.

Blumenberg holds that the turn to active, reconstructive engagement in the world so characteristic of the modern age was first made possible—indeed, was impelled—by a fundamental shift in the character of the world's significance for humanity at the end of the Middle Ages.

95. In response to the question of why self-assertion did not emerge in antiquity, Blumenberg replies that "only after nominalism had executed a sufficiently radical destruction of the humanly relevant and dependable cosmos could the mechanistic philosophy of nature be adopted as the tool of self-assertion" (Blumenberg, *Legitimacy*, 154). For the Greeks the postulate of *ataraxia*—intraworldly composure of mind, the self-sufficient life—was still a possible alternative.

> A 'disappearance of order' [*'Ordnungsschwund'*], causing doubt regarding the existence of a structure of reality that can be related to man, is the presupposition of a general conception of human activity that no longer perceives in given states of affairs the binding character of the ancient and medieval cosmos, and consequently holds them to be, in principle, at man's disposal. . . . The reality that at the end of the Middle Ages comes to be seen as 'fact' [*factum:* something done or made, i.e., a contingent state of affairs] provokes the will to oppose it and concentrates the will's attention upon it.[96]

The modern turn to a self-assertive, self-realizing stance in the world thus presupposes the "facticity of reality" concomitant upon the loss of a cosmos teleologically ordered to human needs. Blumenberg, in turn, traces this *Ordnungsschwund* to the theological absolutism of late medieval nominalism.

Scholars have long recognized an important connection between late medieval nominalism and the emergence of the new science, but this connection has generally been spelled out in terms of the contributions made in the *natural* philosophy of William of Ockham, Nicole Oresme, Nicolas of Autrecourt, and others. Indeed, much excellent work has been done on the way in which nominalist theories of motion, space, matter, and so on anticipate or prepare the way for the new science of Galileo, Kepler, and Newton.[97] While Blumenberg gives some attention to these late medieval anticipations of modern physical theories, he interprets their significance within a broader consideration of the *metaphysical* foundations of modern science laid down by nominalist theological speculation.[98]

96. Ibid., 137–38.

97. See, especially, Anneliese Maier, *Studien zur Naturphilosophie der Spätscholastik, I: Die Vorläufer Galileis im 14. Jahrhundert. II: Zwei Grundprobleme der scholastischen Naturphilosophie. III: An der Grenze von Scholastik und Naturwissenschaft. IV: Metaphysische Hintergründe der scholastischen Naturphilosophie. V: Zwischen Philosophie und Mechanik.* Storia e letteratura 22, 37, 41, 52, 69. 2d ed. (Rome: Edizioni di Storia e letteratura, 1951–1966); Edward Grant, *Much Ado about Nothing: Theories of Space and Vacuum from the Middle Ages to the Scientific Revolution* (Cambridge and New York: Cambridge University Press, 1981) and *A Source Book in Medieval Science* (Cambridge: Harvard University Press, 1974); and Marshall Clagett, *The Science of Mechanics in the Middle Ages* (Madison: University of Wisconsin Press, 1961).

98. Amos Funkenstein (*Theology and the Scientific Imagination: From the Middle Ages to the Seventeenth Century* [Princeton: Princeton University Press, 1986]) has recently turned attention to the role of nominalist theology in providing metaphysical foundations for modern

THEOLOGICAL ABSOLUTISM AND THE DISAPPEARANCE OF THE TRADITIONAL WORLD ORDER

In the wake of the Condemnation of 1277,[99] nominalist theologians of the fourteenth century were concerned to defend the doctrine of divine freedom from any apparent "necessities" philosophically derived from the order of nature. God's absolutely free will was posited as *the* fundamental theological premise, and God's omnipotence was elevated to the rank of the primary divine attribute. This intensifying of the attribute of divine omnipotence had a destructive effect on the medieval cosmos, as the created world came to be grasped by the nominalists as the expression *not* primarily of God's goodness or of his wisdom, but first and foremost of his absolute power.[100] The result was a world whose underlying aspect was no longer its beauty and order, or its rational intelligibility, but its utter facticity, its radically contingent existence as the immediate result of an absolute will.

---

science. Funkenstein describes the transition from medieval to modern world-views as a gradual migration and transformation of the divine predicates of omnipresence, omnipotence, and providence from God to the world. Funkenstein, however, does not attempt to provide a philosophical *explanation* for the cosmological shift that he describes. This is precisely what Blumenberg's reading attempts in the *Legitimacy*. For a critical response to Blumenberg's reading, see Louis Dupré, *Passage to Modernity: an Essay in the Hermeneutics of Nature and Culture* (New Haven and London: Yale University Press, 1993). See also Jürgen Goldstein's (*Nominalismus und Moderne: Zur Konstitution neuzeitlicher Subjektivität bei Hans Blumenberg und Wilhelm von Ockham* [Freiburg/Munich: Verlag Karl Alber, 1998]) recent critique of Blumenberg's reading nominalism's role in the transition to modernity. Goldstein argues, through a philosophical reinterpretation of Ockham, that the modern subject was founded by nominalism and not in opposition to it.

99. See J. Wippel, "The Condemnations of 1270 and 1277 at Paris," *Journal of Medieval and Renaissance Studies* 7 (1977): 169–201; Edward Grant, "The Condemnation of 1277: God's Absolute Power and Physical Thought in the Middle Ages," *Viator* 10 (1979): 211–44; and Blumenberg, *Legitimacy*, 160–62, 346.

100. Thomas Aquinas had already concluded that God's goodness does not direct his creative act, since divine goodness is not in need of anything, and Duns Scotus argued further that God's will must have primacy even over his wisdom. This was the line, of course, followed by William of Ockham and later nominalists. See Aquinas, *De potentia* q.3 a.17; and Duns Scotus, *Ordinatio* 1 d.39 q.u. n.14. See Funkenstein, *Theology and Scientific Imagination*, 131–32. For an alternative reading see Marilyn McCord Adams, "Divine Omnipotence and the Charge of Theologism," vol. 2, chap. 29 in *William Ockham* (Notre Dame: University of Notre Dame Press, 1987), 1233–55.

Blumenberg's reading here is insightful and deserves to be spelled out in a bit more detail. To this end, it will perhaps be helpful to note briefly a few of the central philosophical positions held by William of Ockham (ca. 1290–1349) on the premise of divine omnipotence:

1. God's will is bound only by the principle of non-contradiction. For him anything is possible as long as it does not involve a contradiction.[101]

2. The primary cause (God) can do anything a secondary cause can do. Thus, no event or act at any time determines the next by any intrinsic necessity. At any time God is capable of interrupting the "natural" causal sequence of events and himself directly producing any given effect.[102]

3. Essence and existence can't be separated. If they could be, the essences would constitute an intermediate realm between individuals and God, but nothing mediates between God and the world as he wills it. Every individual is newly created *ex nihilo,* the original and immediate result of God's absolute willing.[103]

4. Each and every entity can exist independently of every other entity by divine power. God can create or destroy whatever he chooses at any moment.[104]

5. There are no formalities existing in the individual of which the last one is the *haecceitas* (Duns Scotus' individual form). There is not intrinsic

101. This principle is, of course, not original to Ockham and had been a commonplace of Scholastic thought since Anselm of Canterbury. It was the use Ockham made of this principle, to intensify the contingency of creation by narrowing what counts as a contradiction, that proved so powerful. See Funkenstein, *Theology and Scientific Imagination,* 127–28.

102. See for example, Ockham, *Quodlibeta* 6, q. 6. Again this principle is not unique to Ockham. Aquinas held that everything which God does with the mediation of secondary causes he can also do immediately without them (*De potentia* q.3 a.7 ad 16); also, this principle had been insisted upon in the Condemnation of 1277 (Proposition 69). Ockham was certainly no skeptic, and he believed that, once chosen, the *potentia ordinata* will be observed. In fact the nominalists generally restricted their discussions of God's intervention in the causal chain to the requisite example of miracles, which presuppose as a backdrop for their exceptionalness the "normal" working of nature.

103. See Ockham, *Scriptum in librum primum Sententiarum Ordinatio* 1, d.2, q.4, D.

104. "Omnis res absoluta, distincta loco et subiecto ab alia re absoluta, potest per divinam potentiam existere alia re absoluta destructa" (Ockham, *Quodlibeta* 6, q.6, in *Philosophical Writings,* ed. P. Boehner, O.F.M., and revised by Stephen F. Brown [Indianapolis and Cambridge: Hackett Publishing Company, 1990], 26).

in a thing any "individual" form, "species" form, "genus" form, etc. Only individual things exist. Intuition of individuals is the foundation of all human knowledge. Universals exist only in the mind as names or terms.[105]

The world picture that emerges is one which is radically contingent on a divine will which is not "bound" by any rational order which would somehow "determine" his production, and which is immediate to each created entity. Amos Funkenstein is correct to underscore that "the difference between Ockham and earlier Scholastic thinkers is *not* that Ockham's world is more contingent than that of his predecessors," as Blumenberg's reading might at first lead one to suppose. "It is rather a difference in the *meaning* of 'contingent orders' and of 'things.'" Funkenstein goes on to explain:

> The radical change in the perception of the world that occurred between the generation of Thomas and that of Ockham is embodied in the latter's principle of annihilation. . . . "Every absolute thing, distinct in subject and place from another absolute thing, can exist by divine power even while [any] other absolute thing is destroyed." Thomas admitted that God could have created other worlds, but each of the worlds that God could have created, much as ours, is such that the singular things that inhabit it are necessarily bound by some mutual reference-structure. For Ockham all things are immediate of God. . . . That which cannot pass the test of being conceived *toto mundo destructo* is not a 'thing' *(res)*.[106]

Hence for Ockham God's omnipotence, understood both in terms of his creative and his destructive power, is immediate to each individual thing in a radical way never before conceived.

This also implies that the "natural" order of things is not a necessary order, but merely an ordained order. God's *potentia ordinata* (the way things are in fact at each moment) is thus only a particular expression of his *potentia absoluta* (God's absolute power to arrange the world however he chooses at any given time).[107] There is no limit to what is possible,

105. See Ockham, *Scriptum in librum primum Sententiarum Ordinatio* 1, d.2, q.7. See also *Ordinatio* d.2, q.8, in *Philosophical Writings*, 41–43, for his earlier position on the nature of universals as thought-objects; and *Expositio super librum Perihermenias*, in *Philosophical Writings*, 43–45, for his later position on universals as acts of the intellect.

106. Funkenstein, *Theology and Scientific Imagination*, 135.

107. For a history of the distinction between *potentia Dei absoluta et ordinata* see

and much that God *could* create he chooses *not* to create. This, according to Ockham, is what distinguishes free creation from natural causality. Only in the case of natural causation does the whole of the possible effect inevitably follow from its cause. Hence, an infinity of possible worlds corresponds to God's *potentia absoluta,* with the principle of non-contradiction acting as the sole limitation on the range of possibilities. And although the *potentia ordinata* represents the divine choice of one actual world, this choice cannot be rationally accounted for. The world is no longer the order of what is possible. It is not the expression of a divine cosmological plan. Individuals in this world are no longer instances or images of an ideal model, parts in an ordered and rational whole. The world ordained by God's unbounded will thus no longer presents itself as ordered to human reason and human needs. It is an indifferent and essentially arbitrary reality, indeed, one in which the term "reality" no longer connotes an order of being or a degree of perfection, but simply comes to mean "that which is the case."

THE TURN TO MODERN WORLDLINESS AND THE RISE OF HUMAN SELF-ASSERTION

The disappearance of a providential, teleologically ordered cosmos, in turn, opened the way for a new conception of man's place—or better, role—in this new contingent world of facts. The "bad" aspects of the world no longer appeared as the marks of a metaphysical principle or punishing justice, but rather as the indifference of the "facticity" of reality to human worldly needs.[108] It is Blumenberg's thesis that it was precisely this alienated and alienating quality of the world that opened up a new horizon of existential possibility: active engagement in the world aimed at the alteration and transformation of this now indifferent reality. This was, needless to say, not at all Ockham's intention, nor that of later nominalist theologians. On the contrary, the radical destabilizing of the medieval cosmos carried out in this school was intended to make the existential

---

Funkenstein, *Theology and Scientific Imagination,* 124–52. See also Adams, *William Ockham,* 1186–1207.

108. See Blumenberg, *Legitimacy,* 138.

choice between engagement in this world and hope in "the next" a foregone conclusion in favor of the "world to come."[109] Ironically, Blumenberg notes, the meaningfulness of that "choice" was blocked by the reappearance of divine omnipotence in the realm of individual salvation as well, where the doctrine of predestination makes the absolute separation of the elect from the rejected itself also a matter of absolute divine willing.[110]

> The escape into transcendence, as the possibility that is held out to man and has only to be grasped, has lost its human relevance precisely on account of the dependence of the individual's salvation on a faith that he can no longer choose to have. This changed set of presuppositions brings into the horizon of possible intentions the alternative of the immanent self-assertion of reason through the mastery and alteration of reality.[111]

In the face of the removal of concern for salvation from the sphere of meaningful human engagement, the facticity of the world became, according to Blumenberg, an irritation and provocation for a rehabilitation of theoretical curiosity[112] and a radical turn toward technicity. The perceived deficiency of nature vis-à-vis human needs became the motive force behind man's activity as a whole, and human "self-assertion" became the existential program of the modern age.

Self-assertion, here, is not to be confused with the basic biological drive toward self-preservation, which has always been with us. Self-assertion designates a new quality of consciousness and orientation to the world, as the scene of radical engagement and mastery, an orientation that first emerges in the modern age. It "does not mean the naked biological

109. Ibid., 151.

110. "[T]he concern for salvation was largely removed from the sphere over which man has disposition, the sphere of his free decision and just desserts. This alienation of the certainty of salvation from self-consciousness and self-realization was accomplished by a theology that traced justification and grace exclusively to the unfathomable divine decree of election, which is no longer bound to man's 'works.' Nominalistic voluntarism, with its central emphasis on predestination, make man's care appear impotent in relation to the requirement that one possess a faith that was no longer initiated by the autonomous summoning-up of human obedience" (ibid., 345).

111. Ibid., 137.

112. See Part III of the *Legitimacy,* "The Trial of Theoretical Curiosity," especially Chapter 7, "Preludes to a Future Overstepping of Limits," 343–60.

and economic preservation of the human organism by the means naturally available to it. It means an existential program, according to which man posits his existence in a historical situation and indicates to himself how he is going to deal with the reality surrounding him and what use he will make of the possibilities that are open to him."[113] Thus "worldliness" (spelled out in terms of self-assertion) became *the* characteristic of the modern age, according to Blumenberg, not as the product of secularizations, but as a result of the fact that it became all but impossible to "choose" the alternative of salvation.[114] In the struggle between the competing claims made on humanity by the world and by transcendence, Blumenberg holds, it was the world that was finally able to make the stronger claim.

The success of modern self-assertion as an existential program, Blumenberg points out, depended on the prior restriction and refocusing of traditional epistemological pretensions carried out by the late medieval nominalists. Confronted by the absolutism of divine omnipotence, "divine reason" could no longer function as a meaningful measure for human knowledge of the world. Theological voluntarism had thus necessarily humbled human epistemological pretension, so that *hypothesis* rather than *theoria* (contemplation) emerged as the appropriate theoretical attitude when faced with the mute facticity of nature. Since nominalist theoreticians still maintained the ancient and medieval cognitive ideal of truth as adequacy to "what is," however, they were compelled to resign themselves to the impossibility of conclusive demonstration in the science of nature. The emergence of modern science depended, according to Blumenberg, on surrendering the theoretical claim to *adaequatio,* and reconceptualizing theory *as* hypothesis.

Aristotelian physical theories, for instance, came to be regarded as

113. Ibid., 138. Just as Blumenberg distinguishes between self-assertion and self-preservation, he emphasizes the difference between traditional tool-making and modern technology. See 138–39, and 234ff.

114. Thus, against the secularization thesis, Blumenberg argues, "The modern age does not have recourse to what went before it, so much as it opposes and takes a stand against the challenge constituted by what went before it. This distinction . . . makes worldliness the characteristic feature of the modern age without its having to be the result of secularization" (ibid., 75).

possible, but not necessary, descriptions of the actual workings of nature. Other accounts had to be admitted as also possible. Hence, the possible world speculation that became so prevalent in fourteenth-century nominalism prepared the way not only for those who (like Copernicus and Galileo) were later to challenge the authority of Aristotelian science in describing the ordained order. It also helped to develop tools of reason that would be applicable in any possible world and which were adopted as the instruments of the new science as well: the *mathematizing* and *materializing* of nature.[115]

Nominalistic explanations of the world thus provided the structural framework, Blumenberg claims, for an understanding of reality which gradually came to be "reoccupied" by early modern materialistic and mechanistic explanations of nature.[116] Whereas the primacy of God's will in nominalism aimed at increasing the binding force of the factually given order over men, the modern mechanistic thesis, by contrast, "established the material substratum of the world as something meaningless in itself, and consequently as a potentiality open to man's rational disposition. The reoccupation that took place between the absolutes *will* and *matter* defined the world as that which is precisely not pregiven, as a problem rather than as an established state of affairs."[117]

115. See Blumenberg, *Legitimacy*, 164. On the mathematizing of nature, see Blumenberg, *Legitimacy*, 348–53. See also Funkenstein, *Theology and Scientific Imagination*, 28–29, 171–74, 311–15. Blumenberg views the atomism of Nicolas of Autrecourt, for example, as the systematic adaptation of a minimal theoretical position least affected by the thesis of divine omnipotence. Here the appearances of nature are due entirely to the changing constellations of identical atoms, i.e. to a minimal homogeneous material substratum. See Blumenberg, *Legitimacy*, 173. See also Blumenberg's discussion of the connection between voluntarism and atomism in the Leibniz-Clarke correspondence, 149–51. See also Funkenstein, *Theology and Scientific Imagination*, 57–72.

116. See also Margaret J. Osler, *Divine Will and the Mechanical Philosophy: Gassendi and Descartes on Contingency and Necessity in the Created World* (Cambridge: Cambridge University Press, 1994). Osler examines the transformation of medieval conceptions about God's relationship to the creation into seventeenth-century ideas about matter and method in early articulations of the mechanical philosophy.

117. Blumenberg, *Legitimacy*, 151. Blumenberg goes on in the same passage to address the question why the turn to self-assertion was not made in late antiquity from the framework of ancient atomism: "[T]he question why atomism could have this significance as the successor of voluntarism, but not in its original situation in the ancient world, leads us to a recognition of the irreversibility of this reoccupation: only after nominalism had executed a sufficiently radical

Since the actual quality of the world remained hidden from human reason, pure (qualityless, homogeneous) matter was postulated as the minimal substrate of nature. And since the postulated matter is meaningless in itself, it presents itself as a malleable substratum subject to human rationality and technical mastery. We may not know how nature actually operates, reasoned the early modern theoretician, but we can construct mathematically sound models which can accurately predict its behavior. The production of desired phenomena then becomes a (sometimes simple, sometimes complicated) matter of the reconstruction of, or artificial intervention in, observed processes.

In this way, hypothesis, experiment, and technicity become tools for human self-assertion in the face of a natural world that is not teleologically ordered with an eye toward human interests. Modern man takes it upon himself to make up for the perceived inadequacies of nature's products through productions of his own. This shift in man's theoretical relation to the world, from the blissful repose of the *vita contemplativa* to that of laborious reconstruction in the *vita activa,* is characterized on the one hand by surrender of the traditional claim to truth as *adaequatio,* and on the other by this new use of theory to "recreate" the world, this time in a human image. "*Hypothesis,* which from one point of view is the formal expression of the renunciation of the claim to truth in the traditional sense of adequacy [*adaequatio*], becomes from another point of view a means of self-assertion, the potential for human production of that which nature makes scarce or does not provide for man at all."[118] When God as measure becomes absolutely transcendent and so unavailable, the words of Protagoras are rehabilitated: Man is recognized as the measure of all things.

Blumenberg claims that modern consciousness is neither directed to nor sustained by a correspondence between our ideas of nature and what actually exists. Instead, our consciousness "depends exclusively on an immanent structure of harmony in what we are given."[119] Insofar as

destruction of the humanly relevant and dependable cosmos could the mechanistic philosophy of nature be adopted as the tool of self-assertion" (151). See *Legitimacy,* Part II, Chapter 3 for "A Systematic Comparison of the Epochal Crisis of Antiquity to That of the Middle Ages," 145–79.

118. Ibid., 199. See also 353.

119. "The question, then, which for the first time achieves its full clarity in Kant's philoso-

Descartes hoped to secure a guarantee of the correspondence between our "clear and distinct ideas" and the real, his very concept of reality, claims Blumenberg, remained tied to the medieval understanding of truth as *adaequatio*. It is only by virtue of his approach to certainty through the *cogito* that Descartes may be said, for Blumenberg, to fundamentally define the character and claims of modern thought. That is, Blumenberg locates the truly modern aspect of Descartes' thought in his reduction of the process of doubt to the final regaining of an absolute fundament in the immanence of the *cogito*. The evil genius appears in this context as a transformation of nominalism's *deus absconditus,* that is, as the embodiment of the requirements that must be met by reason in the face of theological absolutism if it is to find a new ground in itself.[120] The measure of human knowledge is now located within the human mind itself as a "principle of economy."

> Divine spirit and human spirit, creative and cognitive principles, operate as though without taking each other into account. The gratuitousness of the Creation implies that it can no longer be expected to exhibit any adaptation to the needs of reason. Rather than helping man to reconstruct an order *given* in nature, the principle of economy (Ockham's razor) helps him to reduce nature forcibly to an order *imputed* to it by man.[121]

Human classification is set over against the abundance of authentic reality, not in an attempt to prove itself adequate to that reality, but in order to project onto the "given" reality, the "human" reality to be *produced.* This is, finally, the position adopted by Descartes in his *Principles of Philosophy.* There Descartes grants that the scientist as model-builder can

phy," Blumenberg adds, "is that of the conditions of the possibility of this synthetic structure of the given" (ibid., 187).

120. Ibid., 184. For Descartes, although we may be deceived in our apprehension of reality, we are nevertheless free to withhold our assent to judgments we are inclined to make based on these apprehensions. "Under the enormous pressure of the demands made upon it by theology, the human subject begins to consolidate itself. . . . Absolutism reduces whatever is exposed to it, but in the process it brings to light the constants, the no longer touchable kernels. . . . The *ius primarium* [primary right], the primeval right to self-assertion, becomes comprehensible . . . as the essence of the modern age's understanding of itself—that is, as the anthropological minimum under the conditions of the theological maximum" (ibid., 196).

121. Ibid., 154.

have no guarantee that his models of natural processes accurately reflect the *actual* workings of nature. But if they "save the appearances," i.e. give a consistent, plausible account, then they provide a "sufficient certainty for application to ordinary life, even though they may be uncertain in relation to the absolute power of God."[122]

On the assumption of an unlimited or even an indeterminate number of possibilities, the experimental verification of hypotheses can never be conclusive. Since nominalism had still maintained the cognitive ideal of adequacy, it had resigned itself to the impossibility of conclusive demonstration in the science of nature. This restriction lost its significance in the modern age, Blumenberg claims, because the early modern approach to knowledge of nature is characterized by a rational expediency directed at the production of phenomena rather than at a share of the truth possessed by God.

> As an instrument of self-assertion, theory has no need of the luxury of relating its hypotheses to—and taking part in—the truth possessed by divinity itself. The involvement with technique integrates theory and the theoretical attitude into the functional complex of the immanent teleology of human self-assertion, and weakens its—until then—irreducible claim to truth.[123]

Hence both the function and the nature of theory are radically transformed in the modern age. Theory no longer means *theoria*, it is no longer the contemplation of truth, no longer the vehicle for the reception of reality, where reality is the meaningful expression of divine wisdom and order. Once theory's essential and immediate connection to truth was broken in late medieval nominalism, it was freed up to be used as a tool of self-assertion. Theory directed toward nature had already become

122. René Descartes, Principle 205, *Principles of Philosophy*, in *The Philosophical Writings of Descartes*, 3 vols., trans. John Cottingham, Robert Stoothoff, and Dugald Murdoch (Cambridge: Cambridge University Press, 1984–91), 1:289–90. See also Principle 204: "[A]lthough this method may enable us to understand how all the things in nature could have arisen, it should not therefore be inferred that they were in fact made in this way. Just as the same craftsman could make two clocks which tell the time equally well and look completely alike from the outside but have completely different assemblies of wheels inside, so the supreme craftsman of the real world could have produced all that we see in several different ways. I am very happy to admit this; and I shall think I have achieved enough provided only that what I have written is such as to correspond accurately with all the phenomena of nature" (1:289).

123. Blumenberg, *Legitimacy*, 208.

hypothesis, and its adoption as an instrument of self-assertion in the modern age transformed *hypothesis* into a theoretical construct to be tested by manipulating nature in the experiment, and then applied for the betterment of human life in this world.

Once theory is identified with hypothesis in this way, however, it loses its status as an end in itself. For the ancient and medieval theoretician, contemplation of the truth was not a means to some further end, but an end in itself constitutive of human happiness and fulfillment. The modern theoretician, however, no longer finds fulfillment in the quasi-divine life of contemplation, but uses theory instrumentally as a means to world reconstruction.[124] "The [early-modern] investigator of nature," writes Blumenberg, ". . . had to reconstruct the connection between cognitive truth and finding happiness in a different way if, following Francis Bacon's new formula, domination over nature was to be a precondition of the recovery of paradise."[125] Again, however, as Blumenberg is quick to point out, the loss of the immanent value of theory (the bond between the contemplation of truth and human happiness) cannot be viewed as the *result* of theory's instrumentalization; rather, it is its precondition:

> Theory that can no longer be anything but hypothesis has really already lost its immanent value, its status as an end in itself; thus the functionalization of theory for arbitrarily chosen ends, its entry into the role of a technique, of a means, is a process subsequent to the loss of its status as an end in itself.[126]

Be that as it may, the functionalization of theory as a means to the reconstruction of reality clearly raises new and pressing problems for the modern age. What is to be the measure of our making (or remaking) of the world? What the measure of human fulfillment? Can self-assertion, as an existential attitude toward the world, ground meaningful human existence? It is to the problematic raised by these questions that I would now like to turn.

124. "The absolutism of the hidden God freed the theoretical attitude from its pagan ideal of contemplating the world from the divine point of view and thus ultimately sharing God's happiness. The price of this freedom is that theory will no longer relate to the resting point of a blissful onlooker but rather to the workplace of human exertion" (ibid., 200).

125. Ibid., 232.

126. Ibid., 200.

[V]

Arendt's Diagnosis of Worldlessness as the Hallmark of the Modern Age

Hannah Arendt would take issue with Blumenberg's reading of the "worldliness" of the modern age.[127] First of all, Arendt is critical of the general tendency (a tendency which Blumenberg shares) to identify the term "secularization" *(Verweltlichung)* with "worldliness" *(Weltlichkeit).* In fact, she argues, expropriation and world alienation coincide. Even if one admitted that "the modern age began with a sudden, inexplicable eclipse of transcendence, or belief in the hereafter [Blumenberg, of course, sees in the excesses of theological absolutism the foundation for the subsequent eclipse of transcendence], it would by no means follow that this loss threw men back upon the world. The historical evidence, on the contrary, shows that modern men were not thrown back upon this world but upon themselves."[128] Arendt points to the "most persistent

127. Blumenberg himself invokes Arendt at the very beginning of the *Legitimacy* (8–9) but only to bolster his argument that the "worldliness" of the modern age cannot be viewed as a simple recovery of the reality of the ancients (i.e. that "world" can't be understood as a historical *substance* covered over in the Middle Ages and then recovered in the Renaissance). He fails altogether, however, to use Arendt's analysis here as an impetus to question his own assumption that worldliness in some obvious sense is indeed *the* fundamental characteristic of the modern age.

128. Arendt, *The Human Condition,* 253–54. "Whatever the word 'secular' is meant to signify in current usage," Arendt writes in striking contrast to Blumenberg, "historically it cannot

trends" in modern philosophy since Descartes as demonstrating an exclusive concern with the self (as opposed to the soul, the person or man in general) and the attempt to reduce all experiences of the world and of others to "experiences between man and himself."

> The greatness of Max Weber's discovery about the origins of capitalism lay precisely in his demonstration that *an enormous, strictly mundane activity is possible without any care for or enjoyment of the world whatever,* an activity whose deepest motivation, on the contrary, is worry and care about the self. World alienation, and not self-alienation as Marx thought, has been the hallmark of the modern age.[129]

Arendt sees the roots of "modern world alienation" in a twofold flight from the world to the self (Weber's "innerworldly asceticism") and from the earth to the universe (the search for a *universal,* i.e. non-perspectival, non-earthbound, science).

Hence, Arendt would agree with Blumenberg that it is the mentality of *homo faber* (man the maker) which guides the new science, and that this mentality consists precisely in the relinquishing of the measure of truth as *adaequatio* in the modern reconstruction of the world. Arendt would be made uneasy, however, by the apparent readiness with which Blumenberg identifies the instrumentalization of theory with the modern theoretical enterprise as a whole, so that he reads "progress of knowledge" immediately in terms of modern self-assertion, that is, in terms of "the extension of the mastery of reality."[130] Indeed, Arendt thematizes the threat of world-loss that results from the elision of value in the theoretical commitment to universal objectivity guiding the new science, that is, loss of reality as it is given in concrete, context imbedded, meaningful experience.

Like Blumenberg, Arendt emphasizes that the modern age is heralded by a fundamental transformation of the traditional concept of truth and of

---

possibly be equated with worldliness; modern man at any rate did not gain this world when he lost the other world . . . he was thrust back upon it, thrown into the closed inwardness of introspection, where the highest he could experience were the empty processes of reckoning of the mind, its play with itself" (ibid., 320).

129. Ibid., 254, my emphasis. See my paper "Hans Blumenberg and Hannah Arendt on the 'Unworldly Worldliness' of the Modern Age," *Journal of the History of Ideas* 61 (2000): 513–30.

130. Blumenberg, *Legitimacy,* 499.

theory. The traditional assumption that reality is given to the human knower (i.e. that "what truly is" will appear of its own accord to the contemplative beholder, whose capacities are adequate to receive it) gave way to the conviction that only interference with appearance—indeed, only the doing away with appearances altogether—could offer any hope for a "true" science of nature.

Cartesian doubt, in its radical and universal significance, Arendt insists, was first of all a response to the recognition that nature does *not* give itself up to either the eyes of the body or to those of the mind; that being does *not* appear to the contemplative beholder and that, "In order to be certain one had to *make sure,* and in order to know one had to do."[131] Theory became hypothetical and had to be tested in the experimental process. Hence *homo faber,* man the maker and fabricator, came to the aid of the modern theoretician, who could no longer trust reality to appear to the contemplative gaze.

> Where formerly truth had resided in the kind of 'theory' that since the Greeks had meant the contemplative glance of the beholder who was concerned with, and received, the reality opening up before him, the question of success took over and the test of theory became a 'practical' one—whether or not it will work. Theory became hypothesis, and the success of the hypothesis became truth.[132]

Unlike Blumenberg, however, Arendt emphasizes that this standard of success is not tied to practical considerations of the utility or the applicability theoretical knowledge, or to the technical developments which might or might not follow in the wake of specific scientific discoveries. "The criterion of success is inherent in the very essence and progress of modern science quite apart from its applicability."[133] Arendt is quite right, here, to underscore the fundamental independence of theory from technicity, where Blumenberg is too quick to see in the appropriation of theory as a tool of self-assertion an essential connection between the two. Historically, Arendt is surely right to insist that the early modern scientist was guided first of all by theoretical considerations in the active recon-

131. Arendt, *The Human Condition,* 290. See also 273–80.
132. Ibid., 278.
133. Ibid.

struction of nature in the experiment. "It is a matter of historical record," insists Arendt, "that modern technology has its origins not in the evolution of those tools man had always devised for the twofold purpose of easing his labors and erecting the human artifice, but exclusively in an altogether non-practical search for useless knowledge."[134] Even Francis Bacon, the great early modern champion of human self-assertion, who had insisted that the "true ends of knowledge" consist in its usefulness and benefit to human life,[135] warned the scientist not to let his experimentation be guided by external standards of utility. By merely aiming at the production of useful "works," Bacon insisted, the scientist is acting as a mere mechanic, failing to investigate the underlying causes of things generally, and simply halting at a superficial investigation of particulars.[136] Only a methodical search for and commitment to the discovery of truth, Bacon held, would lead to a subsequent harvest of works useful to human life.[137]

Be that as it may, however, Arendt is quick to point out that the fundamental experience behind the modern reversal of the traditional hierarchy between contemplation and action lay in the conviction that the search for knowledge had to be grounded in action. "The point was not that truth and knowledge were no longer important, but that they could be won only by 'action' and not by contemplation."[138] Further, Arendt

134. Ibid., 289.

135. Francis Bacon, Preface to *The Great Instauration,* in *Novum Organum with Other Parts of The Great Instauration,* trans. and ed. Peter Urbach and John Gibson (Chicago and La Salle, Illinois: Open Court, 1994), 15.

136. Bacon, *Novum Organum,* Book 1, Aphorism 99. See also Book 1, Aphorisms 121 and 124.

137. "[F]irst, I propose a natural history that does not so much charm with its variety or gratify by the immediate fruit of experiments, as provide light for the discovery of causes. . . . For though I am principally in pursuit of works and the active part of the sciences, I am nevertheless content to wait for harvest-time, and do not attempt to reap moss or the green corn knowing well as I do that axioms rightly discovered bring with them hosts of works, not in ones and twos but thick and fast" (Bacon, *The Great Instauration,* in *Novum Organum with Other Parts of The Great Instauration,* 25). For a critical assessment of Blumenberg's reading of Bacon, see O. Bradley Bassler, "Theology and the Modern Age: Blumenberg's Reaction to a Baconian Frontispiece," *New German Critique* (Fall 2001).

138. Arendt, *The Human Condition,* 290.

would agree with Blumenberg, that this transformation in the nature of the theoretical enterprise was accompanied by a shift in the measure for the success of theory. Once truth was no longer "given" in contemplation, it had to be actively reconstructed as hypothesis, and then tested—again through more doing—in the experiment. The tremendous power of the theoretical reconstructions generated by the new science resulted from what Arendt metaphorically describes as "the discovery of the Archimedean point,"[139] the ability to reconceptualize our particular, context specific, earthly reality from a *universal* perspective.

For whatever we do today in physics—whether we release energy processes that ordinarily go on only in the sun, or attempt to initiate in a test tube the processes of cosmic evolution, or penetrate with the help of telescopes the cosmic space to a limit of two and even six billion light years, or build machines for the production and control of energies unknown in the household of earthly nature, or attain speeds in atomic accelerators which approach the speed of light, or produce elements not to be found in nature, or disperse radioactive particles, created by us through the use of cosmic radiation, on the earth—we always handle nature from a point in the universe outside the earth. Without actually standing where Archimedes wished to stand *(dos moi pou stō)*, still bound to the earth through the human condition, we have found a way to act on the earth and within terrestrial nature as though we dispose of it from outside, from the Archimedean point.[140]

Crucial here is the "distance" gained from our imbedded, contextual experience in the world, by the modern theoretical commitment to an objectivity which aims at the elimination of sensuously "given" reality as it appears, by reducing the multitude and variety of the concrete to universal patterns and symbols. On Arendt's reading, the conviction that man can know with certainty only what he has himself made[141] lies at the root of the modern understanding of mathematics as the model of certain and

139. Descartes describes his search for certainty in the Second Meditation on analogy to that of Archimedes: "Archimedes used to demand just one firm and immovable point in order to shift the entire earth; so I too can hope for great things if I manage to find just one thing, however slight, that is certain and unshakeable" (Descartes, *The Philosophical Writings of Descartes*, 2:16).

140. Arendt, *The Human Condition*, 262.

141. This reflects interestingly enough a conception of knowledge modeled after what was taken to be the immediacy of God's knowledge for his Creation, a relation not of correspondence but of identity.

transparent knowledge. Descartes, she claims, moved the Archimedean point into man himself. He chose "as ultimate point of reference that pattern of the human mind itself, which assures itself of reality and certainty within a framework of mathematical formulas which are its own products."[142] The search for a mathematical translation of our experience of nature may thus be seen as an attempt to ground our knowledge of nature on a secure foundation. "Here the famous *reductio scientiae ad mathematicam* permits replacement of what is sensuously given by a system of mathematical equations where all real relationships are dissolved into logical relations between man-made symbols. It is this replacement which permits modern science to fulfill its 'task of producing' the phenomena and objects it wishes to observe."[143] Even if one can no longer grasp truth as something given and disclosed to the human mind, the mathematical language of the theoretical reconstruction is itself transparent to the mind which made it.

Further, Arendt underscores, the modern turn toward experimentation as a means of checking theoretical hypotheses itself reflects the modern conviction that we can know only what we ourselves have made. In order to gain knowledge of the natural world, which is clearly not man-made, natural processes must be imitated in the experiment, and nature re-made, as it were, in the laboratory.[144] Hence, the element of making and fabricating is inherent in the experiment itself insofar as it aims at the reconstruction of the processes by which natural phenomena are produced. The modern turn toward experimentation thus reflects a profound shift in the interrogative orientation of the theoretician seeking knowledge of nature. The traditional contemplative questions of "what" or "why" something is, questions which focused on the intrinsic meaning

142. Arendt, *The Human Condition*, 284.

143. Ibid.

144. "The experiment repeats the natural process as though man himself were about to make nature's objects, and although in the early stages of the modern age no responsible scientist would have dreamt of the extent to which man is actually capable of 'making' nature, he nevertheless from the onset approached it from the standpoint of the One who made it, and this not for practical reasons of technical applicability but exclusively for the 'theoretical' reason that certainty in knowledge could not be gained otherwise" (ibid., 295).

and value of things, were left to the side in favor of that asked by *homo faber*, man the maker: the question of "how" something came to be.

Significantly, Arendt assumes, here, that earth alienation is a phenomenon that emerges as a result of the objectivization of reality in the new science. As we have seen however, Blumenberg has given a compelling argument that, on the contrary, late medieval nominalism had already transformed the value-laden medieval cosmos into a mute world of facticity, and that the emergence of modernity was characterized not so much by earth alienation as it was by the human response to an *already* alienated reality. It was the adoption of an active, self-assertive stance in the world that marked the shift to the modern age. The rise of the new science then, should more properly be viewed as an expression of this new existential attitude. But whereas Blumenberg focuses almost exclusively on the *origins* of this epochal shift in self- and world-understanding, Arendt's analysis attends specifically to the existential *consequences* of the rise of the principles and ideals of *homo faber* in the modern age.[145]

Indeed, Blumenberg is too quick to see, in his account of the *origins* of modern worldly self-assertion, an argument for the "legitimacy" of the modern age. Blumenberg has argued compellingly that it was not the new science which first led to the *Ordnungsschwund* which produced a mute, factical reality confronting humanity, and that modern science is not somehow to "blame" for the disappearance of the value-laden cosmos of the ancients. Nevertheless, as Arendt's analysis of modern worldlessness helps makes clear, the turn to self-assertion is itself attended by new and

145. "[A]mong the outstanding characteristics of the modern age from its beginning to our own time we find the typical attitudes of *homo faber:* his instrumentalization of the world, his confidence in tools and in the productivity of the maker of artificial objects; his trust in the all-comprehensive range of the means-end category, his conviction that every issue can be solved and every human motivation reduced to the principle of utility; his sovereignty, which regards everything given as material and thinks of the whole of nature as of 'an immense fabric from which we can cut out whatever we want to resew it however we like' [Henri Bergson, *L'évolution créatrice* (Paris: Presses Universitaires de France, 1948), p. 157]; his equation of intelligence with ingenuity, that is, his contempt for all thought which cannot be considered to be 'the first step . . . for the fabrication of artificial objects, particularly of tools to make tools, and to vary their fabrication indefinitely' [Bergson, p. 140]; finally, his matter-of-course identification of fabrication with action" (Arendt, *The Human Condition*, 305–6).

pressing problems. World loss is tied to the elision of value on the one hand and to the threat of epistemological arbitrariness on the other. Finding a measure for both "practical" and "theoretical" reason in an objectively reconstructed world of facts, then became a defining problem for the modern age.

LOSS OF MEASURE AND THE PROBLEM OF VALUE

As we have seen, the shift from the medieval to the modern age was characterized not only by the loss of the ancient cosmos, but by the loss also of the traditional function of and measure for truth. The elimination of contemplation as it was experienced in the ancient and medieval world led to the loss of the permanent and fixed measures which had traditionally guided human action and judgment. By making *homo faber,* man the maker and fabricator, the measure of all things, the problem of finding meaning and value in the newly reconstructed world became acute.

In the fabrication process, Arendt points out, it is the end which justifies the means. The means are utilized in order to attain the end, and it is the end that guides and justifies the choice of means. The problem with the utility standard inherent in the activity of fabrication, Arendt underscores, is that every end, once realized, may itself become a means to some further end in another context.[146] Utilitarianism, the philosophy of *homo faber* par excellence, is inevitably caught in the potential endlessness of this ends-means chain, and is itself unable to arrive at some principle which would justify its category of utility. That is, Arendt argues, utilitarianism is unable to make sense of the distinction between utility (the "in order to" of an action) and meaningfulness (that "for the sake of" which the action is done). "The 'in order to' has become the content of the 'for the sake of'; in other words, utility established as meaning generates meaninglessness."[147]

The only way to put a stop to this endless chain of ends and means and the meaninglessness which it generates, Arendt argues, is to fall back on the subjectivity of use itself and to declare the human subject, man the

146. Ibid., 154.
147. Ibid.

user and instrumentalizer, an "end in himself."[148] The problem with making mankind the ultimate end of utility, however, is that it robs everything else that exists—the whole of nature as well as the products of human activity—of its own intrinsic worth and independent value. "While only fabrication with its instrumentality is capable of building a world," Arendt points out, "this same world becomes as worthless as the employed material, a mere means for further ends, if the standards [of usefulness and utility] which governed its coming into being are permitted to rule it after its establishment."[149]

Arendt underscores that the issue at stake is not instrumentality as such, which is indeed necessary to build a world, but rather the generalization of the fabrication experience so that the standards and measures of *homo faber* become the ultimate standards for human life. The danger presented in the mentality of *homo faber* is its own lack of self-regulating standards which would curb the tendency toward the limitless instrumentalization of *everything* that exists.

Plato, Arendt argues, recognized and addressed this danger in his argument against Protagoras' apparently self-evident statement that "man is the measure of all use things *(chremata)*, of the existence of those that are, and of the non-existence of those that are not."[150]

> Plato saw immediately that if one makes man the measure of all things for use, it is man the user and instrumentalizer, and not man the speaker and doer or man the thinker, to whom the world is being related. And since it is in the nature of man the user and instrumentalizer to look upon everything as means to an end—upon every tree as potential wood—this must eventually mean that man becomes the measure not only of things whose existence depends upon him but of literally everything there is.[151]

148. Arendt notes that Kant's formula that every human being must be regarded as an end in himself, with which he had hoped to exclude the category of ends-means from the ethical and political realm, has its origin in utilitarian thinking (ibid., 156).

149. Ibid. "The trouble with the utility standard inherent in the very activity of fabrication is that the relationship between means and end on which it relies is very much like a chain whose every end can serve again as a means in some other context. In other words, in a strictly utilitarian world, all ends are bound to be of short duration and to be transformed into means for some further ends" (ibid., 153–54).

150. Arendt, *The Human Condition*, 157–58. Arendt notes that Protagoras did not assert that man is the measure of "*all* things" *(panton)*, as tradition has it, but specifically of things used or needed or possessed by men *(chremata)*.

151. Ibid., 158.

It is for this reason, says Arendt, that at the end of his life (in the *Laws* 716D) Plato replaces "man" with "the god" in the famous saying of Protagoras. Not man, but "the god is the measure [even] of mere use objects."[152] Arendt does not appeal to a god for measure, here, but she does see the need for appeal to a realm that transcends the rules that govern the ends-means mentality of *homo faber*. The tendency toward the limitless instrumentaliztion of everything that exists must be countered, Arendt insists, by an openness to our experience of the earth, and by the human capacity for thought and for action within the political realm—where "political realm" is understood broadly as the space of individual appearance with others. It is here, according to Arendt, that we must look for a measure of value and meaning which transcends the endless chain of ends and means generated by the utilitarianism of *homo faber*.[153]

Blumenberg is not altogether insensitive to the danger of world loss which haunts the modern turn to the active life of self-assertion, the danger that comes with the failure to open ourselves to the richness of our shared experience of the earth. He, too, senses the danger of abandoning our "geocentric" perspective for the objectivity gained by a universal science in the pursuit of the Archimedean point. He concludes his analysis in the *Genesis of the Copernican World*, for example, with the following remarks:

> It is more than a triviality that the experience of returning to the earth could not have been made except by first leaving it. The cosmic oasis on which man lives—this miracle of an exception, our own blue planet in the midst of the disappointing celestial desert—is no longer "also a star," but rather the only one that seems to deserve this name.
>
> It is only as an experience of turning back that we shall accept that for man there are no alternatives to the Earth, just as for reason there are no alternatives to human reason.[154]

152. Ibid., 159.

153. Thus it is not surprising that the "theory of value" emerges as a new field of philosophy.

154. Blumenberg, *The Genesis of the Copernican World*, trans. Robert M. Wallace (Cambridge: The M.I.T. Press, 1987), 685. For an all too brief but suggestive discussion of the need to determine the appropriate limits of the extension of technicity see Blumenberg's Introduction to Part III of the *Legitimacy*.

But does Blumenberg really provide us philosophically with an answer to the problem of finding a measure which would make such a return to *this* earth, the place of human dwelling, possible?

He would perhaps point here to the "modest" project of restricting our intellectual pretensions to those of a "sufficient rationality" *(einer zureichenden Vernunft)*. This phrase is a clever tweaking of the Leibnizian principle of sufficient reason *(Prinzip des zureichenden Grundes)*, where Blumenberg emphasizes the need to accept and embrace *human* (as opposed to divine) reason. It also underscores that the concept of rationality, which he embraces in the *Legitimacy*, is thought in functional, or better, dialogical terms. Sufficient rationality, Blumenberg explains, "is just enough to accomplish the postmedieval self-assertion and to bear the consequences of this emergency self-consolidation." As a result, he emphasizes, "The concept of the legitimacy of the modern age is not derived from the accomplishments of reason but rather from the necessity of those accomplishments."[155] That is to say, the rationalism of the modern age arose as a response to the problem pressure exerted by the theological voluntarism of the late Middle Ages. To the extent that it proved effective as such a historical response, and only to that extent, Blumenberg holds, it "legitimately" grounds the modern age. Yet Blumenberg fails to fully appreciate Arendt's point, here, that the standard of utility inherent in the self-assertive activity of modern theory and fabrication is itself fundamentally incapable of providing a normative measure for that very activity.

To rephrase the question in Blumenberg's terms, it seems that we are here confronted with a peculiarly modern problem, one that arises out of the modern conception of the human condition. Human self-assertion, while it may indeed represent a legitimate historical response to a crisis in existential orientation at the end of the Middle Ages, itself raises new and troubling questions. Hence, the "legitimacy" for which Blumenberg argues is actually quite modest. A more robust and positive sense of modernity's legitimacy can't be gleaned merely from the virtue of historical necessity.[156] Indeed, by responding to the carry-over questions which

155. Blumenberg, *Legitimacy*, 99.

156. Pippin made this same point when he suggested that Blumenberg might have done better if he had called his book "The Historical Appropriateness of Some Elements of the Modern

the modern age had inherited with its characteristic turn toward self-assertion, pressing new problems were produced, which demanded solutions appropriate to the new age. The modern age, I want to argue, then, is the age for which the need for measure becomes a radical problem, and solving (or trying to solve) that problem represents one of its most characteristic struggles.

If man is conceived of as *homo faber,* what will be the measure for his making? This question becomes particularly acute, Arendt points out, when considered in terms of the modern, contructivist conception of politics (Hobbes, Locke, Rousseau, etc.). The Enlightenment ideal of political emancipation would seem to be too empty of content to offer the sort of ethical measure (in the broadest sense of *ethos*) needed to establish a normative context, which would provide orientation for ethical and political judgment.[157] One of the central problems of modernity may thus be expressed as the problem of self- and world-*constitution,* where the possibility of self-determination is constantly in tension with the need to ground our political judgments in a shared conception of a common world. The temptation to seek an artificial closure, to collapse this tension would seem to lie at the heart of the totalitarian impulse.

If Arendt is right to view world loss as an inherent danger in the modern project of self-assertion (and I think she is), then Blumenberg's defense of modernity is only partially successful. More needs to be said about the consequences of the modern turn to self-assertion. This is not to imply, however, that the fundamental orientation of the modern age is then bankrupt. It is simply to identify one of its most existentially press-

Enterprise." "After all," Pippin remarks, "while we are nowhere yet close to realizing, to thinking through to the end, what it means for the 'scientific image' to be the dominant force in 'official culture,' we do know that there are several possible implications of that centrality that have to be assessed (because we must decide whether to pursue them or not). These are vast issues in politics, law, medicine, education, and many other areas. In that context, when the full implications of the modern project are considered, it does not seem helpful to hear that modernity is legitimate *because* of its resolution of late scholastic contradictions." (Pippin, "Modernity Problem," 555–56).

157. Michael Halberstam, for example, has argued (*Totalitarianism and the Modern Conception of Politics* [New Haven: Yale University Press, 1999]) that the modern phenomenon of totalitarianism may be viewed as a response to the "loss of world" and the threat of a descent into nihilism occasioned by the critical project of *political* "self-assertion," or emancipation.

ing questions. Recent ethical and political theories which make appeal to the productive imagination, to a *sensus communis,* to reflective judgment, to the encounter of the other, or to the dialogic structure of narrative, may all be viewed as attempts to respond to the problem of establishing an ethical measure in a manner appropriate to our present condition. Indeed, Arendt's own political philosophy may be seen in precisely this light.

By applying Blumenberg's historical methodology to our current situation, we are freed up from the tendency to view modern world alienation as a sort of inevitable consequence of a "wrong turning" located somewhere in the historical past. The course of the development of the modern age is just as dynamic and dialogical in character as its origin. It is not unilaterally directed by a substantially determined content. The history of the modern age is not only the history of the development of the modern phenomenon of self-assertion, but also the rich, varied, and continuing history of modern attempts to arrive at solutions to the problems generated by this new existential orientation.

THE PROBLEM OF EPISTEMOLOGICAL ARBITRARINESS

Up to this point I have focused on the ethical or "practical" problems posed by the instrumentalization of theory in the transition to the modern world, in particular the problem of finding an ethical measure for human action and judgment. A directly related problem—which interestingly enough *both* Blumenberg and Arendt fail to address—arises concomitantly once *theoria* becomes *hypothesis,* the problem of finding an *epistemological* measure for determining the validity of human conceptual reconstructions of the world. Both Arendt and Blumenberg take for granted that progress in science not only is possible but has resulted in an astounding degree of technological mastery of nature (accompanied, Arendt would say, by an unprecedented loss of world). Yet, both grasp the essence (indeed the productive power) of that mastery in terms of the imposition of human conceptual schemes onto a fundamentally transcendent reality.

Arendt, we recall, spoke of the "reduction" of concrete phenomena to a mathematical order "by translating all that man is not into patterns which are identical with human, mental structures."[158] Modern science, she insists, aims at the reduction of all appearances through the force inherent in distance.

> Under this condition of remoteness, every assemblage of things is transformed into a mere multitude, and every multitude, no matter how disordered, incoherent, and confused, will fall into certain patterns and configurations possessing the same validity and no more significance than the mathematical curve, which as Leibniz once remarked, can always be found between points thrown at random on a piece of paper.[159]

Hence, Arendt argues, the mathematical description arrived at in this way does not reflect an underlying rational order inherent in the phenomena given in experience. It is not an order "discovered in nature," as it were, but one produced by the human mind and imposed from without, from a "universal" perspective which reduces all real relations in the multiplicity and variety of the concrete to abstract patterns woven about a mere collection of objects. The mathematical order arrived at in this way, Arendt claims, has no more ontological significance than the curve generated between points randomly scattered on a page.[160]

Indeed, Arendt insists that our ability to produce a mathematical translation of experience demonstrates neither the inherent beauty and order of nature nor the adequacy of the human mind for grasping the truth about that order. She categorically rejects the idea that the applicability of mathematics to the physical world indicates any sort of harmony between mathematics and physics, between mind and matter, or between man and the universe.[161] To the scientist who would point to technological achievements as concrete proof that science deals with an "authentic

158. Arendt, *The Human Condition*, 266.

159. Ibid., 267.

160. Arendt cites Bertrand Russell, here, who had insisted that if "it can be shown that a mathematical web of some kind can be woven about any universe containing several objects . . . then the fact that our universe lends itself to mathematical treatment is not a fact of any great philosophical significance" (Arendt, *The Human Condition*, 269). Arendt cites Russell as quoted by J. W. N. Sullivan, *The Limitations of Science* (New York: The Viking Press, 1933), 229.

161. Arendt, *The Human Condition*, 286.

order" given in nature, Arendt replies that this "demonstrates no more than that man can always apply the results of his mind, that *no matter which* system he uses for the explanation of natural phenomena he will always be able to adopt it as a guiding principle for making and acting."[162]

But doesn't Arendt move too quickly, here, from the fact that *some* curve can be found between random points on a page, and from the fact that we can always adopt our scientific systems as principles for making and acting, to the conclusion that the pattern discovered on the page or in nature actually resides in the mind and is imposed from a distance which disregards the immediacy and coherence of the concrete? After all, while "some" curve can be found, even between random points on a page, not any and every curve will do the trick. Indeed most will not. The points on the page themselves dictate what curve can or cannot be chosen. Similarly while it may be the case that we can always apply theories about nature to our action in the world, this does not mean that *all* systems are equally successful, either in their explanatory power or in the range and extent of their applicability. The Ptolemaic description of our solar system, for instance, would be decidedly unhelpful when planning the course of a Pathfinder or Voyager. The natural phenomena themselves dictate the "applicability" and "workability" of a given theoretical order.

Early modern theorists were well aware that the decision between hypotheses generated in the search for a universal, objective description of nature was inherently problematic; that any given phenomenon could potentially be explained by any number of equally valid hypotheses. It is for this reason that the early modern theorist turned to experimentation in order to counter this potential for arbitrariness in the application of a given hypothesis.[163] Arendt argues, however, that this recourse to experimentation involves the theorist in a vicious circle: "scientists formulate their hypotheses to arrange their experiments and then use these experiments to verify their hypotheses; during this whole enterprise, they obviously deal with a hypothetical nature."[164] The world of the experiment,

162. Ibid., 287, my emphasis.
163. See, for example, René Descartes, *Discourse on Method,* Part Six.
164. Arendt, *The Human Condition,* 287.

she insists, does not serve to connect theory with nature, but rather "puts man back once more . . . into the prison of his own mind, into the limitations of patterns he himself created."[165]

Once again, however, Arendt ignores the resistance that the natural phenomena themselves offer to these "patterns" which we create and apply in the experimental process. Her suspicion that the entire enterprise is hopelessly caught in a vicious circle, and that our results really have nothing to do with a genuine natural order, but "that we deal only with the patterns of our own mind, the mind which designed the instruments and put nature under its conditions in the experiment,"[166] would be immediately borne out *if* it were the case that every well conceived and executed experiment produced the desired result. Any experimental scientist, however, would be quick to point out that the "hypothetical nature" with which the scientist has to deal in practice is rarely so co-operative. There is a certain recalcitrance to "the material given" in experience. Concepts (however we grasp their origin) cannot be successfully applied arbitrarily, as though the world as it is given in experience were actually homogeneous material to be formed and reformed at will. Indeed, it is the very resistance of the phenomena to the arbitrary imposition of conceptual schemes which drives the experimental process.

Hence Arendt moves much too quickly from the observation, that the modern theoretical enterprise is grounded on the general premise that "we only know what we make," to the conclusion that we therefore know only the man-made, the "patterns of our own minds." In fact, the modern dictum that we know only what we make is an expression of the conviction that the way to knowledge is through making, that truth is not given immediately in contemplation *(theoria)* but must be won through active reconstruction *(hypothesis).* Concern with measurement and experiment arises precisely in order to counter the threat of epistemological arbitrariness, to answer the need for an epistemological measure for the truth of theory, by "checking" the validity of a given hypothesis against the resistance offered by the phenomena in question.

165. Ibid., 288.
166. Ibid., 286.

While Arendt, like Blumenberg, is right to characterize the epochal shift in our theoretical relation to the world from the *vita contemplativa* to the *vita activa* in terms of the transformation of *theoria* into *hypothesis*, both are mistaken when they insist that this transformation in the nature of the theoretical enterprise was accompanied by a fundamental shift in the measure of the success of theory. Both claim that in the modern age adequacy to "what is," as the measure of theoretical success, is relinquished in favor of a new criterion: the successful production of desired phenomena. Hence, both Arendt and Blumenberg view the experimental process as the testing ground for theory's ability to re-produce desired phenomena in the laboratory. "Theory," writes Blumenberg, "projects upon ['the *given* reality'] the reality *to be produced* and checks the latter, once produced, against it."[167] Arendt concurs. She writes, we recall, that in the modern age "the test of theory became a 'practical' one—whether or not it will work. Theory became hypothesis, and the success of the hypothesis became truth."[168]

What is missing from both accounts is a consideration of the extent to which the recalcitrance of the "given reality" serves as a measure for the success or failure of the hypothesis. Further, the "success of the hypothesis" becomes "truth" only in a provisional sense and is always subject to revision. Hence, Blumenberg and Arendt are mistaken when they claim that the measure of theoretical success in the modern age is no longer thought in terms of *adaequatio*. In fact the adequacy of theory to what is remains, in a crucial sense, the measure for truth. This measure, however, has been transformed into a purely *regulative* ideal, constantly directing theory, but never finally attaining that immediate unity of thought and being which had characterized the contemplative conception of truth. The successful hypothesis is always conceived of as provisional relative to the regulative ideal that is projected into nature itself, and experienced in terms of the resistance of natural phenomena to the imposition of theory. Once theory becomes hypothesis, truth is understood as provisional and

167. Blumenberg, *Legitimacy*, 200.
168. Arendt, *The Human Condition*, 278.

conjectural, and *progress* in science is determined (among other criteria)[169] by the relative responsiveness of theory to the recalcitrance of reality.

In order to account for the viability of this process, however, a minimal fit between mind and nature (a harmony of the sort too quickly rejected by Arendt) must be *assumed.* It turns out that faith in a *world*-immanent *logos,* an immanent structure of harmony in the content given in experience, is necessary if there is to be a science *of* nature at all. Norbert Wiener, the philosophically oriented mathematician and inventor of cybernetics, understands Einstein's dictum that "The Lord is subtle, but he isn't mean," to be a statement of just this faith.

> I have said that science is impossible without faith. By this I do not mean that the faith on which science depends is religious in nature or involves the acceptance of any of the dogmas of the ordinary religious creeds, yet without faith that nature is subject to law there can be no science.[170]

That law is precisely this world-immanent *logos,* which serves to ground concept-formation and safeguards the relative accuracy of human conceptualization. Concepts remain infinitely inadequate to the richness of objects "given" in experience. Recognition of this gap motivates our attempts to narrow it, so that our descriptions of reality (though never adequate) may be evaluated as better or worse. It is the very inexponability of reality, the infinite richness and unique nature of each individual, which both counters and grounds human attempts to "name" it.

By ignoring this way in which reality transcends our attempts to describe it and yet remains the measure of the relative accuracy of theory, both Blumenberg and Arendt fail to consider another central problem of the modern age: the need for measure, not only in the practical realm of human action, but also in the scientific pursuit of objectivity. Hence, I

169. A theoretical hypothesis will also be preferred because it is in keeping with generally accepted scientific principles and practices or because it exhibits certain aesthetic criteria such as simplicity or elegance. However, a hypothesis will be considered adequate only to the extent that it is able to account for experimental results, and a proliferation of experimental anomalies which run counter to scientific hypotheses or general scientific principles must ultimately undermine the acceptability of these theoretical commitments.

170. Norbert Wiener, *The Human Use of Human Beings: Cybernetics and Society* (New York: Avon Books, 1967), 262–63.

would argue against Blumenberg's and Arendt's assessment that Descartes' "modernity" consists solely in his approach to certainty through the *cogito.* His attempt to secure a guarantee for the correspondence between our "clear and distinct ideas" and reality by proving the existence of a non-deceiving God may be understood as an attempt to rationalize his faith in the attunement between reason and nature. The circularity of this proof may be understood as an unfolding of this cognitive faith, and the failure of the proof does not serve to discredit that faith so much as to make explicit the fact that this cognitive faith, while not itself "reasonable," is nevertheless a presupposition of reason. Thus the mathematization of nature characteristic of Cartesian science depends on an understanding of the essence of nature as *res extensa.* In this Descartes shares Galileo's faith that God wrote the book of nature in the language of mathematics. Without this presupposition even the Descartes of the *Principles* would be unable to claim that his scientific models are "well-founded" conjectures.

I have suggested that faith in something like a world-immanent *logos* (i.e. faith that the world itself exhibits a rational, law-like structure) is a necessary presupposition of modern science, that without such faith there can be no knowledge *of the world,* no science *of nature.* With the destruction of the old world-order, the ancient *kosmos* at the end of the Middle Ages, it became necessary to provide a *new* account of world-order. Blumenberg points to "the immanent self-assertion of reason through the mastery and alteration of reality." The new world-order would then be precisely that order *to be produced.* The measure of our knowing would no longer be the world with its *logos,* but the coherence, internal necessity and (most importantly) the utility of our conceptual constructs.

Such "epistemological utilitarianism," however, insofar as it is rooted in the mentality of *homo faber,* driven by the demands of the ends-means schema, has no answer to the problems posed by loss of value and the threat of epistemological arbitrariness. Faith in a world-immanent *logos* as measure, I want to assert, is an inescapable need of human reason (practical as well as theoretical). The integrity and richness of the individual person or thing, indeed of the world, of reality, is "given" in experience and is presupposed *by* experience, and remains the paradoxical measure of that experience. Paradoxical, because in our attempts to grasp reality we immediately run up against the paradoxes of unity and plurality, of totality and infinity. Each particular being presents itself as a coincidence of measure and boundlessness. The given experience is itself infinitely rich and every particular utterly unique. And yet the rose itself remains the measure of my naming it "a rose" only because it itself exhibits a *logos*-like structure, is already a determinate thing. Thus we must recognize the philosophical need for a principle of ontological determinacy which would insure the connectedness of human conceptualization and the world. Such a need is precisely that, a need. The positing of such a principle remains an act of (philosophical) faith, faith that nature is indeed subject to law.

PART TWO

The Infinite and the Problem of Measure

IN THE PREVIOUS SECTION I suggested that faith in a world immanent logos, faith that nature is subject to law, is a necessary presupposition of science, and further, that adequacy to "what is" remains in an important sense, even in the modern age, the measure of theoretical success. But theory, here, no longer means *theoria,* the contemplative experience of the unity of thought and being. It has become hypothesis, and the measure of its success has been transformed into a purely regulative idea. The successful hypothesis is always conceived of as provisional relative to the regulative ideal of adequacy, and is experienced in terms of the resistance of natural phenomena to the imposition of human conjectural schemes. Hence, progress in science depends in part on the relative responsiveness of theory to the recalcitrance of reality.

In order to tell the story of the origin of the modern conception of progress in science, much more needs to be said about the transformation of the cognitive measure of adequacy into a regulative ideal which directs the potentially endless pursuit of truth. In what follows, we shall see that the seeds for such a transformation are sewn in the late medieval Neoplatonic tradition, in which Meister Eckhart and Nicholas of Cusa stand.

In this tradition the infinite God is grasped as simultaneously transcendent to and immanent in the world. It is the (immanent) incarnation of the infinite in the finite that acts as the measure of my attempts to know and to name reality. The infinite as manifest in the finite world would serve to ground both our knowledge and our being and yet at the same time remain ever and elusively transcendent. In order to articulate this dual movement of the infinite, these thinkers make recourse to the "mystery" of the Incarnation, a move which Blumenberg considers a pre-modern gesture which hopelessly entangles theory in religious dogmatics. Indeed, he asserts that it is precisely the *possibility* of taking the Incarnation seriously which distinguishes the Middle Ages from modernity.[1] It becomes immediately clear that there is a religious and philosophical distinction to be made here. The fact that these late medieval thinkers made use of the dogmatic belief in Christ as the divine Logos in their speculations on the metaphysical nature of the infinite does not vitiate the *philosophical* import of their innovations. Clearly the notion of a world-immanent logos is far older than Christianity. It already operates as a metaphysical principle in the thought of Plato, Aristotle, and their followers.

What I want to argue is that re-thinking this world-immanent logos *as* infinite led to radical innovations in self- and world-understanding. When the Neoplatonic problem of the relation between the One and the many becomes, in the late Middle Ages, an extension of the problem of the relation of the infinite to the finite, the Neoplatonic notion of unity in the manifold is developed into an understanding of the incarnation of the infinite in the finite. Such a shift implies far-reaching ontological and epistemological consequences, which in turn contribute to the emerging shape of the epochal transition. By ignoring or dismissing the significance of this notion of the incarnate or immanent infinite, Blumenberg's treatment of the character and shape of the epochal threshold between the medieval world and modern world becomes skewed, and the adequacy of his reading of the history leading up to this threshold must then be brought into question.

1. Blumenberg, *Legitimacy*, 480.

[1]

The Infinity of God and the Universe

The pressing question of the late Middle Ages in Blumenberg's view —and here I would agree—is that of the relationship between the infinite God and his finite creation. As we have seen, for Blumenberg it is the tension produced by the single-minded emphasis on the infinite power of God in nominalist theology which led to an acute crisis in the self- and world-understanding of the late Middle Ages. On his reading the gap between God and man—traditionally bridged by the doctrine of creation in the image of God and by the Incarnation—was stretched to the breaking point when the infinity of God was understood first and foremost in terms of his absolute power and will. When salvation came to be experienced as a question of the seemingly arbitrary will of an omnipotent God, the dogmatic link supplied by the doctrine of Incarnation could no longer fulfill its function as an intelligible and dependable bond between God and man. Human "self-assertion"—that is, attention to self-realization of "this-worldly" possibilities—was (on his reading) the early modern response to the problem posed by this extreme form of theological absolutism.

In the wake of nominalism, so Blumenberg's reading goes, the ideal of the contemplative life gave way to that of the active life of modern world re-construction, *hypothesis* replaced *theoria,* and the traditional world order was radically transformed. Crucial for Blumenberg's reading of the epochal transition, here, is the role played by the *infinite* power of the nominalist God in the breakdown of the traditional *finite* cosmos, which in turn prepared the way for the emergence of the *infinite* universe of the new cosmology. This last marks, for Blumenberg, a decisive moment in the emergence of modernity. Indeed, the "epochal threshold" between medieval and modern is thematized in Part IV of the *Legitimacy* precisely in terms of the transferal of the attribute of infinity from God to the world.

The cosmos of the Middle Ages is a finite, well-ordered whole, a closed hierarchy, whose order and value (indeed its very being) is granted by an infinite and benevolent God. In the transition to the modern age, the world comes to "acquire" the divine attribute of infinite being, but only at the price of the destruction of this ancient order and the unmooring of humanity from its traditional place in the meaningful totality. Blumenberg remarked early on in the *Legitimacy,* "If anything deserved to be called secularization, it would be the way this divine attribute comes to be embodied in the world,"[2] and he devotes Part IV to a careful study designed to show why this is not the case.

"THE SUPPOSED MIGRATION OF THE ATTRIBUTE OF INFINITY FROM GOD TO THE WORLD"

At issue ultimately is how to interpret the late medieval / early modern process of the infinitization of the cosmos. Alexandre Koyré's study *From the Closed World to the Infinite Universe* provides what has become a standard reading of this process.[3] Here Koyré outlines the gradual process of the destruction of the medieval cosmos and the infinitization of the universe from the fifteenth to the eighteenth century. In this process the hierarchically ordered, teleologically conceptualized cosmos of the Middle Ages is replaced by a homogeneous, mechanistically determined "infinite" universe. In the new cosmology infinite, eternal, homogeneous space is filled with atomically structured bodies, in turn governed by universal, mathematically articulated laws.

2. Ibid., 79.

3. Alexandre Koyré, *From the Closed World to the Infinite Universe* (Baltimore and London: The Johns Hopkins University Press, 1957).

Implied in this shift, Koyré underscores, is "the discarding by scientific thought of all considerations based upon value-concepts, such as perfection, harmony, meaning and aim, and finally the utter devalorization of being, the divorce of the world of value and the world of facts."[4] Hence, Koyré concludes his study with the following observation:

> The infinite Universe of the New Cosmology, infinite in Duration as well as in Extension, in which eternal matter in accordance with eternal and necessary laws moves endlessly and aimlessly in eternal space, inherited all the ontological attributes of Divinity. Yet only those—all the others the departed God took away with Him.[5]

Blumenberg's reading of the epochal transition challenges Koyré's by now standard interpretation on two important counts. First, Koyré's discussion operated on the assumption that the divorce of the world of value from the world of facts is a consequence of the world-view instituted by the new science. Blumenberg has argued quite compellingly, however, that the reverse is actually the case. That is, it was the transformation of the ancient cosmos into a mute world of facticity in the theological speculation of late medieval nominalism which prepared the way for the emergence of the new science and the new cosmology. Secondly, while Koyré is comfortable with the suggestion that the infinitization of the universe may be viewed as a gradual process of secularization, Blumenberg of course is not, and he instead interprets the transition in terms of a process of "reoccupation."

In Part IV of the *Legitimacy*, Blumenberg situates the epochal threshold between the medieval and the modern world in that period which straddles the Copernican "revolution": the period between Nicholas of Cusa (1401–1464) and Giordano Bruno (1548?–1600). Like Koyré, Blumenberg views the transition between epochs as marked by the process of the infinitization of the cosmos. While Nicholas of Cusa in fact applies

4. Koyré, *Closed World*, 2.

5. Ibid., 276. This is an interesting conclusion, because it serves to underscore the discrepancy between medieval and modern conceptions of reality, that is, in what counts as an "ontological attribute." Koyré presupposes a modern conception of ontology here, which understands the nature of being in material/physicalistic terms. A medieval conception of ontology, on the other hand, would focus on the four transcendentals *(unum, verum, bonum, esse)* and their interrelations.

the attribute of infinity (albeit in a restricted sense) to the world in his metaphysical speculation on the nature of the cosmos, Giordano Bruno makes this notion of the infinite universe (now in an unrestricted sense) the keystone of his philosophy. Neither thinker, for Blumenberg, may claim actual responsibility for the "making" of the new epoch. The point is not to identify the "true founder" of the new world—epochal change is not rooted in this sense in any one thinker or event. The point is rather to distinguish the character of thought peculiar to each thinker in terms of its relationship to the epochal threshold. Thus, in Blumenberg's view, Cusanus (the cardinal) stands just before this threshold in his attempt to salvage the inconsistencies of the medieval world-view, and Bruno (the heretic) is triumphantly aware of having crossed over it in proclaiming the birth of a new age.[6]

Once again, the pivotal issue for Blumenberg is how to account for "the supposed migration of the attribute of infinity" from God to the world without resorting to the secularization hypothesis. That is, Blumenberg wants to show that the infinitization of the cosmos is not simply the *transposition* of an essentially divine attribute—not a surreptitious divinization of "Nature"—but rather a process of the *reoccupation* of "function positions" within a system of self- and world-understanding.

Indeed, as Blumenberg himself points out, this case has singular importance for the viability of his critique of the secularization hypothesis and the account of the epochal transition which he offers in its stead:

> If anything deserved to be called secularization, it would be the way this divine attribute comes to be embodied in the world; judged by its intention, this would undoubtedly be an act of expropriation, if the difficulties that arose in the heart of Christian theology as to how to distinguish between intradivine generation of the Second Person of the Trinity and the act of creation had not paved the way for the "reoccupation" of the Trinitarian position of the Son by the universe to the point of making it inevitable.[7]

Blumenberg's reading of the "epochal threshold" in Part IV of the *Legitimacy* is thus an attempt to describe the process of this reoccupation. That

6. Blumenberg, *Legitimacy*, 469.
7. Ibid., 79.

is, Blumenberg believes that he can demonstrate, in the thought of Cusanus and Bruno, "an identical fundamental system of elementary assertion needs, notions of the self and world, on both sides of the [epochal] threshold."[8] It is therefore at this point that he sees the possibility of illustrating most clearly his own reading of the transition from the medieval to the modern world as a process of confrontation and reoccupation, rather than one of secularization. I will question the adequacy of this reading by taking issue with his claim that the systems of Cusanus and Bruno represent homologous metaphysical "position frames," that is, that they share the same fundamental "assertions needs" and questions.

In particular, Cusanus recognized that the infinitization of the universe brings with it a new problem, that of finding a measure for human action and knowledge. Indeed, by making sophisticated speculative use of the distinction between Christ and the world, and by developing the Neoplatonic conception of the immanence of the infinite in the finite, Cusanus arrives at the notion of truth as a regulative ideal, which functions as a measure for our potentially unending attempts to better approximate reality.

A further and related difficulty with Blumenberg's reading of the epochal threshold is his failure to recognize that the "infinitization" of the cosmos which marks the transition from the medieval to the modern world was not strictly an *extensive,* or quantitative, infinitization into spatial boundlessness, but also an *intensive,* or qualitative, infinitization of the being of each particular entity. This shift in ontology led to a corresponding shift in epistemology, insofar as the infinitization of the real meant, at the same time, an infinitization of the knowable. In the transition to modernity, a gap was opened up between finite human concepts and the infinite richness of the natural world. The very inexponability of reality now demanded a new theory of knowledge. In place of *theoria,* in which the essential and determinate form of the world appeared to the contemplative beholder, *conjecture* emerged as the theoretical approach most appropriate to a reality, which could be adequately measured only

8. Ibid., 469.

by an infinitely rich conceptual scheme. Let me refer briefly to three examples of this development in Descartes, Leibniz, and Kant.

Cusanus' dual infinitization of the universe appears in a somewhat restricted form in Descartes. Like Cusanus, Descartes makes a fundamental distinction between the absolute infinity of God and the indefinitely extended cosmos. Indeed, Descartes reserves the term "infinite" for God alone. The extension of the world, the division of matter, the number of stars, and so on, he terms "indefinite."[9] In the case of these things, he says, we do not positively grasp the absence of a limit, "we merely acknowledge in a negative way that any limits which they may have cannot be discovered by us."[10] But for Descartes, the indefinite plays a crucial role in our attempts to arrive at knowledge of the natural world not only when we consider its spatial extension, or the question of the divisibility of matter, but also when we turn our consideration to the essential properties of particular entities in the world. Here Descartes distinguishes between adequate and complete knowledge of particular entities. "Adequate" knowledge of a thing is exhaustive knowledge of all of the properties of the entity in question. "Complete" knowledge of a thing on the other hand, is not exhaustive knowledge of the entity, but rather sufficient knowledge to recognize that a given entity is a "complete thing," i.e. a substance distinct from other substances. Descartes insists that only God can *know* that he has adequate knowledge of any thing.

A created intellect, by contrast, though perhaps it may in fact possess adequate knowledge of many things, can never know it has such knowledge unless God grants it a special revelation of the fact. In order to have adequate knowledge of a thing all that is required is that the power of knowing possessed by the intellect is adequate for the thing in question, and this can easily occur. But in order for the intellect to know it has such knowledge, or that God put nothing in the thing beyond what it is aware of, it would have to equal the infinite power of God, and this plainly could not happen on pain of contradiction.[11]

9. René Descartes, Principle 26, *Principles of Philosophy*, in *The Philosophical Writings of Descartes*, 1:201–2.

10. Descartes, Principle 27, in ibid., 1:202.

11. Descartes, Fourth Set of Replies to the Objections to *Meditations on First Philosophy*, in ibid., 2:155.

Descartes grasps the indefinite character of the natural world (intensive as well as extensive) as grounded in the limitations of the thinking subject. Leibniz, on the other hand, follows Cusanus in locating the intensive infinity of the particular entity in the being of the entity itself. While Descartes had held that we might in fact possess adequate knowledge of a given entity (but could never be sure that we did) Leibniz insisted that we could never, even in principle, arrive at an adequate concept for a particular entity in the world, because the analysis of its concept would inevitably be infinitely complex. This is because of the fundamental interconnection of all substances in the universe, which are themselves infinite in number. Hence, for Leibniz, the notion of any particular individual is so rich that the entire universe could be deduced from it alone. Indeed, every substance is a mirror of the infinite God, each in its own way. Each and every substance is an expression of the entire universe, each from its own particular perspective.[12]

Kant transfers this conception of the inexponability of the natural world to that of the work of art. In creating a beautiful work, the genius in effect produces an "aesthetical idea," an idea so rich, no concept is ever adequate to it. It is, Kant explains, the counterpart of a "rational idea," a concept of reason to which no intuition or representation of the imagination can be adequate. Ideas, in both cases, "strive after something which lies beyond the bounds of experience."[13] It is the inexponability of the idea that allows it to serve as a regulative principle, which at the same time checks the pretensions of understanding in its attempts to adequately grasp the idea, and also grounds the ambition toward a completeness which can never be attained.[14]

The intellectual prehistory of this modern conception of the inexponability of the natural world, and of conceptual adequacy as a regulative

12. See *Discourse on Metaphysics* (Section 9), and *Monadology* (n. 56), and his Preface to the *New Essays on the Understanding.* For an important discussion of Leibniz's views regarding the nature of the quantitative infinite and the status of infinitesimals see O. Bradley Bassler, "Leibniz on the Indefinite as Infinite," *Review of Metaphysics* 51 (1998): 849–74.

13. Immanuel Kant, *Critique of Judgement,* trans. J. H. Bernard (New York: Hafner Press, 1951), 157.

14. Kant, preface to *Critique of Judgement,* 3.

ideal, has its roots in late medieval Neoplatonic speculation on the nature of infinity. Hence, Blumenberg is quite right to emphasize the fundamental shift in the function and nature of theory in the modern age. He is also right to clarify the role played by nominalism in preparing the groundwork for the modern conception of hypothesis. He fails, however, to account adequately for the shift from the nominalist understanding of hypothesis, which connotes resignation in the face of the impossibility of ever arriving at truth, to the optimism of the early modern use of hypothesis as a tool in a progressive scientific enterprise which aims at the discovery of truth. In the modern age, adequacy to what is remains the measure of knowledge, but it has been transformed into a regulative ideal.

INFINITY AS A METAPHYSICAL TERM

In order to account for this shift in the measure of knowledge, it will be necessary to provide a far more nuanced and complex reading of the role of infinity in the epochal transition—and indeed, in the prehistory leading up to that transition—than Blumenberg advances in the *Legitimacy*. Consider, for example, the following passage, in which Blumenberg quickly outlines his understanding of this history:

> Infinity is an element of extremely worldly metaphysics that found its way into patristic and Scholastic thought by way of Plotinus's speculations. It burdened the medieval concept of God with a quantity of paradoxes that itself can only be described as infinite. The ancient metaphysics of the cosmos was consummated precisely by the success of Plato and above all Aristotle in eliminating the problem of actually infinite space and infinitely numerous worlds. The reappearance of infinity, now in a positive form, was destructive for the medieval Scholastic system above all through its combination with the concept of omnipotence, and had to be so if only because this system was bound to presuppositions of ancient metaphysics in the form given it by Aristotle.[15]

First of all, it is revealing that Blumenberg holds "infinity" to be a concept which belongs, properly, to the metaphysics of nature. "Is the space of the cosmos boundless or bounded?" "Is there one unique cosmos, or multiple or even an infinite number of cosmoi?" These were questions

15. Blumenberg, *Legitimacy,* 79–80.

posed in the ancient world, he notes, and answered authoritatively by Plato and (above all) Aristotle, who held that there is one finite and unique cosmos. Plotinus, Blumenberg holds, took this properly *cosmological* notion, and applied it to the divine One. Patristic and later Scholastic theologians (unfortunately) followed Plotinus' lead, here, and attributed infinity to the divine nature, and in so doing "burdened the medieval concept of God with a quantity of paradoxes that can only be described as infinite."

In other words, Blumenberg seems to imply, it was not so much the universe which appropriated the *theological* attribute of infinity at the end of the Middle Ages, but rather God who took on this properly *cosmological* attribute in late antiquity, to the lasting detriment of theology. By attempting to use this concept in an inappropriate context, Blumenberg implies, theology burdened itself with endless paradoxes, which ultimately came to a head in the theology of late medieval nominalism. The reappearance of divine infinity, in the form of God's absolutely unlimited will, had a destructive effect on the entire Scholastic system, including the Aristotelian assumption of one, finite cosmos. In particular, Blumenberg emphasizes, nominalism's dismantling of High Scholastic Aristotelianism cleared the way for the (re)emergence of infinity in the cosmological realm.

A careful reading of the history of the use of the concept of infinity will show that Blumenberg is mistaken in his assumption that "infinity" is a term which has its proper origin in the metaphysics of nature, and was only subsequently given a theological application by Plotinus. As we shall see, Anaximander had already used the term in both a cosmological and a theological context. And Philo of Alexandria had already described God as infinite, before Plotinus.

Indeed, the interpretive scope of Blumenberg's reading of the history of the metaphysics of the infinite is limited by this assumption, and it is indicative of his general tendency to think of infinity first of all, either as a quantitative term or as a term of privation, i.e. as the *un*limited or the *un*bounded. The term is used in many different ways, however, in the history to which Blumenberg alludes. Indeed, it is frequently intended as a qualitative term to indicate a principle of unity, perfection, or completion. While Blumenberg is well aware of this "absolute" conception of the infinite, he fails to attend to the way in which it is developed in the Neoplatonic tradition, and the significance of the manner in which this tradition associates and intertwines absolute infinity with privative and indeterminate forms. Indeed, it was Cusanus' sophisticated and nuanced reflection on the nature of infinity in its various aspects which led him to posit the (extensive *and* intensive) infinity of the universe.

Before returning to a presentation of Blumenberg's reading of the epochal threshold (in the next two sections of Part Two), and proceeding to my own revised interpretation (in Part Three), it will be helpful first to provide a more nuanced reading of the history of the metaphysics of infinity, which attends specifically to the question of divine infinity.

THE QUESTION OF DIVINE INFINITY

In Book III of the *Physics* Aristotle raises the question of the ontological status of the infinite. Is there or is there not such a thing as the infinite, he asks, and if so what is it?[16] He begins his discussion with a brief survey of positions taken by his predecessors. Here he distinguishes between those thinkers who attempt to treat the infinite itself as a substance or principle (e.g. Plato and the Pythagoreans) and the "physicists" who regard the infinite as an attribute of a substance (e.g. Democritus and Anaxagoras, who made the elements infinite in number). He also refers in passing to Anaximander, who identifies the infinite with the divine.[17]

Anaximander's Apeiron

Anaximander speaks of the infinite (*apeiron*—literally that without *peras,* i.e. without end, limit or boundary)[18] in divine terms. It is eternal and indestructible and exists prior to the emergence of concrete and individual powers. It is the *apeiron* which "secretes" the seeds out of which

16. Aristotle, *Physics* 3.4–7.

17. Aristotle, *Physics* 3.4.203A4–203B15.

18. See Charles Kahn's discussion, in *Anaximander and the Origins of Greek Cosmology* (New York: Columbia University Press, 1960), 232–33.

the opposing principles which constitute the world arise. It itself has no determining quality or form. It is the unbounded, inexhaustible source of living stuff from which all determinate things come and to which they return. Further, Anaximander seems to have understood the *apeiron* to be an enormous mass surrounding the whole of our world. As first principle it encompasses the world in space as well as in time. There has been much discussion as to whether or not Anaximander thought of the *apeiron* as stretching out endlessly in space.[19] Cornford, for example, has suggested that Anaximander may have conceived of his *apeiron* as a vast sphere. In this case the term *apeiron* would signify the absence of any internal boundaries or distinctions.[20]

Pre-cosmic Chaos in Plato's Timaeus

The indeterminate, formless receptacle in Plato's *Timaeus,* the "mother" of all created, sensible things,[21] preserves something of the cosmological function of Anaximander's *apeiron,* but not its divine status. This is accorded rather to the intelligible Form, which provides a definite shape and articulation to reality.[22] The Platonic demiurge, confronted with a receptacle filled with unruly powers, a "tumultuous welter" of proto-elements, does his best to bring this originary chaos into order and harmony.[23] "But at first they were without reason/proportion and meas-

19. This would indeed be typical of the Ionian view of the universe, which descends from Anaximander. It further is retained in both Epicurean and Stoic cosmology. The finite spherical cosmos of Plato and Aristotle offers an alternative conception of the universe that may have its origin in the monistic philosophy of Parmenides. See Kahn, *Greek Cosmology,* 234.

20. See F. M. Cornford, *Principium Sapientiae: The Origins of Greek Philosophical Thought* (Cambridge: Cambridge University Press, 1952), 176–78. Cornford points out that the term *apeiron* was frequently used in Greek to describe both spheres and rings, with the idea that one can go continuously around them without ever coming to a bounding or distinguishing point, no beginning or end. Their surfaces are uniform in every respect. Hence, Cornford argues, "there is no objection to supposing that Anaximander thought of his Unlimited as an immense sphere. It is difficult to believe that any Greek would think of a divine being as of indefinite or strictly infinite extent" (Cornford, *Principium Sapientiae,* 176–77). See also Kahn, *Greek Cosmology,* 235.

21. Plato, *Timaeus* 51A.

22. Plato compares the receptacle to a mother, the Form to a father, and the nature generated to their child (*Timaeus* 50C–51B).

23. Plato, *Timaeus* 69B–C.

ure *(alogos kai ametros)* . . . altogether in such a condition as we should expect for anything when deity is absent from it."[24] Being unbalanced and dissimilar, the contents of the receptacle were in a state of constant disequilibrium, shaking and swaying about, so that the most similar "elements" were forced together and the most distinct forced apart. This haphazard sorting out of "opposites" was the nearest thing to cosmic order that could be attained from the purposeless interaction of dissimilar and unbalanced qualities or powers.[25]

This "pre-cosmic," chaotic state of generation actually resembles Anaximander's *apeiron,* the 'unbounded' mass out of which the cosmos was formed. The Peripatetics report that Anaximander believed an eternal motion in the boundlessness caused the "opposites," or contrary powers, to be separated out from it, generating the visible world. Plato's account, here, may then be understood as an implicit criticism of Anaximander's belief in the divinity of his *apeiron. Before* the heavens were made, Plato assures us, things were in just that condition which we would expect from anything "when deity is absent from it." It is the Demiurge, who (looking to the eternal Forms) first gave measure and proportion to the elements, forming them "by means of shapes and numbers."[26]

The indeterminate "receptacle" of the *Timaeus* has often been linked with the infinite or unlimited of the *Philebus:* "All things . . . that are ever said to be consist of a one and a many, and have in their nature a conjunction of limit and unlimitedness."[27] Here it is the infinite *(apeiron)* which

24. Plato, *Timaeus,* trans. Francis MacDonald Cornford, in *Plato's Cosmology: The "Timaeus" of Plato, Translated, with a Running Commentary, by Francis MacDonald Cornford* (Indianapolis and Cambridge: Hackett Publishing Company, 1997), 53A–B.

25. A. E. Taylor argues that Plato's description of this pre-cosmic disorder is an implicit critique of earlier physical theories: "The main point is that a multitude of such chaotic movements, without the direction of intelligence, could not issue in the formation of what we call an *ouranos* [heaven] or *kosmos,* a system which is in a state of equilibration *(isorropei)* and marked by the prevalence of periodic rhythms of movement" (A. E. Taylor, *A Commentary on Plato's Timaeus* [Oxford: The Clarendon Press, 1928], 352).

26. Plato, *Timaeus* 52D–53B. The "shapes" are those of the regular geometrical solids Plato posits as embodying the four elements. The "numbers" are probably the number of faces and angles of each shape.

27. Plato, *Philebus,* trans. R. Hackforth, in *The Collected Dialogues of Plato,* ed. Edith Hamilton and Huntington Cairns (Princeton: Princeton University Press, 1982), 16C. Plato, it would

receives form and definition, that is, *peras* (limit) and *metron* (measure).[28] Indeed, in the very late thought of Plato, a formless indeterminate principle, the Indefinite Dyad (the Great and the Small), acts together with the One (or the Good) to produce the World of Forms.[29]

Aristotle's Rejection of the Divine Infinite

In Aristotle "primary matter" comes to take on much of the role ascribed to the receptacle of Plato, as that indeterminate "stuff" which is capable of receiving a variety of forms. While Aristotle denies that there is an infinite amount of matter in the world—the infinitely large or cosmic infinite cannot be reconciled with his own conception of a unique, bounded cosmos—still he goes on to relate the infinite *(apeiron)* to matter. He does this by considering the relation of the infinite to the whole. The "physicists," he says, connect the infinite with the universe and the whole. And he says, "it is from this they get the dignity they ascribe to the infinite—its containing all things and holding the universe in itself."[30] But in this they err, for in relation to a complete magnitude (i.e. one with a proper form) the infinite is matter: a whole only potentially (i.e. when given form or limit). The infinite that Aristotle has in mind here (indeed the only sort he is prepared to recognize) is the quantitative infinite of a con-

seem, is alluding to the Pythagoreans, here, who according to Aristotle "thought finitude and infinity were not attributes of certain other things, e.g. of fire or earth or anything else of the kind, but that infinity itself and unity itself were the substance of the things of which they are predicated" (Aristotle, *Metaphysics,* trans. W. D. Ross, in *The Complete Works of Aristotle,* 2 vols., ed. Jonathan Barnes [Princeton: Princeton University Press, 1984], 987A15–19).

28. Plato, *Philebus* 25Aff.

29. A. H. Armstrong notes, "At the end of his life it appears that Plato came to think of the Forms in more strictly Pythagorean terms, holding that the nature of each of them could be expressed by a 'number' or mathematical formula, the Good, the first principle of all, being One; and he would seem to have analyzed out the ultimate principles of the World of Forms, again in a Pythagorean manner, as the principle of limit or definite number and the unlimited on which it is imposed, the One and the Indefinite Dyad (the number two, the first even number, and so according to Pythagorean ideas, infinitely divisible and therefore indefinite and unlimited)" (A. H. Armstrong, *An Introduction to Ancient Philosophy* [London: Methuen, 1947], 46). See also W. K. C. Guthrie, *A History of Greek Philosophy,* vol. 5 (Cambridge: Cambridge University Press, 1978), 428–35.

30. Aristotle, *Physics,* trans. R. P. Hardie and R. K. Gaye, in *The Complete Works of Aristotle,* 3.6.207A17ff.

tinuous magnitude, divisible *ad infinitum.*[31] Extension without definite dimensions is unknowable. It is like matter without form. Its "infinity" is merely a potential condition. Every actual magnitude is finite and has a definite length. It can be infinitely divided, just as primary matter can receive an endless series of substantial forms.[32] Thus the infinite is not to be identified with the All, as that which contains everything else, "but, in so far as it is infinite, is contained. Consequently, also, it is unknowable, *qua* infinite; for the matter has no form. (Hence it is plain that the infinite stands in the relation of part rather than of whole. For the matter is part of the whole, as the bronze is of the bronze statue.)"[33]

Thus, for Aristotle, infinity is the privation of wholeness and perfection. The infinite, as continuum, is by nature formless; it is the incomplete, the always outstanding. Thus he writes, "The infinite turns out to be the contrary of what it is said to be. It is not what has nothing outside it that is infinite, but what always has something outside it."[34] By contrast, the cosmos is finite because it is a "uni-verse," that is, a complete, all-inclusive, perfect whole.[35]

Aristotle's insistence on recognizing only the quantitative infinite (as that which can "go on" *ad infinitum,* e.g. division,[36] counting, etc.) makes

31. See Friedrich Solmsen's discussion of this passage in *Aristotle's System of the Physical World* (Ithaca, N.Y.: Cornell University Press, 1960), 161–65.

32. See Leo Sweeney's discussion in *Divine Infinity in Greek and Medieval Thought* (New York: Peter Lang, 1992), 4f.

33. Aristotle, *Physics* 3.6.207A24ff.

34. Aristotle, *Physics* 3.6.206B32–207A2.

35. Solmsen remarks, "Since both matter and the infinitely small must be contained by Form and cannot themselves contain anything, Aristotle is in a position to challenge the original concept of the Infinite. Anaximander was thoroughly mistaken when he described it as 'containing everything.' The Infinite, once the all-encompassing principle, has become the formless and the purely material; what originally was its strength—that it is nothing determinate or particular—has become its weakness. It exists insofar as it exists at all, below the level of full reality, in the Platonic as well as the Aristotelian meaning of the word" (Solmsen, *Aristotle's System,* 164–65).

36. For Aristotle any magnitude can potentially be infinitely divided. Because he denies the possibility of an infinitely large body, however, a magnitude can be multiplied *ad infinitum* only in a restricted sense: by adding the progressively smaller parts of one finite magnitude to another finite magnitude, that is, by dividing up the one *ad infinitum* and adding these pieces to another determinate magnitude. That is, Aristotle does recognize in this form of "infinite addition" the possibility of an infinite series converging to a finite sum. See, for example, *Physics* 3.6.206B3–12.

it impossible for him to consider the possibility of an infinite cosmos. That is, he tends to imagine an "infinite Universe" as if it were a Platonic-Aristotelian cosmos expanded to infinity, a move that inevitably leads to contradictions and impossibilities. He also refuses to take seriously the notion of a qualitatively indefinite first principle, infinite because all-encompassing. For Aristotle unity and totality must arise from a *formal* principle, a principle of determination. Reality is the actual, and the actual is the determinate and thus the knowable. In this he follows Plato, for whom the Forms, and later the One,[37] provide limit. What "is" *is* determinate and determined. Given this metaphysics, a pre-cosmic indeterminate, all-encompassing, divine first principle would be nonsensical. Hence, Aristotle follows Plato's lead in rejecting the association of divinity and infinity. Perfection implies completeness and completeness requires form and limit. Thus, not only did Plato and Aristotle move to exclude the attribute of infinity from the cosmos, as Blumenberg notes, they also moved (on similar grounds) to exclude it from association with the divine.

The One and the Infinite in Plotinus

Plotinus, on the other hand, while still maintaining a *formal* conception of Being, makes his first principle (the One) *prior* to Being. In doing so he makes the identification of the infinite with the divine once again possible.[38] Plotinus speaks of the One, or the Good, as infinite by the unboundedness of its power.[39] This infinity of power lies in its inexhaustibility and in its all-pervasive character. The One is the ultimate source of a ceaseless succession of recurring world cycles. Further, the power of the divine nature is omnipresent. Thus he speaks of the Divine Intellect as "universal power, extending to infinity, and powerful to infinity," and adds that "god is so great that his parts have become infinite. For what place can we speak of where he is not there before us?"[40] Or, "again, if we say that that [divine] nature is unbounded—it cer-

37. See Plato, *Parmenides* 158B–D, 164C–165C.
38. In this he was anticipated by Philo of Alexandria.
39. See for example Plotinus, *Enneads* 6.9.6.1–13.
40. Plotinus, *Enneads,* trans. A. H. Armstrong, in *Enneads,* 7 vols., Loeb Classical Library

tainly is not limited—what could this mean other than that he will not fall short? But if he is not going to fall short, does this mean that he is present to each and every thing? Yes."[41]

When Plotinus speaks of the inexhaustibility of the power of the One in producing infinitely recurring world-periods, he is using the term "infinite power" in the quantitative sense of 'that which continues without end' recognized by Aristotle.[42] In describing the divine nature as infinite by virtue of its omnipresence, however, the stress is laid once again on its all-encompassing character.[43] Omnipresence is here understood not in a spatial sense—being present at every point in space—but in a metaphysical sense. In his treatise *On the Omnipresence of Being,* for example, Plotinus describes the omnipresence of Divine Intellect as follows:

It [the Divine Intellect] is not like stone, like a great block of stone which lies where it lies and takes as much room as it is large, and cannot go beyond its own bounds because it is measured to a definite size both by its bulk and by the stone-power circumscribed in it; it is the first nature and is not measured and limited to a particular prescribed size; on the contrary, other things are measured by it; it is all power which is nowhere limited to a definite quantity.[44]

(Cambridge: Harvard University Press, 1966–88), 5.8.9.25–28. All translations of Plotinus are taken from this edition unless otherwise noted.

41. Plotinus, *Enneads* 6.5.4.13–15.

42. See, for example, *Enneads* 4.3.12.12ff. This form of attribution is similar to that used by Aristotle when he describes the prime mover as "infinite" by virtue of its power to sustain the eternal motion of heavenly bodies. See Sweeney's discussion of this use (Sweeney, *Divine Infinity,* 195–219). Sweeney argues that Plotinus' use of the term "infinite" in describing the power of the divine is strictly "extrinsic," i.e. it refers only to the power to produce an infinite effect, not to the nature of the power source itself. I disagree with this interpretation. True, the product of this power (endless world-periods) is infinite, but Plotinus clearly grounds this in the character of the power itself, which is both inexhaustible *and* omnipresent.

43. A. H. Armstrong notes that Plotinus uses the term "infinite" in a similar way of the lower Hypostases, the Divine Intellect (*Enneads* 5.8.9) and Soul (*Enneads* 6.5.9)—though not of the absolutely partless One. It is applied to them "in the sense of *to adiastaton,* complete and simultaneous unity, the state proper to eternal and non-spatial spiritual being in which there is absence of limit by division in the sense that one part is not *here* and another *there,* one does not exist *now* and another *then*" (A. H. Armstrong, "Plotinus' Doctrine of the Infinite and Christian Thought," *Downside Review* 73 [Winter 1954–55]: 52).

44. Plotinus, *Enneads* 6.5.11.8–15, trans. A. H. Armstrong, in "Plotinus' Doctrine," 52.

The divine nature is not circumscribed by anything else, but is itself the unlimited, immeasurable measure of all other things.

For Plotinus, only the One is absolutely unbounded, the primal source and measure of all else.[45] Just as Divine Intellect or Being is not omnipresent in the sense of occupying all points in space, the One is to be understood as all-inclusive not in the sense of being the sum total of all that is, but rather as the source of all that is. For "if he was all things, he would be numbered among beings."[46] But the One is prior to Being, that is to say, prior to all form or measure, prior to all determination. To borrow a description from A. H. Armstrong, the First Principle may be understood to be "infinite" or "unbounded" in the sense of being "without limit as being all-inclusive and so unincluded, immeasurable as having nothing outside to measure it and as being itself the absolute standard or measurement."[47] The One is the indeterminate, the all-encompassing source of, and first principle of, the real and the intelligible.

> [T]he One must be without form. But if it is without form it is not a substance; for a substance must be some one particular thing, something, that is, defined and limited; but it is impossible to apprehend the One as a particular thing: for then it would not be the principle, but only that particular thing which you said it was. But if all things are in that which is generated [from the One], which of the things in it are you going to say that the One is? Since it is none of them, it can only be said to be beyond them. But these things are beings, and being: so it is "beyond being". This phrase "beyond being" does not mean that it is a particular thing—for it makes no positive statement about it—and it does not say its name, but all it implies is that it is "not this". But if this is what the phrase does, it in no way comprehends the One: it would be absurd to seek to comprehend that boundless nature.[48]

Plotinus is able to reverse Aristotle's rejection of this notion of the infinite or indeterminate as all-encompassing first principle—while maintaining the link between Being, Form, and limit—because he conceives of the One as metaphysically prior to Being. Indeed, it is interesting to note

45. Plotinus, *Enneads* 5.5.4.13–14. When Plotinus uses the term "unlimited" in reference to things within the realm of Being, he usually uses it in a relative sense, speaking of things as unbounded in one sense and limited in another. See Armstrong, "Plotinus' Doctrine," 53.

46. Plotinus, *Enneads* 5.1.7.21–22.

47. Armstrong, "Plotinus' Doctrine," 52.

48. Plotinus, *Enneads* 5.5.6.5–15. See also 6.7.17.12–18; 6.7.32; and 6.8.9.37ff.

that Plotinus also refers to matter and to evil as "infinite" or "unbounded" insofar as they, too, are identified with a sort of formlessness or nonbeing.[49] But while the One is infinite because it is "above" being, evil and matter are infinite because they are "below" the threshold of being. As in Plato and Aristotle, the infinite is a negative term of privation and imperfection when it is applied to matter (and evil), signifying the lack of measure and form when these are necessary to complete the perfection of a substance.[50] Only in the case of the One is infinity understood in an absolute sense, as a mark of perfection and utter completeness. Indeed, by so carefully discriminating between the different forms of infinity Plotinus himself helped precipitate the eventual breakdown of the traditional Greek association of unboundedness and evil and so actually helped bring Greek philosophical thought into a form far easier for Christian theologians to assimilate and make use of than any that had come before it.[51]

Still, although Plotinus does speak of the One itself as infinite, he is rather reluctant to do so. He speaks without hesitation of its *power* as unbounded, or of the One as the Source of infinity, but prefers to express the infinity of the One indirectly in terms of "negative theology," denying that it can be defined in any way with our concepts or names, which necessarily limit or delimit that to which they refer.[52] Even the terms "the One" and "the Good" strictly speaking are misleading if taken in a positive sense and are meant only as a sort of negative designation of the fundamentally unnamable. The "transcendent" exists, says Plotinus, but can never be defined. Its definition, in fact, could only be "the indefinable."

49. On matter as infinite see, for example, Plotinus, *Enneads* 2.4.11.36ff; 2.4.15.1ff. On evil as infinite see, for example, 1.8.3.1ff; 1.8.6.32ff. See also Sweeney's discussion, *Divine Infinity*, 176ff.; and Armstrong's discussion, "Plotinus' Doctrine," 49–50.

50. Sweeney notes that infinity of a similar sort occurs even in the realms of Intelligence and Soul: "In the dynamic relationships which Intelligence and Soul have to their respective sources, initial intervals of comparative nonbeing or nonformation occur. Hence Intelligence and Soul are both infinite and finite—infinite insofar as each is without definite form and entity on the initial stages of its journey from its principle, but finite when each is completed and perfected by turning back to its source" (Sweeney, *Divine Infinity*, 219–20).

51. The "Platonic" or "Neoplatonic" heritage of many of the Church Fathers is something of an irony in the face of Plotinus' own determined anti-Christian attitude.

52. Armstrong, "Plotinus' Doctrine," 53.

[W]e in our travail do not know what we ought to say, and are speaking of what cannot be spoken, and give it a name because we want to indicate it to ourselves as best we can. But perhaps this name "One" contains [only] a denial of multiplicity. . . . But if the One—name and reality expressed—was to be taken positively it would be less clear than if we did not give it a name at all: for perhaps this name [One] was given it in order that the seeker, beginning from this which is completely indicative of simplicity, may finally negate this as well, because, though it was given as well as possible by its giver, not even this is worthy to manifest that nature.[53]

Plotinus thus radically departs from Aristotle by developing a notion of infinity that may be understood as a divine perfection. He is able to make this move because he conceives of his divine first principle as beyond (prior to) Being and Form and thus undetermined and unlimited by them. It is precisely by transcending any formal determination that the One demonstrates its absolutely perfect and unlimited nature.

The Infinite God and the Divine Logos in Philo

Philo of Alexandria, a Jewish Middle Platonist (born about 25 B.C. and dead by A.D. 50), actually anticipates much of the thought of Plotinus (A.D. 204/5–270), including this identification of the infinite with the divine. For Philo, God is infinite in a threefold way: as incomprehensible, as infinitely good, and as omnipotent.[54] Philo followed his contemporaries in holding that the infinite cannot be comprehended by the mind. Following the scriptural prohibition against likening God to anything in heaven or on earth, Philo holds that God is absolutely unique and so belongs to no class of universals. Thus no concept for God's essence can be formed. It remains unnamable and ineffable.[55] The infinite goodness of God follows

53. Plotinus, *Enneads* 5.5.6.26–35.

54. See H. A. Wolfson, *Religious Philosophy* (Cambridge: Harvard University Press, 1961), 5–11. See also Henri Guyot, *L'Infinité Divine depuis Philon le Juif jusqu'à Plotin* (Paris: Alcan, 1906).

55. See *De specialibus legibus* 1.32; *Legum Allegoria* 1.91; *De mutatione nominum* 11ff., and 29; *Quis rerum divinarum heres sit* 170. Philo holds that human knowledge of God is only a knowledge of his existence, not of his essence, which he asserts remains "unnamable," "ineffable," and "incomprehensible." Wolfson notes, "This distinction between the knowability of God's existence and the unknowability of his essence does not occur in Greek philosophy prior to Philo. In fact, in none of the extant Greek philosophic literature prior to Philo do the terms 'unnamable,' 'ineffable,' and 'incomprehensible,' in the sense of incomprehensible by the mind,

from the fact that he acts freely by will and design and for a purpose, and the fact that he exercises individual providence over human beings (as opposed to the universal and general providence of the Stoics). God is omnipotent because he created the world and its laws *ex nihilo* in a free act of will, because he can override its laws at any time and produce miracles, or destroy this world and its laws altogether and create another (though Philo is certain on scriptural grounds that he will not do so). Thus world order is neither fixed and unalterable by eternal necessity, as some Greek philosophers would have it, nor the product of chance, as others hold. For Philo it is the work of an omnipotent and providential deity.

Philo's thought is the first great synthesis of biblical revealed religion and Greek philosophy, and his writings had an enormous impact on Greek and Latin patristic theology[56] and so also on the subsequent medieval tradition. For Philo God is immutable, infinite, and self-sufficient.[57] He is the One, the ultimate ground of Being beyond all multiplicity, supremely transcendent. Creation is the result of a benevolent emanation or giving, in which matter is created and then given form and order, stamped with the mark of his Logos. The created world is patterned after the intelligible realm of Ideas, which are God's thoughts, the preexistent Wisdom or divine Logos.[58] Once created, the world is arranged in a great

occur as predications of God. . . . [Philo arrived at this view] by a combination of the scriptural teaching of the unlikeness of God to anything else and the philosophic teaching that the essence of a thing is known through the definition of the thing in terms of genus and specific difference." (H. A. Wolfson, "Philo Judaeus," in *Studies in the History of Philosophy and Religion,* vol. 1 [Cambridge: Harvard University Press, 1973], 66).

56. Certainly Philo's differences with the early Christians are no less striking than the similarities. See Harry Austryn Wolfson, *Philo: Foundations of Religious Philosophy in Judaism, Christianity, and Islam,* 2 vols. (Cambridge: Harvard University Press, 1962), 2:395ff. Still, the history of Philo's influence lies primarily in Christianity, and it is because of this influence that his writings have been preserved. See Chadwick's article, "Philo and the Beginnings of Christian Thought," in *The Cambridge History of Later Greek and Early Medieval Philosophy,* ed. A. H. Armstrong (Cambridge: Cambridge University Press, 1967), 157.

57. On God as immutable, see Philo, *De Cherubim* 19; *Quaestiones in Genesim* 1.93. On God as infinite, see Philo, *Legum Allegoria* 3.206; *De fuga et inventione* 8; *Quis rerum divinarum heres sit* 229. See Chadwick, "Beginnings," 142. On God as self-sufficient, see Philo, *De migratione Abrahami* 27, 46, and 183.

58. Philo, *De confusione linguarum* 63; *Legum Allegoria* 3.96; *Quod Deus sit immutabilis*

hierarchy, a continuum of grades of being, held together by the vital power of the now immanent Logos, which acts as the omnipresent instrument of God's providence. There also exists in the world, according to Philo, an incorporeal being created in the likeness of an idea contained in the Logos. This is the prophetic spirit of God, whose function is to serve as mediator between God and man. It was this Divine Spirit, for example, who appeared at the burning bush, and who dwelt in Moses and the prophets.[59] It is easy to see why Philo's doctrine of the divine Logos—as mediator between the divine infinite and the finite world of multiplicity—was readily adapted for use by the early Church Fathers.[60] As we shall see, this conceptual connection between the divine infinite and the world immanent logos will play a crucial role for Eckhart and Cusanus in their developing conceptions of the intensive infinity of the cosmos.

Divine Infinity in the Middle Ages

The Latin and Greek Church Fathers followed Philo and Plotinus in attributing infinity to God as a divine perfection. Both traditions understood divine infinity in terms of God's omnipotent, omnipresent, incomprehensible, incorporeal, and eternal nature. There is no limit to God's power as creator and sustainer of all creatures, and it is the ubiquity of his presence which confers being and life to the world. God remains conceptually beyond the grasp of finite, created intellects just as he transcends

57. Chadwick notes: "Philo is the earliest witness to the doctrine that the Ideas are God's thoughts. The notion, which is certainly earlier than Philo, that the Ideas are analogous to a human designer's plans, could naturally arise from a fusion of Platonism either with the Stoic doctrine of seminal principles *(logoi spermatikoi)* in nature or with the Aristotelian conception of the divine self-thinking mind" (Chadwick, "Beginnings," 142).

59. Philo, *De somniis* 1.69; *De vita Mosis* 1.66; *De sacrificiis Abelis et Caini* 8; *De mutatione nominum* 128. For a discussion of Philo's conception of the Divine Logos, see H. A. Wolfson, *The Philosophy of the Church Fathers*, vol. 1 (Cambridge: Harvard University Press, 1964), 177; and Chadwick, "Beginnings," 143–44.

60. For a history of the origin and development of the early Christian doctrine of the Christ Logos, see Wolfson's *The Philosophy of the Church Fathers*, vol. 1, chapters 10–18. See also his discussion in "Greek Philosophy in Philo and the Church Fathers," in *The Crucible of Christianity*, ed. Arnold Toynbee (New York: World Publishing Company; London: Thames and Hudson, 1969), 309–16, 354.

physical location in space or time.[61] The Greek Fathers, who remained more strictly Neoplatonic in their outlook, tended to view these characteristics as following directly from God's absolute transcendence of Being.[62]

With the notable exception of John Scottus Eriugena—who, under the influence of the Greek Fathers, held an almost wholly Neoplatonic doctrine of divine infinity—Christian theologians from the ninth to the middle of the thirteenth century appear to have shown little interest in the nature of divine infinity.[63] Indeed, some early-thirteenth-century theologians rejected the notion of divine infinity altogether.[64] After 1250, however, divine infinity once again became an important topic of discussion, and it was given a new interpretation by Scholastic theologians making new use of Aristotelian metaphysics. These thinkers followed their contemporaries in accepting Aristotle's conception of quantitative infinity with regard to lines, numbers, etc. They also accepted the Aristotelian view of the cosmos as unique and finite. They broke with Aristotle, however, by predicating infinity of God, as divine first principle, but they used a form of Aristotelian substance metaphysics in order to account for this attribution.

61. Augustine, for example writes, "What is in your mind and heart when you think of a certain substance which is living, perpetual, omnipotent, infinite, everywhere present, everywhere complete, nowhere enclosed? When you think of that, you have a conception of God in your heart" (Augustine *In evangelium Iohannis* 1.1.8, trans. John W. Rettig, in *St. Augustine: Tractate on the Gospel of St. John 1–10, Fathers of the Church,* vol. 78 [Washington: The Catholic University of America Press, 1988], 48–49). For a discussion of the evolution of Augustine's conception of divine infinity see Sweeney, *Divine Infinity,* chapter 17.

62. John Damascene, for example, held that God is above Being, transcends essence and so also knowledge. Divinity is thus both infinite and incomprehensible (*De fide orthodoxa* 1.4). See also his statement of faith, which reads: "We believe in one God: one principle, without beginning, uncreated, unbegotten, indestructible and immortal, eternal, unlimited, uncircumscribed, unbounded, infinite in power, simple, uncompounded, incorporeal" (John Damascene, *De fide orthodoxa* 1.8., trans. Sweeney, in *Divine Infinity,* 9).

63. Sweeney notes, for example, that the term "infinite" rarely even appears in lists of divine attributes in this period. Although it is occasionally applied to God's power or equated with eternity or God's incomprehensibility, nowhere is it discussed at length (See Sweeney, *Divine Infinity,* 9 and 321ff.).

64. These thinkers—referred to by the author of the *Summa Fratris Alexandri,* Thomas Aquinas, and Bonaventure only as the "quidam"—tended to use arguments which understood

Thomas Aquinas, for example, understood the infinity of God in terms of the "absolute subsistence" of the divine Being itself. That is, God's essence or Being is infinite by virtue of its freedom from the determining limitation of matter and potency.[65] Thus infinity, here, is a perfection tied to the pure actuality of divine Being. God's existence is not derived from without, his essence *is* his existence, and he exists in a state of complete fulfillment and realization.[66] Again, also for Aquinas, God's perfection and infinity are tied to his incomprehensibility: being infinite, God is unnamable (since every denomination is a limitation).[67]

Late medieval nominalists, following Ockham, exploded the traditional (Scholastic) balance of divine attributes (most importantly between God's goodness, knowledge, and power) which was still found in Duns Scotus, and grounded their philosophical and theological speculation in the primordiality of God's infinite power, his omnipotence. It is on the basis of this thesis of omnipotence, as we have seen, that Ockham did

infinity to be a strictly quantitative term (thus *only* God's power could be conceived of as infinite), and associated perfection with finitude and determination, or held that only the finite is knowable (and since the blessed in heaven are promised a direct vision of the divine essence, that essence must itself be finite). See Sweeney, *Divine Infinity*, 337–63.

65. Bonaventure argues for the infinity of God on a similar basis. In his commentary on *The Sentences of Peter Lombard* (1, d.19, q.3) he denies that there is matter in God. He notes that there are those who have argued the contrary. They claim that finitude in creatures comes from form but infinitude from matter. God, they assert, is infinite, so there must be a material principle in God. Bonaventure counters this argument by distinguishing between two kinds of infinitude: one arises from lack of perfection or incompleteness, and belongs to matter but not to God. The other kind of infinity arises from the absence of limitation, and belongs to God and pure form but not to matter. It is interesting to note that Bonaventure's distinction is similar to that made by Plotinus, except that Plotinus would never describe the One as pure form.

66. On God as Being and as thus infinite, see also Duns Scotus. Scotus starts by considering being and then deduces a first uncaused cause endowed with will and intelligence which embraces the infinite. Since this intelligence is identical to its essence, its essence also envelops the infinite: *Primum est infinitum in cognoscibilitate, sic ergo et in entitate.* (Duns Scotus, *Opus Oxoniense* 1, d.2, q.1–2, sect. 2, art. 2., as quoted by Etienne Gilson in *The Spirit of Mediaeval Philosophy* [Notre Dame: University of Notre Dame Press, 1991], 57.) Further, for Scotus, both God's essence and his attributes are infinite in their mode of being, and by virtue of this infinity are in reality identical. That is, God's attributes (infinite goodness, infinite power, infinite knowledge, etc.) are formally (or definitionally) distinct, but really identical. They are one and the same in their common mode of existence, which is infinity. See *Opus Oxoniense* 1, d.8, a.4, n.23.

67. See Thomas Aquinas, *Compendium theologiae* Cap. 20.

away with the whole hierarchy of forms and essences that mediated between God and his creatures. This move radicalized simultaneously the sense of divine transcendence (vis-à-vis human reason) and divine immanence (insofar as every aspect of the world is absolutely contingent on God's "groundless" will). Hence, divine immanence is no longer spelled out in terms of the inhering presence of the divine Logos or Reason in the world, but rather by the immediacy of God's inscrutable power.

Blumenberg focuses on the way in which the nominalist radicalization of divine transcendence served as a provocation for the "modern" turn to worldly self-assertion. It is my view, however, that it was an intensification of *both* God's absolute transcendence *and* his absolute immanence that proved so productive in the epochal transition at the end of the Middle Ages. Such intensification is evident not only in the nominalist tradition which follows Ockham, but also (in a significantly different way) in the Neoplatonic tradition of medieval mysticism in which Eckhart and Cusanus stand.

This latter tradition, while not uninfluenced by the "Scholasticism" of Aquinas and the realist and nominalist controversies which followed in its wake, formulated a notion of divine infinity from Neoplatonic and Patristic sources which tended to emphasize the omni*presence* of the One in the multiplicity which constitutes the universe. Here the Neoplatonic notion of unity in the manifold is developed into an understanding of the incarnation of the infinite in the finite. Each created being, for Cusanus, thus comes to be viewed as a "finite infinity," as the "contraction" *(contractio)* of the divine infinite into each unique individual. Perhaps most illustrative of this double intensification of divine immanence and transcendence in this latter tradition is the image of God as an infinite sphere, whose center is everywhere (God as ubiquitous) and whose circumference is nowhere (God as beyond any determinate boundary).[68] Of particular interest for my reading of the epochal transition to the modern age is, of course, the way in which Cusanus transfers this characterization of

68. For an account of the history of the metaphor of the infinite sphere, see Dietrich Mahnke's *Unendliche Sphäre und Allmittelpunkt: Beiträge zur Genealogie der Mathematischen Mystik* (Halle: Max Niemeyer Verlag, 1937).

God as an infinite sphere to the physical universe. The cosmos then comes to be viewed as infinitely extended in space (unlimited by a bounding periphery) and infinitely enriched in its many parts (the center is everywhere).

ABSOLUTE, INDETERMINATE, AND PRIVATIVE CONCEPTIONS OF THE INFINITE

It will be helpful to distinguish between the various "negative" and "absolute" conceptions of the infinite encountered thus far, in order to throw light on their significance in what follows. Blumenberg all too consistently fails to make distinctions between these differing conceptions, but they are crucial for my own reading of the epochal threshold. Insofar as the infinite is understood as indeterminate, unending, or inexhaustible, it is conceived of "negatively," as that *without* end, limit, or boundary. Insofar as it is understood as a principle of unity, totality, perfection, or completion, it is conceived of "absolutely."

The negative conceptions of infinity may be further distinguished into two broad categories: the indeterminate and the privative. The indeterminate, is precisely that which is *not* determined (*not* limited) by anything else. It is that which transcends all finite measure. It is that which is either prior to all form and determination, or else is simply lacking in form, being essentially formless. The *apeiron* of Anaximander, Plotinus' One, Philo's God, and the God of the Christian Neoplatonists are indeterminate in the first sense, and Plato's receptacle, Aristotle's primal matter, and the matter of Plotinus and subsequent Christian philosophers are indeterminate in the second sense.

The "negative theology" espoused by Plotinus, Philo, and subsequent thinkers is based on the *indeterminate* (and so "unnamable" and "incomprehensible") nature of the deity, or on the inherent limitations of a finite intellect. In both cases there is an implicit understanding of the incommensurability of the infinite to be grasped and the finite nature of the forms of the understanding.

The nominalist conception of God's omnipotence, spelled out in terms of an absolute will, unlimited or undetermined by the dictates of reason or a prior conception of the good, provides another example of a negatively defined conception of the infinite. Like Plotinus' One which is not determined by form in a prior ontological order, the absolute will is not determined to act by an intellectual or ethical order prior to and separate from it.

Privative infinity (that which continues endlessly, or without terminus) is also conceived of negatively. Here the infinite is that which always already oversteps any possible boundary. The notion of a continuous or continuing magnitude, divisible or progressive *ad infinitum* (e.g. a line or the series of whole numbers) is clearly of this sort. This is the notion of the infinite as the essentially incomplete, the always outstanding, that which can go on and on indefinitely. Anaximander's *apeiron* and the One of Plotinus both exhibit this quantitative or "privative" infinity insofar as they are conceived of as the inexhaustible source or wellspring of reality. There is no end or limit to their bountiful giving. Plotinus also speaks of the infinite power of the One, i.e. the power to produce infinitely recurring world periods. Aristotle's prime mover is infinite in this sense by virtue of its power to sustain the motion of the heavenly bodies over an infinite period of time. In the Middle Ages, God's omnipotence is sometimes similarly spelled out in terms of the power to produce an infinite effect. Duns Scotus, for example, understands God's omnipotence in terms of his capacity to produce an infinite number of beings; further, he describes God's intellect as infinite since he is capable of first of all conceiving of an infinite number of entities.

"Absolute" conceptions of the infinite, on the other hand, tend to grasp the infinite as a principle of unity, totality, perfection, or completion. Thus not only is Anaximander's *apeiron* understood as the indefinite and inexhaustible source of all things, it is also that which "contains everything," holding the universe in itself. Aristotle, we know, criticized the "physicists" for connecting the infinite with the universe and the whole. Since Aristotle is an ontological finitist, he holds this position to be absurd. The infinite for him can be a whole only potentially (that is, when given form or limit). Aquinas, in contrast, understood God to be pure act, and so he conceived of the infinite in terms of the absolute subsistence of divine Being. Here the term "infinity" is used "qualitatively." It is meant to articulate a certain intensity or fullness of being, a notion of plenitude, a state of complete fulfillment and realization. Thus Aquinas' conception of God's infinity is "negative" if considered in terms of its freedom from the determining limitation of matter and potency, but "absolute" when considered as pure actuality, where divine perfection is tied to the fullness of being and form.

For Plotinus, too, the infinity of the One is not simply a designation of indeterminacy. The infinite nature of the One is further conceived of as a true mark of perfection and signifies its utter completeness, its all-embracing nature. When Plotinus speaks of the One as all-inclusive, the sense is not that of being the sum total of all that is, but rather as the ground and measure of all that is. The inexhaustible power of the One reaches to everything and is everywhere present, not spatially but metaphysically, as the unifying principle of all that is. These "negative" and "absolute" aspects of the infinity of the One are intimately connected for Plotinus: the One is all-inclusive (absolute) and so unincluded (negative). It is immanent in the series of determinate, multiple entities as their source and measure (absolute) and so transcends the series itself—the ground and measure is not itself a being among beings or a form among forms, but is "beyond" the series of determinate things (indeterminate).

Even quantitative, or "privative," infinity is often thought of in the Platonic tradition as having its ground in an absolute infinity (usually connected to a notion of absolute unity). Plotinus' One is thus understood to be the *source* of unending world systems. (Neo)platonic conceptions of number and of time exhibit a similar structural relation between unity (as source) and multiplicity. Eternity is not unending time, or the totality of the temporal continuum; rather, for Platonists, time is derived from eternity as its source. Time is defined in the *Timaeus* as the "moving image of eternity."[69] Similarly for Boethius, and the subsequent tradition, the num-

69. "Now the nature of the ideal being was everlasting, but to bestow this attribute in its fullness upon a creature was impossible. Wherefore [the demiurge] resolved to have a moving image of eternity, and when he set in order the heaven, he made this image eternal but moving according to number, while eternity itself rests in unity, and this image we call time" (Plato, *Timaeus*

ber series is generated by the unfolding of unity. The emphasis, here, is on the One/Unity not as *beyond* multiplicity but as the source of multiplicity.

In another vein, Philo understands the infinite goodness of God in terms of his providential care of the world. Creation is the result of a benevolent emanation in which matter is stamped throughout with the mark of Logos (the image of God). The Logos is the omnipresent instrument of God's providence. Logos is God immanent, a living power holding together the hierarchy of being. In the Christian tradition God's infinity is consistently tied to his ubiquity. It is God's presence which confers being and life on the world.[70]

It is significant that these "absolute" conceptions of the infinite involve either a notion of intensive presence (pure actuality, plenitude, completeness) or a notion of omnipresence (as unifying principle, ground, providential care, cosmic Reason or Logos, ubiquity). That is, they are conceptually tied to various notions of immanence. On the other hand, the "negative" conceptions of the infinite emphasize or are thought in terms of transcendence. The indeterminate, for example, is that which is *beyond* measure, form, definition, articulation, or determination. The unintelligible or ineffable eludes thought, the unnamable transcends language, the indefinite transcends being or form, the all-inclusive is not itself included in the all, the absolute will transcends reason, etc. Similarly, the quantitative or privative infinite is that which always oversteps any possible boundary, generating a possible or actual series in which each element is surpassed by the next. There is no spatial boundary which can't be crossed, no magnitude which can't be further divided, no number which can't be surpassed, no moment which isn't overtaken by the next, etc.

As we have seen, these aspects are interwoven, and for the most part, those who hold a doctrine of divine infinity understand this infinity in a number of ways, both absolute and negative, connoting in turn both

---

37D). For an exposition of this aspect of Plato's view of time see chapter 1 of John F. Callahan's *Four Views of Time in Ancient Philosophy* (Cambridge: Harvard University Press, 1948).

70. For a short history of medieval interpretations of God's omnipresence, see Funkenstein, *Theology and Scientific Imagination*, 42–72.

God's immanence and God's transcendence. The late medieval nominalism of William of Ockham is a notable exception. For Ockham even God's omnipresence is spelled out in terms of his omnipotence—his absolute power to create or destroy or otherwise directly intervene in the course of nature.

It is precisely the radical transcendence of the nominalist God which, for Blumenberg, is mirrored in the subsequent (extensive) infinitization of the universe. Let us turn now to Blumenberg's account of the emergence of the infinite universe, and in particular his interpretation of the historical preconditions for the Copernican revolution in astronomy.

[11]

Historical Preconditions for the Emergence of the New Astronomy

Copernicus is often hailed as the "father" of the modern world, and indeed, by adopting a heliocentric world-picture he radically undermined the traditional medieval cosmos, which was defined by fundamental Aristotelian physical and cosmological principles. According to Aristotle, geocentricism is demanded by the natural motions of both terrestrial and celestial matter. The four terrestrial elements move, by nature, either toward the center of the cosmos (earth and water) or away from the center toward the periphery (air and fire). They will always seek their natural place and rest there unless dislodged by some violent motion. The four terrestrial elements are unstable and exist in a never-ending process of mutation, one into the other, making possible the generation and corruption characteristic of all earthly existence. Celestial matter (aether), on the other hand, is fundamentally different in kind from terrestrial matter. It is immutable and incorruptible, and moves, by nature, eternally in a circle. It is this immutability of aether which accounts for the constancy and regularity observed in the heavenly bodies. It is also this perfect immutability and regularity which allows for mathematical description of the celestial realm—an impossibility for terrestrial change because of its inherently unstable and imperfect character.

Aristotle rejects the possibility of an infinite universe or a plurality of worlds, since either would make the supposition of natural motions and natural places impossible. If the world were infinite, there would be no natural (i.e. absolute) "up" or "down," no center or circumference for terrestrial matter to move toward. All place would merge into homogeneous space.[71] Further, the celestial realm must also be finite or the circular motion of the heavenly bodies would be impossible, because then the heavens would have to transverse an infinite distance in a finite time.[72] A plurality of worlds is similarly unthinkable, for this assumption, too, would make natural motion impossible. On the assumption of a plurality of worlds, all the matter in the universe would be simultaneously drawn to multiple centers and circumferences.[73] Rational order thus demands that there be only one, unique, finite, geocentric cosmos.

By removing the earth from the center of the world, and bestowing on it the dignity of a "heavenly body," Copernicus radically undermined the entire foundation of the Aristotelian world-order with its absolute ontological distinction between the superlunar realm of immutable celestial matter and the sublunar region of unstable mundane matter. By thus homogenizing the "space" and matter of the cosmos, he was able to subject the earth to the laws of celestial physics and so ascribe circular motions to the spherical earth. In doing so, however, he undermined the entire foundation of terrestrial physics which had depended on the notion of "natural place" spelled out in terms of a finite geocentric cosmos.

Copernicus was also forced by his theory to vastly expand the outer boundaries of the cosmos, making the sphere of the fixed stars enormously remote from the earth, in order to account for the "non-observation" of the displacement of the positions of the stars one would expect due to the

71. See Aristotle, *Physics* 3.5.205A8–35.

72. Aristotle, *On the Heavens* 1.5.272B29–273A1.

73. On the supposition of more than one world, "The particles of earth . . . in another world would move naturally also to our centre and its fire to our circumference. This, however, is impossible, since if it were true, earth must in its own world, move upwards, and fire to the centre; in the same way the earth of our world must move naturally away from the centre when it moves toward the centre of another universe. This follows from the supposed juxtaposition of worlds" (Aristotle, *On the Heavens,* trans. J. L. Stocks, in *The Complete Works of Aristotle,* 1.8.276B10ff).

earth's orbit around the sun. Although Copernicus stopped short of proclaiming the universe infinite, his innovation removed the most common objection to the possibility of an infinite cosmos: the empirically "obvious" fact that the motions of the stars trace a circular path in a finite time.[74]

Copernicus' successors moved relatively quickly to explode the now functionless sphere of the "fixed stars" and scatter them throughout a boundless, homogeneous space.[75] Indeed, within a period of less than 150 years—Copernicus' *De revolutionibus* appeared in 1543 and Newton's *Principia* in 1687—the "new science" had arrived at the necessary foundations for a unified physical theory to describe this new infinite universe.[76]

The systematic correlation between Aristotle's theory of terrestrial motion and his cosmology goes a long way in explaining why it was that, despite the many difficulties that naturally arose as astronomical systems became more and more sophisticated, astronomers continued to assume that the earth had to be the unmoving center of a finite universe. For centuries the general acceptance of Aristotelian physics had dictated the cosmological constraints within which astronomy developed its theories.[77] Had the authority granted to the Aristotelian world system not been challenged long before Copernicus, Copernicus himself could never have tak-

74. Aristotle (*Physics* 1.5.272B29–273A1) argued that since an infinite space cannot be traversed in a finite time, and the heavens revolve around the earth in a twenty-four-hour time-span, the celestial realm cannot be conceived of as infinite.

75. For an analysis of this process see Koyré, *Closed World,* especially chapters 2 and 5.

76. Newton's laws of motion and theory of universal gravitation united the sciences of astronomy and physics, providing a physical, dynamical basis for the merely descriptive laws of planetary motion worked out mathematically by Kepler. The new conception of inertia introduced by Galileo and Descartes anticipated Newton's first law of motion, just as Kepler's causal explanation of planetary motion in terms of "non-natural," "violent" forces emanating from the sun and planets anticipated Newton's universal laws of gravity.

77. As Thomas Kuhn has pointed out, "though difficulty in solving the problem of [the eccentric motions of] the planets might have provided an astronomer with a motive for experimenting *in astronomy* with the conception of a moving earth, he could not do so without upsetting the accepted basis of terrestrial physics in the process" (Thomas S. Kuhn, *The Copernican Revolution: Planetary Astronomy in the Development of Western Thought* [Cambridge: Harvard University Press, 1957], 85).

en the hypothesis of a heliocentric cosmos seriously,[78] much less have been convinced of its truth.[79] The fact that he was able to entertain the possibility at all, Blumenberg maintains,must, as we shall see, be accounted a result of the conceptual free space that had been opened up by medieval theological reflections on the omnipotence of God.[80]

Copernicus' conviction in the *truth* of his hypothesis, however, appears within the framework provided in the *Legitimacy* as an utterly anachronistic holdover from an earlier age. Blumenberg's inability—at least initially[81]— to make sense of the early modern renewal of confidence in the human ability to grasp the truth about the world, stems in large part from his mistaken assumption that modern self-assertion entails the rejection of the cognitive ideal of adequacy. I will have more to say about this in what follows. Let us turn first, however, to a consideration of Blumenberg's nevertheless insightful reading of the role played by medieval theological concerns in the eventual breakdown of the Aristotelian world-order.

THE BREAKDOWN OF THE ARISTOTELIAN WORLD-ORDER

Blumenberg's account of the prehistory of the Copernican revolution in the *Legitimacy* begins with an assessment of the impact of the Condemnation of 1277[82] on the reception of newly available texts in Aristotelian natural philosophy and metaphysics. The first half of the thir-

78. It should be noted that Copernicus was not the first thinker to have advocated a heliocentric cosmos. Aristarchus of Samos had already proposed essentially the same theory in the middle of the third century B.C., explaining the apparent motions of the heavenly bodies in terms of the earth's rotation about the sun. Yet Aristarchus' proposal had virtually no effect on the subsequent course of cosmological speculation until the revival of his theory at the hands of Copernicus in the sixteenth century.

79. I am indebted in the following discussion to Karsten Harries' reading of both of these moments in *Infinity and Perspective* (Cambridge: MIT Press, 2001).

80. See, for example, Blumenberg, *Legitimacy*, 346–47. See also Blumenberg, *Genesis*, 163–64.

81. As we shall see, Blumenberg felt compelled to rethink his account of the prehistory of the Copernican revolution in the *Genesis*.

82. For a text of the propositions that were condemned see Heinrich Denifle and Aemilio Chatelain, eds., *Chartularium Universitatis Parisiensis* (Paris, 1889–1897; reprint, Brussels:

teenth century saw the rapid absorption of a tremendous amount of recently translated philosophical and scientific literature, previously unavailable in the Latin West, including almost all of the Aristotle known to us,[83] several important Neoplatonic texts, and major philosophical commentaries by Muslim and Jewish thinkers. As the century progressed the arts faculty at the University of Paris became increasingly focused on philosophy and, in particular, on the newly available works of Aristotle and his non-Christian commentators. Indeed, in 1255 study of all the known works of Aristotle was made a mandatory part of the arts curriculum.[84] Not all of the arts masters who taught at the University of Paris went on to the theological program of study, nor were they all theologically oriented. Siger of Brabant and Boethius of Dacia, for example, were particularly interested in Aristotle's natural philosophy, relied heavily on the great Muslim interpreters of Aristotle, Avicenna and Averroës, and had famously insisted on the autonomy and independence of philosophy even in matters that ran counter to the faith.

On March 7, 1277, three years after the death of Thomas Aquinas, the Bishop of Paris, Étienne Tempier, issued a condemnation of 219 propositions taken to be inimical to the Christian faith.[85] The condemned propo-

Culture et Civilisation, 1964), 1:543–561. For a listing in systematic ordering, which I have followed here, see P. Mandonnet, ed., *Siger de Brabant et l'averroïsme latin au XIIIme siècle.* 2d ed., 2 vols. (Louvain: Institut supérieur de philosophie de l'Université, 1911, 1908), 2:175–91. For an English translation following the Mandonnet ordering see E. Fortin and P. O'Neill, in *Medieval Political Philosophy: A Sourcebook,* ed. Ralph Lerner and Muhsin Mahdi (New York, 1963), 337–54. For a discussion of the historical context, see J. Wippel, "The Condemnations of 1270 and 1277 at Paris," *Journal of Medieval and Renaissance Studies* 7 (1977): 169–201.

83. The works of Aristotle reached the Latin West through two channels in the twelfth and thirteenth centuries. "From the twelfth century on, scholars in Spain and Italy, where Christians were in contact with Muslim learning, prepared Latin translations of the Arabic texts of Aristotle which, at an earlier time, had been translated from the Greek and Syriac. In the first half of the thirteenth century, when the often better Byzantine texts became available to the West, new and often more accurate translations were made from the original Greek. After varying periods of dissemination, this new learning appeared at the universities" (Arthur Hyman and James J. Walsh, *Philosophy in the Middle Ages* [Indianapolis: Hackett Publishing Company, 1983], 452).

84. See Wippel, "Condemnations of 1270 and 1277," 172.

85. Bishop Tempier had already condemned thirteen propositions on December 10, 1270, taken from the work of scholars influenced by Averroistic interpretations of Aristotle. These theses included the doctrine of the unity of the intellect (denying the individual intellect and so

sitions were primarily drawn from the teachings of arts masters like Siger of Brabant and Boethius of Dacia, but it also included a few positions drawn from the writings of Thomas Aquinas.[86] In particular, propositions were censored which implied that God's absolute power could in some way be subject to a rational necessity grounded in nature. "This document," asserts Blumenberg, "marks the exact point in time when the interest in the rationality and human intelligibility of creation cedes priority to the speculative fascination exerted by the theological predicates of absolute power."[87]

Proposition seventeen, for example, was condemned for asserting that what is impossible absolutely speaking cannot be brought about by God. This was held to be erroneous if "impossible" is understood as "impossible according to the laws of nature," i.e. given Aristotelian physics. The condemnation of this proposition was intended to keep open the possibility that God can perform miracles that are contrary to the known laws of nature. Indeed if miracles occur—and faith teaches that they do—then the laws of nature are not absolutely binding. This in itself would seem to imply that other worlds, governed by other laws, are at least possible. This implication is brought home in proposition twenty, which was condemned for holding that God *of necessity* makes what comes from him. This proposition was held to be erroneous insofar as it denies divine freedom and implies that God cannot change the laws of nature if he so chooses.[88] Proposition sixty-nine was condemned for asserting that God is unable to produce a given effect except through the mediation of secondary causes.[89] This was held to be erroneous because it would deny the possibility of a virgin birth and, interestingly enough, the possibility more generally of action at a distance. Proposition sixty-six asserted that

---

immortality), the necessity of natural events, the eternity of the world, the denial of divine knowledge of singulars, the denial of divine providence, the denial of human freedom, and so on. These themes reappeared in the Condemnation of 1277.

86. The Thomistic propositions have mainly to do with issues concerning the individuation of particulars by matter and the relation of intellect to will.

87. Blumenberg, *Legitimacy*, 160.

88. See also Proposition 23.

89. See also Propositions 16, 67, and 68.

God could not move the cosmos in a straight line because then there would be a vacuum (which Aristotle had shown to be impossible). This proposition was condemned on the grounds that it seemed to limit God's infinite power. To assert, on the contrary, that God *could* move the universe in a straight line, forces one to rethink space as potentially empty, and so to reject the Aristotelian equation of space with physical place.

Indeed, reflections on the infinity of God's will challenged thinkers, in the wake of the Condemnation of 1277, to imagine other possible worlds that would not be governed by Aristotelian physical principles.[90] Such "thought experiments" were meant to show that things supposedly ruled out as impossible by the laws of nature were in fact possible in the face of God's omnipotent will. As a result, a space was opened up in which thinkers were conceptually freed to consider, as at least hypothetically possible, alternatives to the generally accepted Aristotelian world-view.

Possible world speculation in the nominalist tradition following Ockham, moreover, led to the development of (at least partial) alternatives to Aristotelian physics. Without this groundwork having been laid, it is inconceivable that Copernicus would have been taken seriously by his peers, or indeed that he himself could really have believed in the truth of his hypothesis. Two of the most important ideas generated in the process of possible world speculation were those of the *impetus* of objects in motion and the conception of the *appetitus partium* (striving of parts) to cohere. The *impetus* theory of motion held that when an object is set in motion, a force or *impetus* is imparted to it that keeps it in motion. In lieu of the concept of inertia, this theory helped explain why, in a heliocentric cosmos, terrestrial objects like thrown stones and flying birds would not be left behind by the rotation of the earth as would be the case on the assumption of an Aristotelian theory of motion. The idea of *appetitus partium,* that similar parts strive to form a whole, also helped to explain why (in lieu of a concept of gravity) the component parts of the earth do not fly apart as it gyrates, since on the Copernican theory recourse could no

90. For a more detailed account of the Condemnation of 1277 and the manner in which it challenged the hierarchy and order assumed by the Aristotelian cosmos see Harries, *Infinity and Perspective,* 128–47.

longer be made to "natural" motion toward or away from the center of the cosmos.

The possible world speculation of late medieval nominalism led to further important innovations in natural philosophy, including the rejection of final causes (on the basis that we can no longer pretend to know God's will for the universe) and the homogenization of cosmic regions. Blumenberg stresses:

> For the 'trial' of theoretical curiosity, it is decisive that this index of the prohibited [the Condemnation of 1277] actually functioned as the source and documentation of the license not to identify the traditionally received knowledge about the cosmos with the plan of creation. What was intended as a defense of theology against physics became in its turn an authority for what was not well established, an authority to which a new physics could appeal in defense of its right to 'play through' constructive hypotheses and thus to criticize a world model that had served High Scholasticism as the incontestable key to its rational theology.[91]

Hence, the Condemnation of 1277, while representing a victory for "conservative" theologians vis-à-vis the new Aristotelianism, had the unexpected effect of "authorizing" the possible world speculation of the late Middle Ages. This last helped, in turn, to clear up the intellectual space for the emergence of the new physics and the new astronomy.

THE OVERCOMING OF EPISTEMOLOGICAL RESIGNATION

Blumenberg is quick to point out, however, that the dominant theme of God's omnipotence, which led to possible world speculation, also led to a form of epistemological resignation. If, in the face of God's inscrutable will, Aristotle cannot pretend to know the absolute truth about nature, neither can anyone else. If the natural world can no longer be conceived of as a rationally necessary order, the truth about creation would seem to be unavailable to the human knower. "The assumption of God's infinite power means above all that finite reason cannot determine that any of its hypotheses should correspond to the actual constructive principle of nature *(generalis totius huius mundi constructio)*."[92]

91. Blumenberg, *Legitimacy*, 346–47.
92. Ibid., 206.

In order to overcome the impasse of this cognitive resignation, Blumenberg holds, there had to be a shift in the goal or telos of human knowledge from the search for truth (as *adaequatio*) to the more modest end of "theoretical efficacy."

> This is at bottom the . . . solution of the modern age—a program of rational expediency, which is opposed to viewing reality as transcendent and renounces the cognitive ideal of adequacy [*adaequatio*] . . . it required the Scholastic system no longer to accept transcendence but rather to compensate for it with an artificial universality of human convention.[93]

Blumenberg thus sees in Descartes' method the beginnings of a move away from the pursuit of truth as correspondence and toward an emphasis on the internal consistency of a system of clear and distinct propositions. This move was given its characteristically "modern" form, Blumenberg claims, in the *Principles of Philosophy,* where Descartes remarks that hypothesis has the same serviceability in life as secure truth. Descartes goes further in the French version by adding that hypothesis is perfectly sufficient for the manipulation of natural causes to produce a desired effect. On the assumption that any number of hypotheses *could* explain the given phenomena with equal predictive power, it becomes impossible to definitively verify a given hypothesis experimentally. This difficulty, however, loses its significance, Blumenberg holds, if knowledge of nature has as its telos not the ascertainment of the truth possessed by God, but rather "the production of phenomena."

Once again, however, Blumenberg fails to take into account the fact that, although a given hypothesis may never find definitive experimental confirmation, the hypothesis is nevertheless formulated with an eye toward reproducing the natural phenomenon it is meant to explain. The "internal consistency" of a theory is valueless if it is unable to account for the phenomena *given* in nature. In this sense nature remains the transcendent measure of our human attempts to grasp it. Indeed theory, even as an instrument of self-assertion, cannot do without the need to relate its hypotheses to the phenomena given in nature. It is precisely the recalcitrance of those phenomena to the application of theory which provides

93. Ibid., 353.

the measure for the viability of a particular hypothesis, and it is this viability which is tested in the experiment. Blumenberg wants to claim that the success of a theory is in its ability to produce "desired" phenomena, that is, to mold nature to our will. This may well be the case for technicity, but theoretical science aims not at the production of "desired results," but at the re-production of the phenomena that occur in nature. Even in the case of technicity, we control nature, not by the arbitrary intervention of our will, but by using our experience of *its* (law-like, predictable) behavior to our own advantage.

Since Blumenberg ignores this element of the "transcendence of reality" in the modern project of self-assertion, he views late medieval cognitive resignation and the industry of early modern science as systematic correlates: "*Hypothesis,* which from one point of view is the formal expression of the renunciation of the claim to truth in the traditional sense of adequacy [*adaequatio*], becomes from another point of view a means of self assertion."[94] Hence Blumenberg views the mathematizing and materializing of nature as the "systematic correlate of theological absolutism,"[95] and early modern mechanistic explanations of the world as the simple "reoccupation" of nominalist voluntarism. He thus claims without further ado that "the scientific progress of the early modern age is based on the destruction of the Aristotelian dogmas, on the one hand, and the new legitimization of interest in nature on the other—both of which had been substantially accomplished by nominalism."[96]

On this reading of the emergence of self-assertion as "the process of the disassociation of theoretical efficacy from the idea of truth,"[97] Copernicus' claim for the *truth* of his astronomical system must appear utterly anachronistic. In *The Legitimacy of the Modern Age* Blumenberg can only describe it as "an episode of metaphysical contradiction, which failed to block the overall process that is [the] subject here." While Blumenberg admits that this "monumental recurrence of the anthropocentrically as-

94. Ibid., 199.

95. Ibid., 173. See also 164: "The search for a set of instruments for man that would be usable in any possible world provides the criterion for the elementary exertions of the modern age: The *mathematizing* and the *materializing* of nature."

96. Ibid., 348.

97. Ibid., 205.

sured claim to truth" was "of incomparable importance" for the actual history of science, he holds nonetheless that it "had no direct effect on the theory of science."[98]

Perhaps it was in part because of the need to think through this "episode of metaphysical contradiction" that Blumenberg took *The Genesis of the Copernican World* as the theme for his next major reading of the origins of modernity. In any case it is certainly telling that when Blumenberg focuses on the historical preconditions of the Copernican revolution in this later work, he feels the need to substantially supplement his original reading of the epochal transition to modernity. In the *Legitimacy* all that had seemed necessary in order to account for the epochal shift had been supplied by nominalism's dismantling of Aristotelian Scholasticism and the shift to hypothetical forms of reasoning. In the *Genesis,* however, Blumenberg feels compelled to account for the early modern renewal of faith in the human ability to arrive at truth, and so introduces a new player to the field: Renaissance Humanism. Hence, in the *Genesis of the Copernican World,* Blumenberg redescribes the epochal crisis of the Middle Ages as "falling apart into Nominalism, on the one hand, and Humanism, on the other."[99]

On this revised reading, the destruction of the Aristotelian cosmos, and the opening up of a space for the possible emergence of a Copernicus, is linked to nominalism's dismantling of High Scholastic Aristotelianism. And the renewal of faith in the human capacity for truth is linked to Humanist anthropocentric reflections on the dignity and "ubiquity" of man.[100] Just as the world has its center and foundation in God, so the known cosmos has its center and foundation in the human being. Man has no "natural" place in the cosmic hierarchy, but appropriates all

98. Ibid., 205–6.

99. Blumenberg, *Genesis,* 200.

100. See Harries, *Infinity and Perspective,* 200–223. See also in this context Louis Dupré's book *Passage to Modernity: An Essay in the Hermeneutics of Nature and Culture* (New Haven: Yale University Press, 1993). Dupré provides a reading of the transition to the modern age which attends both to the role of nominalist theology and to the impact of Italian humanism in shattering the traditional synthesis that had united cosmic, human, and transcendent components in the medieval conception of Nature. See also his essay, "Nature and Grace in Nicholas of Cusa's Mystical Philosophy," *American Catholic Philosophical Quarterly* 64 (1990): 153–70.

of nature in his intellect.[101] Knowledge thus comes to be viewed in this tradition as a second act of world "creation."

In the *Legitimacy* this reading is already nascent in Blumenberg's interpretation of Cusanus. "If the Cusan can be regarded as a forerunner of Copernicus in any respect at all," he writes, "then it is surely in the fact that, for him, man's cosmological placement gives no information as to what he can credit himself with and regard as his worth."[102] Indeed, Cusanus holds man's most god-like characteristic to be the infinitely creative power of his mind:

> Human being *(humanitas)* is a unity, and that means that at the same time it is infinity realized in a human manner *(infinitas humaniter contracta)*. Now, however, it is the nature of such a unity to unfold beings from itself *(ex se explicare entia)*, for it contains in its simplicity a multiplicity of beings. So man has the capacity *(virtus)* to unfold everything from himself into the circle of the region he inhabits *(omnia ex se explicare intra regionis suae circulum)*, to make everything arise from his power as the center (of that circle) *(omnia de potentia centri exercere)*.[103]

Thus in his theory of knowledge Cusanus interprets human beings as essentially creative. Blumenberg claims that this immanent creation of a cognitive world would appear as truly modern if "this daring" had not been "blunted by the requirement that what man projects must be appropriate to the divine creation."[104] Once again Blumenberg fails to recognize that although we create the measures by which we conjecture about reality, it is the recalcitrance of the given reality itself which serves as the measure for the relative applicability of those conjectures.

Cusanus would surely accuse Blumenberg of neglecting the distinction between theory which aims at descriptions of reality and cognitive free-play. The playful invention of a game ("as a reality closed in itself, a 'world' that unfolds itself with its own elements according to a set of

101. See for example, Giovanni Pico della Mirandola's *De hominis dignitate (Oration on the Dignity of Man)* and Juan Luis Vives' *Fabula de homine (A Fable about Man)*. Both are translated in *The Renaissance Philosophy of Man*, ed. Ernst Cassirer, Paul Oskar Kristeller, and John Herman Randall, Jr. (Chicago: The University of Chicago Press, 1948).

102. Blumenberg, *Legitimacy*, 524. Blumenberg follows up on this immediately with a short gloss on Pico della Mirandola's *Oration on the Dignity of Man* (524–5).

103. Nicholas of Cusa, *De coniecturis* II, 14. Cited in Blumenberg, *Legitimacy*, 533.

104. Blumenberg, *Legitimacy*, 533.

rules")[105] must be fundamentally distinguished from the craftsman who is able to aid deficient vision with eyeglasses and so correct the errors of sight by the art of perspective.[106] Man is the measure in an unrestricted sense in the invention of a game. Human measures are in turn measured by the phenomenon of refraction, etc., in the invention of eyeglasses.

In order to account for this latter sense of nature as a transcendent and yet guiding measure of knowledge, Cusanus made use of the notion of the immanence of the divine infinite in the world. Hence, much more remains to be said about the way in which late medieval Neoplatonic reflections on the infinity of God not only contribute to the destruction of the Aristotelian cosmological picture, but also help to lay the ontological and epistemological foundations for the modern notion of progress in science.

On the one hand Neoplatonic conceptions of the omnipresence of God serve to disrupt the hierarchically structured world picture of Aristotelian cosmology. On the other hand the notion of an immanent or "incarnate" infinite, as the ontological ground of reality, prepares the way for an understanding of nature as the perpetually elusive but concrete measure for human knowledge of that reality. In other words, the early modern understanding of scientific progress as the never-ending pursuit of knowledge, as a process of unending approximation to "the truth," depends on an ontology that understands nature as itself exhibiting not only an "extensive," but an "intensive" or "intrinsic" infinity as well.

At issue is not merely the "indefinite" or "boundless" extension of the space of the real. Nor is it simply a new awareness of the way in which nature always transcends our conceptual grasp because in some sense there is "always more of it," so that "progress" in science is itself strung out indefinitely on the temporal plane. What is crucial to recognize here is that nature also transcends our power to conceptualize it at the local level, by virtue of what I am calling an "intensive" infinity. Each oak tree presents itself as infinitely rich and utterly unique, conceptually inexponable in its intensive unity. Thus the "infinitization of the universe," which occurs at the end of the Middle Ages and marks the transition into the modern world, must be understood intensively as well as extensively.

105. Ibid., 535. See Nicholas of Cusa, *De ludo globi.*
106. Blumenberg, *Legitimacy,* 535. See Nicholas of Cusa, *Compendium* VI.

[III]

Blumenberg's Reading of the Epochal Threshold

We recall that in Part IV of the *Legitimacy,* Blumenberg situates the "epochal threshold" between medieval and modern in that period which straddles the Copernican "event": the period between Nicholas of Cusa and Giordano Bruno. Both thinkers apply the attribute of infinity to the universe, but Cusanus does so only in a restricted sense. He still distinguishes between the expression of God's infinite nature as it is mirrored in the Second Person of the Trinity and in the created universe. Bruno, on the other hand, abandons this dogmatic distinction between the intra-divine generation of the Trinity and the extra-divine creation of the world, and so views the universe as God's unrestricted self-revelation.

Blumenberg understands this shift as a systematic "reoccupation" of the Trinitarian position of the Son in the thought of Cusanus by the universe in that of Bruno.[107] Hence, he believes that he can demonstrate, in their respective systems of interpretation, "an identical fundamental system of elementary assertion needs, notions of the self and world, on both sides of the [epochal] threshold."[108] As I have already indicated (pp. 100–102), I find this interpretation fundamentally unconvincing.

The universe, for Nicholas of Cusa, is an imperfect expression *(explicatio)* of God—imperfect because it is an unfolding in the realm of multiplic-

107. Blumenberg, *Legitimacy,* 79.
108. Ibid., 469.

ity and determinacy of what is fundamentally an intensive unity *(complicatio)* in God. Every singular thing in the world is a "contraction" *(contractio)* of the divine infinite into this unique particular. Cusanus makes recourse to the Neoplatonic Christian conception of the "intradivine" generation of the Second Person of the Trinity (the Christ Logos), in order to account for the possibility of this "contraction" of the infinite in the finite.

For Cusanus the world is generated through the "unfolding" of the unity which is "enfolded" in God, who may be thought of as the absolutely Maximum, or infinite, in whom all oppositions (all determinateness) must coincide. Cusanus uses the analogy of the generation of number from unity to describe the creation of the world by God. Here the double role of the number one (as both generating principle of unity and first number) is crucial. The creative "Word of God" (the Son) fulfills an analogous role. "One" *(unum)* is a concrete repetition of unity *(unitas)* and thus a wholly adequate image, "perfect equality," but also, as absolute minimum, is the unit measure of the generated sequence, of the procession of multiplicity.[109] If God is to be thought of as absolute unity *(unitas),* the Son of God, his creative word, must be understood as absolute equality *(aequalitas).*[110] Cusanus follows the tradition, here, in distinguishing the process in which God reveals himself in his Son through intradivine generation and that in which he unfolds himself in the creation of the world.

Bruno, on the other hand, dispenses with this middle term (the moment of the *contractio* or the intensive infinite), and proclaims the created universe to be the complete and perfect expression of God. Indeed, for the Nolan, the infinite universe *is* in fact the actualized complete revelation and exhaustion of the infinite God. Blumenberg welcomes this move in Bruno, and views the distinction Cusanus makes between intradivine generation and extradivine creation as so much excess baggage, the legacy of centuries of accumulated dogmas, distinctions, and provisos aimed

109. Ultimately this paradigm is too weak to serve as a sufficiently satisfying metaphor for the intensive infinite. In the section on Cusanus I will discuss his use of the metaphor of the infinite sphere, and the inscribed polygon, and how they figure for him an understanding of the immanence of the infinite in the finite, which gives measure and meaning to existence.

110. Nicholas of Cusa, *Nicholas of Cusa on Learned Ignorance: A Translation and Appraisal of "De Docta Ignorantia"* by Jasper Hopkins (Minneapolis: Arthur J. Banning Press, 1985), 57.

at producing a synthesis of finally incommensurable elements. Bruno is for him the thinker who is finally able to clear the field, as it were, and respond to what is essential:

Bruno did not go along with one of the most obscure distinctions in the history of dogma, the distinction between *generatio* and *creatio:* the production of the Son of God as "generation," the production of the world as "creation." He holds to the Cusan's fundamental idea that the absolute "ability" must manifest itself in the arising of *aequalitas* from *unitas*—but the position of *aequalitas* in Bruno is occupied by not the Son but the infinite universe.[111]

For Blumenberg to claim that the infinite universe simply reoccupies the position held by the Son in Cusanus' system is to fail completely to grasp the "elementary assertion need" this position fulfills for Cusanus, the need for an epistemological measure in the newly infinite universe. And as I have already indicated, this is not a need that disappears in the transition to the modern age but one that comes to be felt with increasing force. By constructing his system with an eye to the need for such a principle of ontological determinacy, Cusanus' system is actually far more sophisticated than that of Bruno, and it reveals an awareness of what would become one of the fundamental problems of modernity.

It is not simply Bruno's rejection of the Incarnation, however, which motivates Blumenberg to situate the epochal threshold where he does. At issue for him is the emergence of a robust conception of progress in science: one which entails both reflection on the surpassability of the state of knowledge at any point, and an awareness that such progress in knowledge depends on the institution of a community of scientists, spanning generations.[112]

From this perspective, it becomes apparent why Blumenberg wants to place Cusanus and Bruno on opposite sides of the epochal threshold. Cusanus' doctrine of "learned ignorance" appears in this light as a premodern gesture toward "method" in that it constitutes a commitment to reflect on the surpassability of the state of knowledge at any given time.

111. Blumenberg, *Legitimacy,* 664 n. 26.

112. It became rapidly apparent in the new boundless universe of the early modern age, that no one individual could ever hope to know "all there is to know" about the world. Even Descartes' initial optimism for the new science was moderated when it became increasingly clear that truth in its totality is not, in fact, at the disposition of any one individual. As a result the

The "trace of God in the world" is experienced, by Cusanus, as a track to be pursued in a never-ending hunt for wisdom.[113] Nevertheless, as Blumenberg rightly points out, Cusanus fails to combine this preliminary idea of method with that of a community of scientists, related to one another over centuries, building upon past achievements in their common pursuit of knowledge. Bruno, on the other hand, embraced the notion of progress over time in his vision of a scientific community capable of spanning generations, and so, according to Blumenberg, was able to overstep, self-consciously and "joyously," the epochal threshold into the new age.

Yet in this analysis Blumenberg fails to consider the way in which the modern notion of unending progress in science (in particular the ability to grasp one theoretical construct as in fact "better" than another) depends on an understanding of nature as itself the ever-elusive measure for human theorizing. Absolutely crucial, here, is the emergence of the early modern conception of truth as a regulative ideal, the perpetually deferred, but ever-present goal of infinite progress in knowledge. This conception of adequacy to "what is" as the regulative ideal of human knowledge, presupposes not only the *privative* conception of infinite progress in knowledge, which endlessly approaches but never arrives at its goal, but also the *absolute* conception of infinity, thought precisely as the completion or limit of this never-ending approach. Hence, the notion of the regulative ideal, here, is thought as the convergence of two orders of infinity.

Blumenberg fails to recognize this dual aspect of infinity at the heart of the modern conception of the regulative ideal. Indeed, he is content to view the shift to the modern age as characterized by the reduction of the notion of infinity to a predicate of indefiniteness.[114] The ancient cosmos is expanded into boundless, homogeneous space. The theoretical enterprise is spread out temporally in unending progress. The indefinite nature of this modern reality is, for Blumenberg, the systematic correlate

"end" of knowledge had to be projected as the ideal goal of a community of scientists, related to one another over centuries.

113. See Nicholas of Cusa, *De venatione sapientiae*.

114. Blumenberg notes that whereas Descartes had still understood the finite as a negation of the (positive) concept of the infinite, Hobbes rejected the presupposition that we have any positive concept of the infinite whatsoever. He insists that when we speak of something as infinite, "we signify nothing really, but the impotency in our own mind; as if we should say, we know not

of the reduction of divine infinity to omnipotence (*un*limited power) in nominalist theology.

As I have already indicated, this interpretation of the role of infinity in the epochal transition is inadequate and misleading. The infinitization of the universe at the end of the Middle Ages is intensive as well as extensive in character, and the emergence of the modern conception of progress is tied to that of truth as a regulative ideal. The historical preconditions for the emergence of these aspects of modern cosmology and epistemology lie not in the nominalist tradition, but rather in that of late medieval Neoplatonism.

Blumenberg's analysis of the emergence of the modern age is distorted by his failure to grasp the significance of the notion of an *incarnate* infinite in this transition, as is his treatment of the character of the "epochal threshold." As an alternative to the threshold pair, Cusanus-Bruno, with which Blumenberg presents us, I will shift the focus instead to the pair, Eckhart-Cusanus, not in order to move the threshold back in time and more accurately "locate" the turning point of epochal change, but rather in order to reexamine the character of this change from another point of view. While I agree with Blumenberg that Cusanus develops a genuinely modern understanding of method, I believe that we must take seriously the way in which this "method" is inextricably rooted in a sophisticated ontology of the infinite. When the Neoplatonic problem of the relation between the One and the many becomes an extension of the problem of the relation of the infinite to the finite, the Neoplatonic notion of unity in the manifold is developed into an understanding of the incarnation of the infinite in the finite. Such a shift implies far-reaching ontological and epistemological consequences, which in turn contribute to the emerging shape of the epochal change.

whether or where it is limited" (Thomas Hobbes, *De cive* XV, 14, trans. Thomas Hobbes, in *Man and Citizen*, ed. Bernard Gert [Garden City, N.Y.: Doubleday, 1972], 299). Blumenberg then concludes, "The infinite serves from this point onward less to answer one of the great traditional questions than to blunt it, less to give meaning to history than to dispute the claim to be able to give it meaning" (Blumenberg, *Legitimacy*, 85). But how is Blumenberg justified in singling out Hobbes' position as somehow definitive for modernity? In fact, the debate over whether or not the concept of the finite is a negation of the infinite, or whether the infinite is a negation of the finite, is a characteristic of early modern metaphysics. Leibniz and Descartes take the first view, whereas Hobbes and Locke take the second.

PART THREE

Meister Eckhart and Nicholas of Cusa on the Immanence of the Infinite

THE EPOCHAL TRANSITION from the late medieval to the early modern age is marked by the "infinitization" of the medieval cosmos. Traditionally this process has been studied by focusing on the prehistory and the aftermath of the Copernican revolution, that is, by describing the transition from the finite, hierarchically ordered medieval cosmos to the infinite and homogeneous universe of the new astronomy. As I have already indicated, however, this process of infinitization must be understood *intensively* as well as extensively. Nature, in the modern age, is thought of not only as infinitely extended in space, but also as exhibiting an infinite richness in all of its parts. Each particular, each individual being is grasped as utterly unique, as infinitely rich and consequently as conceptually inexponable. Thus the infinitization of the real leads to an infinitization of the knowable—the radical shift in ontology grounds a corresponding shift in epistemology, so that the progress of human knowledge is understood as an unending project infinitely extended over time. In this third section I will consider the theological origins of this dual infinitization of reality, intensive as well as extensive. I will do so by focusing on the way in which a single metaphor, that of the infinite sphere, is unfolded historically in the thought of Meister Eckhart (1260–ca.1328) and in that of Nicholas of Cusa (1401–1464) in order to articulate these changing notions of self and world.

[1]

Meister Eckhart: The Mystical Interpretation of the Infinite Sphere

EARLY SOURCES OF THE INFINITE SPHERE METAPHOR

The metaphor of the infinite sphere[1] makes its first appearance in the pseudo-hermetic *Liber XXIV philosophorum (Book of Twenty-Four Philosophers),* a short text in the literary form of an *opus propositionum* which, in twenty-four propositions, describes the ineffable essence of God in the mystical language of Neoplatonic theology. It is in the second proposition of this book that we find for the first time the formulation, "God is an infinite sphere, whose center is everywhere, whose circumference is nowhere."[2] This formulation represents a significant development

1. See Dietrich Mahnke's general history of the metaphor in *Unendliche Sphäre,* and especially Karsten Harries' essay "The Infinite Sphere: Comments on the History of a Metaphor," *Journal of the History of Philosophy* 13 (January 1975): 5–15, which explores the philosophical link between medieval mysticism and the emergence of modern cosmology. Harries focuses on the *extensive* infinitization of the cosmos and on the way in which the construction of the metaphor itself reveals the capacity of the human intellect to project the ideal of a genuinely a-perspectival understanding of the world. See my article, "Transitions to a Modern Cosmology: Meister Eckhart and Nicholas of Cusa on the Intensive Infinite," *Journal of the History of Philosophy* 37 (1999): 575–600.

2. *Liber viginti quattuor philosophorum, Corpus Christianorum Continuatio Mediaeualis,*

in the history of the Neoplatonic conception of intensive unity, and in the Christian understanding of divine infinity. The Neoplatonic One is here identified with God as infinite being. As a result the relationship between the One and the many, between God and the world, comes to be viewed in a new light, through the lens of "infinite unity."

The metaphor of the infinite sphere is a paradoxical formulation, which pictures the coincidence of divine immanence with divine transcendence. That is, it expresses a double infinity: both intensive and extensive. God's center is located at every point, as it were, indicating the plenitude and infinite richness of God's being, while there is no limit, no boundary to the extent of God's all-encompassing reach. The infinite sphere figures the divine nature as an intensive plenitude without end or bounds. The third and next proposition in this same work goes on to strengthen this sense of divine intensity, by asserting that God *in his entirety* is present in every part ("Deus est totus in quolibet sui").[3] The divine nature is not spread out compositionally, as it were, but is *wholly* present throughout. Proposition 18 describes God as a sphere which has just as many circumferences as points ("Deus est sphaera, cuius tot sunt circumferentiae, quot sunt puncta"),[4] once again, an exploding image which can make sense only in the case of an infinite sphere. These three propositions taken together provide us with a springboard for considering the nature of infinite unity. The exploding paradox of the infinite sphere provides a rubric for thinking the coincidence of transcendence and immanence, a way of conceptualizing infinite unity, which cannot be "grasped" with finite concepts or through discursive reasoning. The metaphor of the infinite sphere finds its meaning precisely in the *way* in which the infinite overruns the limitations inherent in its visualization and concretization in the *figure* of the sphere.[5]

---

vol. 143a, edited with introduction by Françoise Hudry (Turnholt: Brepols, 1997). Proposition 2 reads: "Deus est sphaera infinita, cuius centrum est ubique, circumferentia vero nusquam" (7).

3. Ibid.

4. Ibid.

5. In the context of his discussion of Nicholas of Cusa's use of mathematical metaphors, Blumenberg aptly describes the infinite sphere as a "Sprengmetapher" (exploding metaphor), whose "explosive material" is the concept of infinity itself. Such metaphors illuminate the divine

The metaphor of the infinite sphere is used by the author of the *Book of Twenty-Four Philosophers* to describe God's creative power. God, as the first cause of all things, is likened to a living center of creative efficacy. In its simplicity this center contains unending possibilities, realized in the ever-expanding divine sphere. There is no limit to the reach of the divine efficacy which extends to all of creation, and in this sense the "circumference is nowhere." On the other hand there is no specific beginning point of this all-encompassing, unlimited sphere. Its creative origin, which is wholly unextended and contains the whole of the divine creative power, may be found at any and every point within this realm. In this way, we may say that the "center is everywhere." God's infinity is thus pictured in two ways: as infinitely concentrated in an unextended, minimal, ubiquitous "center" and as infinitely expansive in an all-encompassing sphere of limitless unfolding.[6]

Clemens Baeumker, who published the first modern study of the complete text of the *Book of Twenty-Four Philosophers,* considered the work to be that of an unknown medieval author who composed the text at the turn of the twelfth to the thirteenth century. On the basis of the first known manuscripts, which attributed the text to Hermes Trismegistus, Baeumker placed the text within the pseudo-hermetic tradition.[7] It was no doubt this attribution in the manuscript tradition to the legendary

---

infinite precisely by exploding the boundaries of discursive thought. It is the experience of this explosion that brings with it an intuition of the divine infinite in which opposites coincide. See Blumenberg, *Legitimacy,* 490–91, 495, 510, 514, 539, and 572. Blumenberg tends to read the infinite sphere metaphor as a technique for experiencing infinite transcendence as the limit of conceptualization. He misses, however, the significance of the fact that this is a metaphor whose function is to figure *both* the transcendence *and* the immanence of the infinite.

6. See Mahnke, *Unendliche Sphäre,* 174–75.

7. Clemens Baeumker, "Das pseudo-hermetische 'Buch der vierundzwanzig Meister' (Liber XXIV philosophorum): Ein Beitrag zur Geschichte des Neupythagorismus und Neuplatonismus im Mittelalter," *Studien und Charakteristiken zur Geschichte der Philosophie insbesondere des Mittelalters. Beiträge zur Geschichte der Philosophie und Theologie des Mittelalters* 25 (Münster, 1928), 194–214. Hudry's subsequent research on the manuscript tradition has revealed that this attribution to Trismegistus is far from consistent. Only 13 of the 25 preserved manuscripts attribute the text to Trismegistus. Of the other 12, four offer no title or attribution, four only a descriptive title, and four give various other titles and attributions. See Hudry, ed., *Liber XXIV philosophorum,* CVIII–CIX.

Egyptian sage which favored the text's broad dissemination, since Trismegistus had long been considered a pagan theologian with imperfect but certain knowledge of the Trinity.[8] Along with the writings of Pseudo-Dionysius the *Hermetica* was an authority of great weight for the Neoplatonism of the time. More recently Françoise Hudry has argued that the doctrinal content of the *Book of Twenty-Four Philosophers* should actually be dated to the beginning of the third century, and that the medieval manuscript tradition represents a Latin translation of an Alexandrian school text, which itself was a condensed theological tract drawn from a much larger source (once extant in both Greek and Arabic).[9]

Interestingly, the first two propositions in the *Book of Twenty-Four Philosophers* appear (with slight variation) as Rules 3 and 7 in the *Theological Rules* of Alan of Lille (c.1116–c.1202), a fact which has encouraged the idea that the author of the *Book of Twenty-Four Philosophers* might be an unknown member of the Chartrian movement.[10] This suggestion, though supported by the fact that the manuscript tradition of the *Book of Twenty-Four Philosophers* dates to the same period, seems unlikely, given Hudry's recent research which indicates a much earlier origin.[11] In any case, the *Theological Rules* was more widely read than the *Book of Twenty-*

8. Hermes Mercurius Trismegistus was the legendary author of the *Corpus Hermeticum*, the *Asclepius*, and other excerpts and fragments known collectively as the *Hermetica*. This body of work was compiled by a number of unknown authors of Hellenistic Egypt during the third or fourth century A.D. On the history of the attribution of the *Book of Twenty-Four Philosophers* to Hermes Trismegistus, see Hudry, *Liber XXIV philosophorum*, XXV–XXXII.

9. See Hudry, *Liber XXIV philosophorum*, V–XXIII.

10. M.-T. D'Alverny, "Un témoin muet des luttes doctrinales du XIIIe siècle," in *Archives d'histoire doctrinale et littéraire du moyen âge* 17 (1949): 231–32. See Hudry, *Liber XXIV philosophorum*, V–VI. The first proposition of the *Book of Twenty-Four Philosophers* appears as Rule 3 in *Regulae theologicae*, and that of the "sphaera intelligibilis" appears as Rule 7. See *Alani de Insulis Opera omni* in J.-P. Migne, ed., *Patrologiae cursus completus. Series Latina* (Paris, 1855), 210: 624, 627. See also Alan's *Sermo de sphaera intelligibili*, in *Alain de Lille: Textes inédits*, ed. M.-T. D'Alverny (Paris: Vrin, 1965), 297.

11. Although Alan does not cite a source for Rules 3 and 7 in the *Regulae theologicae*, Mahnke points out that he does cite the first proposition from the *Book of Twenty-Four Philosophers* as the saying of another philosopher ("Unde et philosophus ait: 'Monas gignit . . .'") in *Contra haereticos*, lib. 2, cap. 4, *Patrologia Latina* 210: 405. The addition "Mercurius Trismegistus" which appears in the *Patrologia* is not in the manuscript. In chapter 3, however, Mercurius is named three times. See Mahnke, *Unendliche Sphäre*, 172–73.

Four Philosophers, and so it was through this work of Alan of Lille that many of the major Scholastic thinkers of the thirteenth century became familiar with the geometrical symbolism of the divine sphere. The formulation which appears in the *Theological Rules,* however, deviates from that given in the *Book of Twenty-Four Philosophers* by naming God an "intelligible sphere" rather than an "infinite sphere."[12] Alan's seventh rule reads: "Deus est sphaera *intelligibilis,* cuius centrum ubique, circumferentia nusquam," and this is the version found in Bonaventure, Alexander of Hales, and Thomas Aquinas, among others.[13] Indeed, it was apparently not until the time of Meister Eckhart that the original formulation of the "*infinite* sphere" metaphor resurfaced,[14] and it did not become widely known until Nicholas of Cusa—after discovering the saying of the *infinite* sphere in Eckhart's writings—transferred the metaphor from God to the cosmos.

In fact, the restoration of the designation "infinite" is demanded by the metaphor itself. An "intelligible" sphere whose "center" is every-

12. Mahnke argues that Alan's formulation here is not merely an inconsequential deviation in terminology, but rather indicates that he did not fully grasp the significance of comparing God to an *infinite* sphere, since his elucidation of the metaphor shows that he is thinking primarily in terms of the attributes of a finite though immaterial sphere. God is comparable to the circumference of the sphere, Alan says, because his eternal nature has no beginning or end, just like a circle that returns upon itself, and because his omnipotence contains everything. He interprets the extensionless center, on the other hand, as comparable to creatures because in comparison to God they are mere points or moments. He does add that in a metaphorical sense God can be thought of as a sphere because the center of his effective power is everywhere and its limit nowhere, whereas in a physical sphere, the center, due to its minuteness, is hardly anywhere, while the circumference passes through many places. But this addition, Mahnke argues, is a rather superficial gloss on the metaphor of the divine sphere as compared to the rich and original elucidation provided in the *Book of Twenty-Four Philosophers,* which stresses in detail the infinite breadth and richness of the divine nature. See Mahnke, *Unendliche Sphäre,* 173–75.

13. Alan of Lille, *Regulae theologicae* in *Patrologia Latina,* 210: 627. See also Bonaventure, *Itinerarium mentis in Deum,* chap. 5, n. 8; Alexander of Hales, *Summa theologica,* pars. 1, qu. 7, m. 1; Aquinas, *De veritate* qu. 2, art. 3, obj. 11. See Mahnke, *Unendliche Sphäre,* 171–72; and Herbert Wackerzapp, *Der Einfluß Meister Eckharts auf die ersten philosophischen Schriften des Nikolaus von Kues (1440–1450),* Beiträge zur Geschichte der Philosophie und Theologie des Mittelalters XXXIX/3 (Münster: Aschendorff, 1962), 141–42.

14. Mahnke notes (*Unendliche Sphäre,* 176) that Eckhart and his contemporaries Jean de Meun and Thomas Bradwardine are the first thinkers he is aware of to return to the notion of the "unlimited" or "infinite" sphere.

where and whose "circumference" is nowhere must in fact be conceived of as infinite. Any finite sphere, as such, has a definite circumference and a fixed center. The designation "infinite" thus serves here to make explicit what is already implicitly conceptually contained in the image of a sphere with its center at every point and with no bounding periphery. The (finite) circle and sphere had, of course, long been used as symbols for divine perfection, to figure the eternal, self-sufficient, all-encompassing nature of divine unity.[15] The duality between eternity and time, being and becoming, creator and creation, mind and thought, is readily mirrored in the relation between the center and circumference of a circle or sphere. Only in the case of the infinite sphere, however, is the *coincidence* of unity and plurality, of minimum and maximum, of inner and outer, of immanence and transcendence explicitly thematized.[16]

Meister Eckhart makes this coincidence a central feature of his thought and so it is not at all surprising to witness the readiness with which he makes use of the paradoxical figure of the divine sphere. Eckhart, who was familiar with both the *Theological Rules* and the *Book of Twenty-Four Philosophers,*[17] uses the symbol of the divine sphere six

15. See O. J. Brendel, *Symbolism of the Sphere: A Contribution to the History of Earlier Greek Philosophy* (Leiden: Brill, 1977); and J. Gaus, "Circulus mensurat omnia," in *Mensura, Mass, Zahl, Zahlensymbolik im Mittelalter,* vol. 2, ed. A. Zimmermann and G. Vuillemin-Diem (Berlin and New York: W. de Gruyter, 1984), 435–54.

16. See Georges Poulet, "Le symbole du cercle infini dans la littérature et la philosophie," *Revue de métaphysique et de morale* 64, no. 3 (1959): 257–75. See also his *The Metamorphoses of the Circle,* trans. Carley Dawson and Elliott Coleman (Baltimore: The Johns Hopkins University Press, 1966).

17. Eckhart made extensive use of the *Book of Twenty-Four Philosophers,* a work he clearly held in high esteem. Eleven of the twenty-four propositions (1, 2, 3, 6, 7, 8, 14, 16, 18, 19, 22) appear in his Latin works and six more in his German Sermons (11, 17, 20, 21, 23, 24). For the importance of the *Book of Twenty-Four Philosophers* in the work of Eckhart see Heinrich Denifle, "Meister Eckharts lateinische Schriften und die Grundanschauung Seiner Lehre," *Archiv für Literatur- und Kirchengeschichte des Mittelalters* 2 (1886): 427–29. See also Mahnke, *Unendliche Sphäre,* 149–50, 169–71; and Wackerzapp, *Einfluß Meister Eckharts,* 142.

Interestingly, Hudry speculates that the unknown author of the commentary (2b) on the *Book of Twenty-Four Philosophers,* discovered by Marie-Thérèse d'Alverny, was the fourteenth-century Dominican Nicolas Trivet. If that is the case, Eckhart and Trivet would likely have met in Paris during Eckhart's second *magisterium* there between 1311 and 1313, and Hudry suggests

times in various works, sometimes with the designation "infinite sphere," sometimes "infinite intellectual sphere," and sometimes "intelligible sphere."[18] In all cases he uses the figure to reflect a central theme in his thought: the simultaneous transcendence and immanence of God vis-à-vis creation. In what follows we will see how, through his peculiar brand of image mysticism, Eckhart develops the pseudo-hermetic conception of divine omnipresence as an intensive infinity present even in the least part of creation. Secondly, we will see how for Eckhart the human soul, in particular, mirrors the infinite nature of the divine.

THE UBIQUITY OF GOD IN THE WORLD

I would like to turn first to a specific text in which Eckhart cites the three propositions from the *Book of Twenty-Four Philosophers* discussed

---

that it might have been Eckhart who commissioned Trivet—a specialist in the explication of ancient texts—to write a commentary on the *Book of Twenty-Four Philosophers.* She notes the appearance of several common themes in both commentary 2b and Eckhart's Predigt 9, which makes heavy and explicit use of the *Book of Twenty-Four Philosophers.* If Eckhart was indeed drawing on commentary 2b in his Predigt 9, Hudry notes, then the dating for that sermon would have to be revised and situated after his second *magisterium* in Paris. It would then likely have been preached in Strasbourg, perhaps to the Dominican nuns—perhaps to beguines—under his spiritual direction. This connection would further explain, Hudry notes, why the *Book of Twenty-Four Philosophers* is transmitted in the fourteenth century with texts of piety and preaching. See Hudry, *Liber XXIV philosophorum,* XLVIII–L.

18. Eckhart's German Works and Latin Works (designated as "DW" and "LW" respectively are cited from *Meister Eckhart. Die deutschen und lateinischen Werke: Herausgegeben im Auftrage der Deutschen Forschungsgemeinschaft* (Stuttgart: W. Kohlhammer, 1936–).

According to Joseph Koch's compilation, the metaphor of the divine sphere appears six times in Cusanus' manuscript of Eckhart's writings, the Codex Cusanus 21. See Mahnke, *Unendliche Sphäre,* 147 n. 2; and Wackerzapp, *Einfluß Meister Eckharts,* 142.

- "sphaera infinita": fol. 14, col. 4 = *Expositio libri Genesis,* n. 155 (LW I, 305, 3–8)
- "sphaera intellectualis infinita": fol. 47, 3 = *Exp. Exodi,* n. 91 (LW II, 94, 17–95, 3)
- "sphaera intellectualis infinita": fol. 80, 1 = *Exp. Eccli.,* n. 20 (LW II, 248, 2–4)
- "sphaera intelligibilis": fol. 124, 4 = *Exp. Joh.,* n. 604 (LW III, 527, 4)
- "sphaera intelligibilis": fol. 158, 2 = Sermo XLV, n. 458 (LW IV, 379, 13)
- "sphaera intelligibilis": fol. 170, 1 = Sermo LV, 3, n. 546 (LW IV, 457, 5)

In the commentaries on Exodus and Ecclesiasticus, Eckhart uses "intellectualis" rather than Alan of Lille's "intelligibilis." Mahnke takes this as an indication that Eckhart was aware of both the *Book of Twenty-Four Philosophers* and Alan's *Rules of Theology* as well as a reference to the divine sphere in Bartholomaeus Anglicus. See Mahnke, *Unendliche Sphäre,* 150 n. 3. Perhaps the

above. In his *Commentary on Exodus,* in the context of describing God's omnipresence in the world, Eckhart writes:

With his whole being God is present whole and entire as much in the least thing as in the greatest. Thus the just person who loves God in all things would seek in vain for something more or greater when he has some little thing in which the God whom he loves alone to the exclusion of everything else is totally present. There is no 'greater' or 'less' in God nor in the One; they are below and outside God and the One. And thus someone who sees, seeks, and loves what is more or less is not as such divine. This is the meaning of the axiom in the *Book of Twenty-Four Philosophers:* 'God is the infinite intellectual sphere with as many circumferences as centers and whose center is everywhere and circumference nowhere. He is entire in his least part.'[19]

In this passage Eckhart stresses both the absolute transcendence and the absolute immanence of the divine. "God and the One," as infinite, transcend all relative relations of more or less, greater or smaller, which are applicable only to things of finite determination. All creatures insofar as they are relative, finite beings "are below and outside" the divine One which knows no such distinction. In this sense God as infinite unity transcends all finite multiplicity. Eckhart goes further and asserts in one of his German sermons that all creatures, with respect to their creaturely nature, and considered apart from God, are mere nothings. "All creatures are a pure nothing. I do not say that they are insignificant or are only a little something: they are a pure nothing. Whatever has no being *is* not. Creatures have no being because their being depends on God's presence.

---

term serves also to underscore Eckhart's understanding of God as pure Intellect *(intelligere)* as well as absolute Being *(esse).* See Ruedi Imbach, *Deus est Intelligere. Das Verhältnis von Sein und Denken in seiner Bedeutung für das Gottesverständnis bei Thomas von Aquin und in den Pariser Quaestionen Meister Eckharts* (Freiburg, Switzerland: Univeritätsverlag), 1976.

19. *Commentary on Exodus,* chapter 16, verse 18 (LW II, 94, 17–95); translated in *Meister Eckhart: Teacher and Preacher,* ed. and trans. Bernard McGinn with the collaboration of Frank Tobin and Elvira Borgstädt, The Classics of Western Spirituality (New York: Paulist, 1986), 75. (References to this translation will hereafter be designated by "*TP*" followed by the page number.) Eckhart refers to the same three sentences in his first commentary on Genesis (chapter 2, verse 2) in order to explain why "the smallest work in God is equal to the greatest." The quotes are not exactly the same, however. In the commentary on Genesis we find: "Et hoc est quod in Libro XXIV philosophorum dicitur: 'deus est totus in quolibet sui'; et iterum: 'deus est sphaera infinita, cuius centrum ubique est et circumferentia nusquam'; et rursus: 'deus est sphaera, cuius tot sunt circumferentiae quot sunt puncta'" (*In Gen.* I n. 155 [LW I, 305, 3–8]).

If God were to turn away from creatures for an instant, they would turn to nothing."[20] Here the extremes of transcendence and immanence meet as transcendence flips over into immanence, for it is God who serves as the very ground of their existence, so that all creatures derive the whole of their being from God. God is present "in" all creatures as the principle of their being, indeed in such a way that God "is present whole and entire" in each and every entity.

It is interesting to note, here, that Eckhart does not quote his source exactly, but with an interesting interpolation. The third sentence in the *Book of Twenty-Four Philosophers* reads: "Deus est totus in quolibet sui." Eckhart strengthens this in his commentary on Exodus when he asserts that God is entire in his *least* part ("totus est in sui *minimo*"), and even more in his commentary on Ecclesiasticus, in which he emphasizes that this complete presence of God is to be found in "any *creature* whatsoever," indeed, "in one just as in all" ("Sic deus totus in qualibet creatura, in una sicut in omnibus").[21]

This conception of divine omnipresence is not to be confused with pantheistic divinization of the world as totality. God or "the One" is all-inclusive, not in the sense of being the sum total of all that is, but rather as the ground of all that is. God is immanent in the series of determinate, multifarious entities as their source and ground and so transcends the series itself. That is, God is not a being among beings, but is "above" or "beyond" the series of relative and determinate entities. In another German sermon, for example, Eckhart writes, "God touches all things and re-

20. Predigt 4: *Omne datum optimum* (DW I, 69–70; *TP,* 250). See also A. Daniels, "Eine lateinische Rechtfertigungsschrift des Meister Eckhart," *Beiträge zur Geschichte der Philosophie des Mittelalters* 23 (1923): sections IX, 1 and IX, 50. C. F. Kelly explains: "The link between the finite and the Infinite, or between the individual manifestation and unmanifested God, is that the finite is in its principle Infinite, while the finite as such is not" (C. F. Kelly, *Meister Eckhart on Divine Knowledge* [New Haven: Yale University Press, 1977], 229). On the nothingness of creatures in themselves see also Vladimir Lossky, *Théologie négative et connaissance de Dieu chez Maître Eckhart* (Paris: Vrin, 1960), 59, 76, 82, 105, 177, 218, 286, and 340. See also Émilie Zum Brunn and Alain de Libera, *Maître Eckhart: Métaphysique du verbe et théologie négative* (Paris: Beauchesne, 1984), 170, n. 27.

21. *Sermones et Lectiones super Ecclesiastici,* chapter 24, verse 23 (LW II, 248, 7–8). See also *Comm. Gen.* 155 (LW I, 305).

mains untouched. . . . God is above all things an instanding in Himself, and this standing in Himself sustains all creatures. . . . He is the ground and the encirclement of all creatures."[22] In this Eckhart follows the traditional Neoplatonic conception of the relation between the One and the many. Of interest to us is the appropriation of the theme of the One in the many expressed here in the metaphor of the infinite sphere: the notion of an *infinite* God present *whole and entire* in each and every part of creation. Here, I believe, we may discover the roots of the "intensive infinitization" of the cosmos, which occurred in the transition from the medieval to the modern age.

Indeed, for Eckhart the symbol of the infinite sphere expresses the "principle of solidarity," the notion that everything is contained in some sense in everything else, that the whole is present or reflected in each part. In this, too, he anticipates a theme that finds expression in modern thought from Leibniz to Whitehead, a theme that may once again be traced back to its theological origins.[23] In his commentary on Ecclesiasticus, Eckhart maintains, "In divine things each and every thing is in every other, the maximum is in the minimum" *(in divinis 'quodlibet est in quolibet' et maximum in minimo).* Eckhart explains this principle of solidarity in the divine by referring to the saying of "a wise man" *(sapiens),* who

22. Predigt 13a: *Sankt Johannes sah in einer Schau* (DW I, 483); translated in M. O'C. Walshe, *Meister Eckhart: Sermons and Treatises,* vol. 1 (Shaftesbury, Dorset: Element Books, 1979), (Walshe Sermon 24b), 193. (This translation will hereafter be designated "W" followed by the volume number, Walshe's sermon number, and the page number.)

23. See O. Bradley Bassler's "Leibniz on Universal Harmony," Section 3 of "Labyrinthus de compositione continui: The Origins of Leibniz' Solution to the Continuum Problem 1666–1672" (Ph.D. diss., University of Chicago, 1995). Here Bassler discusses the role which J. H. Bisterfeld's concept of *immeatio* had in the development of Leibniz's notion of harmony. Bisterfeld abstracts the term *immeatio* from its original theological context—the term had previously been used only to discuss the interrelation of the three Persons of the Trinity—and uses it to designate a much broader metaphysical conception of the relation and connection of all things with all things. Leibniz goes on to develop this principle of solidarity in his own philosophy of universal harmony, and it is this metaphysical foundation which underlies his physical and mathematical treatment of the continuum problem. It is interesting to note, in a similar vein, that Newton's universal law of gravity may be viewed as a physical analogue of the solidarity thesis. Since gravity is described by an inverse square law, everything in the universe exerts some influence on everything else.

says, "'God is an infinite' intellectual 'sphere, whose center together with its circumference is everywhere,' and 'which has just as many circumferences as points.'"[24] Note that here again Eckhart has shifted the sense of the metaphor in a subtle way. He modifies the original saying of the infinite sphere by asserting the ubiquity of *both* center and circumference.[25] This image of the ubiquity of an infinite number of centers and peripheries serves on the one hand to further underscore the coincidence of minimum and maximum, of divine immanence and transcendence, and on the other to emphasize the assertion that God is present—in his entirety—in every part of creation. Thus the image evoked is that of the entire divine sphere, center and circumference alike, simultaneously present in each and every part of the world.[26]

24. The Latin reads: "Ratio, quia 'deus,' ut ait sapiens, 'est sphaera' intellectualis 'infinita, cuius centrum est ubique cum circumferentia,' et 'cuius tot sunt circumferentiae quot puncta,' ut in eodem libro scribitur" (*In Eccl.* n. 20 [LW II, 248, 2–4]). Similarly in Eckhart's commentary on John, where he once again cites the infinite sphere as a metaphor for God (*Comm. Jn.* n. 604 [LW III, 527]), he emphasizes the intensity of God's divine presence: "in parte est totum et optimum."

25. Eckhart's assertion of the ubiquity of the circumference as well as the center amounts to an assertion that God is present not only as an entirety in all of creation, but that God is present *as an infinite sphere* in all of creation. Eckhart combines Propositions 2 and 3 from the original source.

26. Mahnke emphasizes the novelty and significance of Eckhart's variation on the original source. "For [Eckhart] does not say only that the entire divine sphere is contained in each part of the *divine*, as his source [says], but rather [he says] that the entire divine sphere—both its center *and its infinite circumference* alike—is contained in each minimal part of the world" (Mahnke, *Unendliche Sphäre*, 150; my translation).

This move strikes me as quite natural, however, and as a less radical departure from the intention of the *Book of Twenty-Four Philosophers* than Mahnke seems to think. At issue is how to interpret the *"sui"* in the original formulation of the third proposition in the *Book of Twenty-Four Philosophers* ("Deus est totus in quolibet sui"). Mahnke interprets this as God being present as a whole in any given part *of himself*, but this strikes me as an awkward reading. More natural would be to understand it as God being present as a whole in any given part *of his creation*. In any case, whatever the original meaning, Eckhart explicitly intends every single person and thing as the locus of God's absolute and total presence, and develops this notion far beyond what was articulated in the terse statement of his original source. And Mahnke is quite right to recognize in this new emphasis an interpretation which is further developed in the writings of Nicholas of Cusa and later Renaissance thinkers, especially Ficino and Bruno.

ECKHART'S IMAGE MYSTICISM

Eckhart holds that the infinite God is "present" in every finite part of creation. But in what sense? Clearly he intends not a physical but a metaphysical presence. God is present in all things as their ontological ground. Eckhart's understanding of God's omnipresence is thought on analogy to Platonic formal participation. The just man *is* just insofar as (and only insofar as) he participates in the form of Justice; similarly, all things exist insofar as they participate in, or are grounded by, infinite Being. In his *Commentary on John*, for example, Eckhart explains that God is the Being *(esse)* and principle or source *(principium)* of all the many beings which are.[27] They all receive their being, insofar as they are, from God immediately; for there is no medium between Being *(esse)* and a being as such *(ens ut ens)*.[28]

Hence, God is present in all that is by virtue of the fact that God is the Being of all beings. At same time, it is precisely because God is the Being of all beings that God transcends all finite entities. For God is not a being among many beings, all of which are distinct one from the other. Indeed, it is God's utter indistinction from all that is which distinguishes the infinite God from finite beings.[29] Hence, Eckhart writes:

> God is in each being insofar as that being is, but in none insofar as it is *this* being; indeed God is in all beings insofar as those beings are, but outside of all and in none of them insofar as they taste of . . . time, division, continuous quantity, the more or less (also of degree), distinction, this and that, particularity; in short generally [God is] in nothing where there is lack, deformity, evil, privation or negation.[30]

This is because there is no negation or limitation in God and all these terms signify a negation or deprivation of being. But God is absolute and infinite fullness of Being *(esse plenum)*, lacking nothing. In this sense God must be understood to be the "negation of negation" in an absolute

27. On God as *Esse omnium* see Lossky, *Théologie négative*, 298–312; See also Francis Bertin's commentary in *Nicolas de Cues: Sermons eckhartiens et dionysiens* (Paris: Les Éditions du CERF, 1998), 281–92.

28. *Comm. Jn.* n. 205 (LW III, 172).

29. See also *Comm. Ex.* n. 16 (LW II, 46), and *Comm. Wis.* nn. 144–57 (LW II, 481–94).

30. *Comm. Jn.* n. 206 (LW III, 174), my emphasis, my translation.

sense.[31] A creature, on the other hand, is a particular finite being precisely because it exits as this and *not* that, here and *not* there, now and *not* then. Each finite being is the particular that it is by way of a negation or a limitation of its being. Insofar as it exists at all, each finite being participates in God's infinite Being, but God's perfect fullness of Being is received by no particular entity *as* a particular.[32] (If God were in Thomas *as* Thomas God could not also be in John.)

Thus Eckhart appropriates the Platonic structure of formal participation in order to describe the relationship between God and creation (Being and beings) without, however, conceiving of divine Being as determinate in any way. Thus, the analogy to the just man sharing in Justice holds good insofar as the participated term (Justice) is conceived of as present in the just man as his essential being, and insofar as the just man stands in relation to Justice itself as image to exemplar. The analogy is misleading, however, when applied to the relationship between God and creation, to the extent that Justice is understood to be a determinate Form, giving determinate being to the participating term. Indeed, the traditional Platonic conception of participation in a divine Form is effective in describing the manifestation of a determinate reality (Justice, Beauty, Equality and so on). But Eckhart is concerned to describe the inherence of the infinite in the world. Indeed, the infinite in its entirety is understood to be present in each particular. This relation cannot be easily articulated by using the traditional model of the inherence of a Form, since the infinite, as such, explodes all forms. It is perhaps for this reason that Eckhart conceives of the participating relationship between the divine infinite and manifest reality as one of *imaging*, of the presence of the exemplar in its image.[33]

Initially the language of image and exemplar would seem to be just as limiting as that of the Platonic Forms. After all, an image, it would seem, is

31. On God as *negationis negatio* see Lossky, *Théologie négative*, 67, 135, 304–6, 357; and Zum Brunn and de Libera, *Métaphysique du verbe*, 149–50.

32. *Comm. Jn.* n. 207 (LW III, 174–75).

33. On Eckhart's "image mysticism" see Alois Haas, *Sermo mysticus: Studien zu Theologie und Sprache der deutschen Mystik* (Freiburg, Switzerland: Universitätsverlag, 1979), 209–37; and Wolfgang Wackernagel, *Ymagine denudari: Éthique de l'image et métaphysique de l'abstraction chez Maître Eckhart* (Paris: Librairie Philosophique Vrin, 1991).

merely a representation of some determinate reality. It is, however, precisely the representational structure of the image/exemplar relation which Eckhart uses in order to arrive at his mystical recognition of the infinite unity of all that is. When pushed to its extreme the image/exemplar relation approaches one of identity: the *perfect* image cannot be thought of as "other" than its exemplar. This is the insight, as we shall see, which drives Eckhart's image mysticism.

The Emanation and Return of All Things to God

The communication of the totality of God's infinite unity to each being in the world is understood by Eckhart in terms of a process of imaging with two "stages" in which all things flow forth from their divine ground. The first is the inner emanation of the three Persons of the Trinity from the absolute unity that is the Godhead. Eckhart describes this first emanation as a *bullitio* (a boiling). The second emanation is the creation of all things in the world, or *ebullitio* (a boiling over), which is itself modeled on the first emanation.[34] These two stages are distinguished in terms of a metaphysical, not a temporal, priority. Both emanations occur in the same, simple "now" of eternity.[35]

The "first" emanation or *bullitio* is an intra-divine emanation, an inner "boiling" of the Godhead giving rise to the Trinity. This is a self-reflexive process in which the effusion results in something which remains the same as itself. Eckhart describes this as a purely "formal emanation" or production which results in a perfect image. A perfect image is not merely "like" its exemplar but one and identical with it.[36]

34. See for example Sermo XXV: "God as good is the principle of the 'boiling over' on the outside; as personal notion he is the principle of the 'boiling within himself,' which is the cause and exemplar of the 'boiling over.' Thus, the emanation of the Persons in the Godhead, the cause and exemplar of creation, is prior" (LW IV, 236; *TP*, 218). See also *Comm. Gen.* n. 7, *and Comm. Ex.* n. 16.

35. Nicholas of Cusa defends Eckhart's teachings on the eternity of creation in his Sermo CCXVI, nn. 21–25.

36. "The One acts as a principle *(principiat)* through itself and gives existence and is an internal principle. For this reason, properly speaking, it does not produce something like itself, but what is one and the same as itself. For what is "like" entails difference and numerical diversity, but there can be no diversity in the One. This is why the formal emanation in the divine Persons

Note that an image properly speaking is a simple formal emanation that transmits the whole pure naked essence. The metaphysician considers it in abstraction from the efficient and final causes according to which natural scientists investigate things. The emanation [of the Trinity] then is from the depths in silence, excluding everything that comes from without. It is a form of life, as if you were to imagine something swelling up from itself and in itself and then inwardly boiling without any 'boiling over' yet understood.[37]

Eckhart describes this dynamic, formal emanation of the three Persons of the Trinity in his *Commentary on Exodus* in similar terms, referring for support to the first proposition in the *Book of Twenty-Four Philosophers:*

Note that the repetition [in Exodus 3:14] (namely that it says "I am who am") indicates the purity of affirmation excluding all negation from God. It also indicates a reflexive turning back of his existence into itself and upon itself, and its dwelling and remaining fixed in itself. It further indicates a "boiling" *(bullitio)* or giving birth to itself—glowing in itself, and melting and boiling in and into itself, light that totally forces its whole being in light and into light and that is everywhere totally turned back and reflected upon itself, according to that saying of the sage, "The monad gives birth to" (or gave birth to) "the monad, and reflected love or ardent desire back upon itself." Therefore, John 1 says, "In him was life" (Jn. 1:4). "Life" expresses a type of "pushing out" by which something swells up in itself and first spreads out totally in itself, each part into each part, before it pours itself forth and boils over on the outside *(ebulliat).*[38]

The second "emanation", this "boiling over on the outside" or *ebullitio,* exhibits a structure parallel to the first. "What is produced or proceeds from anything is precontained in it. This is universally and naturally true, both in the Godhead . . . and in natural and artificial things."[39] What is produced in divine emanation (intra and extra) is contained, as Eckhart says, *in principio.* Eckhart uses this term to mean both "in the beginning" (i.e. from eternity) and "in the principle" or ground. Here we

---

is a type of *bullitio,* and thus the three Persons are simply and absolutely one." *Comm. Jn.* n. 342 (LW III, 291); translated in *Meister Eckhart: The Essential Sermons, Commentaries, Treatises, and Defense,* ed. and trans. Edmund Colledge, O.S.A., and Bernard McGinn, The Classics of Western Spirituality (New York: Paulist Press, 1981), 37. (References to this translation will be designated by *"EE"* followed by the page number.) See *EE,* 303 note 74, concerning the term *bullitio* here.

37. Sermo XLIX (LW IV; *TP,* 236). See also *Comm. Wis.* n. 283 (LW II, 615–16), and Bernard McGinn's discussion in his "Theological Summary" in *EE,* 37–38.

38. *Comm. Ex.* n. 16 (LW II, 21–22; *TP,* 46).

39. *Comm. Jn.* n. 4 (LW III, 5; *EE,* 123).

encounter one of the main themes running throughout Eckhart's writings, that of the "principial" relation of all that is to its source. "What proceeds is in its source; it is in it as a seed is in its principle, as a word is in one who speaks; and it is in it as the idea in which and according to which whatever proceeds is produced by the source."[40]

Thus, just as the Second Person of the Trinity, the divine Word or Logos, exists "in principio" as the perfect image of the Father, so too that divine Logos acts as the exemplary, or "principial," cause by which all the world comes into existence.[41] Here Eckhart makes the traditional tie between Genesis 1:1 ("In the beginning God created the heaven and the earth") and John 1:1 ("In the beginning was the Word and the Word was with God and the Word was God"). This second world-engendering emanation from the principle does not produce a "perfect image" as in the case of the procession from the Father to the Son, but in the speaking of the divine Word, the *multiplicity* of created nature is formed. Again, this "act" of creation is not to be understood as a temporal event, for the Godhead persists in an unmoving, eternal "now."[42] In this "eternal now" God utters his "Only Begotten Word" with the breath of life, or the Holy Spirit, and the Eternal Word is the *exemplary*[43] principle and cause by which God creates all things.

In speaking the divine Word, God creates the world. This is because,

40. *Comm. Jn.* n. 4 (LW III, 6; *EE,* 124).

41. For a discussion of the parallel structure of *bullitio* and *ebullitio* see Bernard McGinn's "Theological Summary" in the introduction to *EE,* especially 30–45.

42. "It is false to picture God as if he were waiting around for some future moment in which to create the world. In the one and the same time in which he was God and in which he begot his coeternal Son as God equal to himself in all things, he also created the world. 'God speaks once and for all' (Jb. 22:14). He speaks in begetting the Son because the Son is the Word; he speaks in creating creatures, 'He spoke and they were made, he commanded and they were created' (Ps. 32:9). This is why it says in another Psalm, 'God has spoken once and for all and I have heard two things' (Ps. 61:12). The 'two things' are heaven and earth, or rather 'these two,' that is, the emanation of the Persons and the creation of the world, but 'he speaks' them both 'once and for all'; 'he has spoken once and for all.'" *Comm. Gen.* n. 7 (LW I, 1, 190–91; *EE,* 85). On Eckhart's conception of time and eternity, see Niklaus Largier, *Zeit, Zeitlichkeit, Ewigkeit: ein Aufriß des Zeitproblems bei Dietrich von Freiberg und Meister Eckhart* (Bern and New York: P. Lang, 1989).

43. See *Comm. Gen.* nn. 7–8 (LW I, 190–92; *EE,* 85), *Par. Gen.* n. 16 (LW I, 486–87; *EE,* 99), and *Comm. Jn.* n. 73 (LW III, 61; *EE,* 148).

unlike with us, God's speaking *is* his making.[44] That is, in the divine ground there is no distinction between word and object, idea and thing. Thought and being coincide in perfect equality. The emanation of the Persons and the creation of the world must be understood as a two-fold self-manifestation of the divine: "The Father speaks the Son out of all his power, and he speaks in him all things. All created things are God's speech. The being of a stone speaks and manifests the same as does my mouth about God. . . . Therefore the Father speaks the Son always, in unity, and pours out in him all created things."[45]

Three Modes of Divine Imaging: Emanatio, Factio, Creatio

As we have seen, Eckhart describes the relationship between the divine principle of all things and that which emanates from it as a kind of imaging, as a relationship between exemplar and image. What does Eckhart mean by the term "image"? He does not intend a representation that is merely similar to its exemplar. He has in mind here a sort of "iconic" relationship between image and exemplar, that is, the actual *presence* of the imaged in the image itself. In his *Commentary on John* Eckhart describes the nature of a perfect or true image. He lists nine characteristics:

1. "An image insofar as it is an image receives nothing of its own from the subject in which it exists, but receives its whole existence from the object it images."
2. "It receives its existence only from the object."
3. "It receives the whole existence of the object according to everything by which it is an exemplar. For if the image were to receive anything from another source or did not receive something that was in its exemplar, it would not be an image of that thing but of something else."
4. "The image of anything is one in itself and is the image of one thing alone."
5. "The image is in its exemplar, for there it receives its whole existence. On the other hand, the exemplar insofar as it is an exemplar is in its

44. *Comm. Gen.* n. 8.
45. Predigt 53: *Misit dominus manum suam* (DW II, 535–37; *EE,* 205).

image because the image has the whole existence of the exemplar in itself."

6. "The image and that of which it is an image, insofar as they are such, are one."

7. "Such an expression or begetting of the image is a kind of formal emanation."

8. "The image and the exemplar are coeval . . . in such a way that the exemplar cannot be understood without the image and vice versa."

9. "Only the exemplar knows the image and the image the exemplar. . . . The reason is because their existence is one and nothing of one is alien to the other. The principles of knowing and of existence are the same, and nothing is known through what is alien to it."[46]

The image receives its being immediately, and in an exclusive and singular manner, from its exemplar.[47] The generation of the image is explained as a process of formal emanation, the formal expression, or effusion, of the pure and complete being of the exemplar.[48] It is a "simple pouring out according to form, through which the whole, pure being (of the exemplar) is imparted."[49] Nothing is held back in the transmission of essence, or the image would not be an image *of* the exemplar, but of something else. Further the image can image only the exemplar, or again it would have some element of difference with its exemplar and again would not be a true image. Clearly for an image to be a perfect image, it cannot merely resemble its exemplar, but must be one and the same with it. This pouring forth of the image out of the exemplar is further characterized by simultaneity, so that the image and exemplar mutually imply each other and are eternally coextensive. Since both have one and the same being, they have the same epistemological content, and so are self-reflexively "known" to each other.[50]

46. *Comm. Jn.* nn. 23–26 (LW III, 19f.; *EE,* 129–30).

47. The image takes its being "âne mittel an dem, des bilde ez ist, und hât ein wesen mit im und ist daz selbe wesen" (Predigt 16b [DW I, 270, 5f.]). See also Sermo XLIX.3 (LW IV, 425–28).

48. *Expositio libri Sapientiae* n. 143 (LW II, 481).

49. Sermo XLIX,3: *Imago* n. 511 (LW IV, 425).

50. See Sermo XLIX,2–3 nn. 509–12 (LW IV, 424–28; *TP,* 236–37.), and Predigt 16b: *Quasi vas auri solidum* (DW I, 270, 1–6; *TP,* 275).

These nine determinations of the exemplar-image relation are all referred directly to the intra-divine relation of Father to Son. Only the Son stands in this relation of perfect image to its exemplar.[51] Eckhart makes use of scriptural sources and doctrinal teaching about the Trinity to support his reading of the image relation. The Son receives his entire being from the Father. All that the Father is, is passed on to the Son; nothing is held back. The relationship is exclusive: the Son is the "only begotten Son" of the Father. The result is a mutual, internal abiding of Father and Son: "I am in the Father, and the Father is in me" (Jn. 14:11). Father and Son are one, because of the identity of their nature, but distinct in person: "'The Father and I are one' (Jn. 10:30). He says 'we are' insofar as there is an exemplar that is expressive and begets and an image that is expressed or begotten; he says 'one' insofar as the whole existence of the one is in the other and there is nothing alien to it there."[52] Further the imaging process is one of the timeless transmission of essence. Father and Son are co-eternal: "In the beginning was the Word and the Word was with God" (Jn. 1:1). Father and Son are co-extensive. One cannot be thought without the other, and only the one is able to know the other: "He who sees me also sees my Father" (Jn. 14:9), and "No one knows the Son except the Father, nor does anyone know the Father except the Son" (Mt. 11:27).

Just as the intra-divine generation is understood in terms of this imaging process, so too is the extra-divine production of the world. The difference between the two lies in the way the image proceeds from its source. The intra-divine *bullitio* is a formal and natural emanation, which produces a perfect image and proceeds by means of formal causality alone. The extra-divine *ebullitio* is a willed production, which proceeds by way of efficient and final causality as well, and produces something different in number and in reality from its principle. The connection between the two imaging processes is to be found in the Second Person of the Trinity, the divine Logos, the perfect Image, which also functions as

51. Note that it is the Son who is the bearer of the image of God and not the Holy Spirit. See, for example, Predigt 16b (DW I, 267, 3–8).

52. *Comm. Jn.* n. 24 (LW III, 20; *EE,* 129).

the Ideal, or exemplary principle and "predestination," of all created things in the world.[53]

In the extra-divine production of creatures, Eckhart distinguishes between those with and those without reason. Non-rational beings are created according to a likeness of something that is *in* God, namely his ideas. Rational beings, on the other hand, have God himself as their likeness.[54] "God is in all things as being, as activity, as power. But He is fecund in the soul alone, for though every creature is a vestige of God, the soul is the natural image of God."[55] The non-rational world is a divine "footprint" or "vestige," whereas the human soul is made in the image of God.

Eckhart thus distinguishes three different modes of imaging: *emanatio* (the intra-divine generation of the Trinity), *factio* (the creation of rational beings) and *creatio* (the creation of non-rational beings).[56] In the latter

53. See Eckhart's *Comm. Jn.* nn. 23–27 (LW III, 19–22) on the Word as the Father's image; nn. 28–31 (LW III, 22–25) on the Word as Principle; n. 32 (LW III, 26) on the Idea as definition; and nn. 36–37 (LW III, 30–32) on the Word as Exemplar. Eckhart follows here in a long Neoplatonic tradition. Maximus Confessor, for example, assimilated the pagan triad being-life-intellect to a unified Godhead, by equating Being and Life with what he termed "logoi," the divine reasons of all things embraced within the Christ-Logos. These "logoi" or "paradigms" are the ideas or forms of all things, and also their predestinations. For in and through them, all things that have been or will be created were simultaneously predestined, by the will of God. All things in the natural and celestial world (material or conceptual) subsist by participation in them as their ground and reason. And they in turn subsist by participation in the cause of all things, the Godhead itself. (*Ambig.* 7.1084B, cited in Steven Gersh's *From Iamblichus to Eriugena* [Leiden: E. J. Brill, 1978], 156. See also Eriugena's analogous doctrine in his *Periphyseon,* trans. Sheldon-Williams and John J. O'Meara [Montreal: Éditions Bellarmin, 1987], 615D–616B.)

54. *Comm. Gen.* n. 115 (LW I, 270), *Comm. Jn.* n. 549 (LW III, 479), and Predigt 24 (DW I, 415). See also Sermo XLIX: "Augustine says that likeness is found in every creature, but image only in intellectual beings" (LW IV, 422, n. 506; *TP,* 235). See Haas, *Sermo mysticus,* 218.

55. "Got ist in allen dingen weselich, wükelich, gewalteclich. Aber er ist alleine geberende in der sêle, wan alle crêatûre sint ein fuozstapfe gotes, aber diu sêle ist natiurlich nâch gote gebildet." (*Ubi est qui natus est rex Judaeorum?* Pfeiffer Sermon 2 in *Deutsche Mystiker der Vierzehnten Jahrhunderts,* vol. 2, *Meister Eckhart,* ed. Franz Pfeiffer (Göttingen: Vandenhoeck and Ruprecht, 1857; reprint, 1906), 11; Quint Sermon 58 in *Meister Eckehart: Deutsche Predigten und Traktate,* ed. and trans. Josef Quint (Munich: Carl Hanser Verlag, 1963); W I (2), 15.

56. For an important discussion of the three types of production, see Sermo XLIX.3 (LW IV, 424–26). Compare also with *Par Gen.* n. 9 (LW I, 1, 479–81; *EE,* 96). Shizuteru Ueda explains the distinction as follows: "The *emanatio* is a natural (*non voluntate, sed natura sive naturaliter*—not by the will, but by nature or naturally) production, in which a being produces something from itself (*a se*—what concerns the originator), out of itself (*de se ipso*—what concerns the

two cases the mode of likeness *(similitudo)* is quite different. The process of imaging in the case of non-rational creation is by way of vestiges *(per modum vestigii)*, and in the case of the human soul by way of image *(per modum imaginis)*. That is, the human soul proceeds from God in the likeness of divine substance itself *(homo procedit a deo, 'in similitudinem' divinae 'substantiae')*.[57]

The Perfection of the Image of God in the Human Soul and the Return of All Things to God

Just as humanity flows forth from God as created image, so too, it is in the perfecting of that image that the human soul returns to its divine origin. Indeed, Eckhart emphasizes that in the Incarnation, the Word of God assumed human nature in general, not simply that of one particular man, so that the divine image in the soul of each human being might be perfected through grace.[58]

> [T]he first fruit of the Incarnation of Christ, God's Son, is that man may become by the grace of adoption what the Son is by nature, as it says in the text here, "He gave them the power of becoming sons of God" (Jn. 1:12–13), and in the third chapter of Second Corinthians, "with faces unveiled reflecting as in a mirror the glory of the Lord, we are being transformed in the same image from glory to glory" (2 Co. 3:18).[59]

---

material of the production) and in itself (*in se ipso*—what concerns the place of the production), in that it pours forth its bare nature according to form (***naturam nudam formaliter profundens***—bare nature pouring forth formally). In distinction to ***emanatio, factio*** and ***creatio*** are willful productions. More specifically, they are ***ebullitio sub ratione efficientis et in ordine finis*** (a boiling over by way of efficient cause and in the order of ends), in which a being produces something from itself but not out of itself, but rather either out of something else *(de alio quolibet)*—that is *factio*—, or out of nothing *(de nihilo)*—that is *creatio;* in both cases what is produced stands outside of that which produces" (***Die Gottesgeburt in der Seele und der Durchbruch zur Gottheit: Die mystische Anthropologie Meister Eckharts und ihre Konfrontation mit der Mystik des Zen-Buddhismus*** [Gütersloh: Mohn, 1965], 52–53, my translation).

57. ***Comm. Gen.*** n. 115 (LW I, 271).

58. "[T]he first fruit of the Incarnation of the Word, who is the natural Son of God, is that we should be God's sons through adoption. It would be little value for me that 'the Word was made flesh' for man in Christ as a person distinct from me unless he was also made flesh in me personally so that I too might be God's son." ***Comm. Jn.*** n. 117 (LW III, 101–2; *EE*, 167). See also Predigt 5b: ***In hoc apparuit caritas dei*** (DW I, 85–88).

59. ***Comm. Jn.*** n. 106 (LW III, 90–91; *EE*, 162).

Eckhart stresses emphatically that it is by the very same image that Christ is the Son of God, that the godlike man, too, may become a son of God.[60] Indeed, Eckhart understands the Incarnation as an eternal event which is repeated whenever the Word is given birth in the human soul.[61] As has often been pointed out, Eckhart is not always careful to make the distinction between Christ, as Son of God, and the divine sonship which is the end and perfection of the human soul. This is no doubt a result of the fact that he is, more often than not, speaking from the mystical standpoint of the *unio,* of image and imaged.

The locus of this union, Eckhart says, is to be found in the "highest part of the soul," in the soul's "inmost nature," in an uncreated "something" or divine "spark" in the soul.[62] Eckhart tends to identify this highest part (or deepest ground) of the soul with the intellect, though that is not always exclusively the case.[63] Eckhart's tendency to privilege the intellect as the locus of the perfection of the divine image results from his conception of its nature as both fundamentally receptive and essentially unitive.[64]

60. See *Comm. Jn.* n. 119 (LW III, 104; *EE,* 169): "We should not falsely suppose that it is by one son or image that Christ is the Son of God and by some other that the just and godlike man is a son of God, for he says, 'We are being transformed into the same image.' Furthermore, just as when many mirrors held up to a person's face and countenance are all informed by the same one face, so too each and every just person is completely and perfectly justified by the same justice. They are formed, informed and transformed into the same justice. Otherwise they would not be just in a univocal sense, and no single just person would be truly just if justice were one thing in itself and another in the just person."

61. See especially *Comm. Jn.* nn. 116–21 (LW III, 101–6). See also Haas, *Sermo mysticus,* 224, and Ueda, *Gottesgeburt,* 53–54.

62. See LW IV, 422, n. 507; DW I, 268; LW I, 272, n. 116; and DW I, 198.

63. See, for example, Predigt 2, in which the "little castle" described as the locus of the breakthrough to the divine ground of the Trinity is thought of as beyond both the will and the intellect, understood as powers of the soul. See also Predigt 52 (*EE,* 210) on the poverty of the godlike soul: "Now the actions proper to a man are loving and knowing. The question is: In which of these does blessedness most consist? Some authorities have said that it consists in knowing, others say that it consists in loving; others that it consists in knowing and loving, and what they say is better. But I say that it does not consist in either knowing or loving, but that there is that in the soul from which knowing and loving flow; that something does not know or love as do the powers of the soul."

64. Hans Hof (*Scintilla animae: Eine Studie zu einem Grundbegriff in Meister Eckharts Philosophie* [Lund: Gleerup, 1952], 196ff.) has pointed out that in Eckhart the intellect has two

On the one hand, Eckhart derives from Aristotle the idea that the intellect is potentially capable of knowing all things precisely because it has no specific form itself. It is literally "nothing of all the things that are." Just as the eye cannot possess some color if it is to see color,[65] just so "the intellect has no actual existence of its own *(nihil omnium est)* so that it can understand all things . . . it has nothing of itself, nothing of its own, before it understands. Understanding is a reception. The formal property of what receives something is to be naked."[66] It is precisely in this naked purity and indeterminacy of the intellect, in its no-*thing*-ness, that it is "like" the divine nature. Indeed, as we shall see, to the extent that the intellect is emptied of the many images of created things, to that extent it is filled with God.[67]

On the other hand, and at the same time, Eckhart appropriates the Neoplatonic conception of the intellect as a unifying or "revertive" power, able to draw the scattered multiplicity of created beings back into the original unity from which they flowed. "All creatures enter my understanding that they may become rational in me. I alone prepare all creatures for their return to God."[68] Indeed, as we shall see, to know all things

modes of being: as created and as an uncreated "something" in the soul. That is, Eckhart distinguishes the intellect as a power of the soul, the organ of human knowledge, and the intellect as such. In the first case it is created being: it has the 'signum' of 'hoc et hoc,' and is of the order of created things. The intellect as such, however, is not an entity at all, and is free of all determinations. It is of course the intellect as such that functions as the locus of the perfection of the divine image. See Haas' discussion, *Sermo mysticus,* 224–25. Wackernagel (*Ymagine Denudari,* 131) associates the reflected presence of the divine intellect in the human intellect with that uncreated "something," that divine "spark" in the soul.

65. Aristotle, *On the Soul* 2.7, 418b26.

66. *Comm. Jn.* n. 100 (LW III, 86–87; EE, 160). This doctrine is based on Aristotle's *On the Soul* 3.4. See especially 429a24–b31. See also Thomas Aquinas' *Commentary on Aristotle's De Anima,* Chapter III, Lecture 7. See also Eckhart's *Comm. Gen.* n. 115, where Eckhart cites Aristotle's *On the Soul* 3.5, 430a14, and 3.8, 431b21, in support of his contention that humanity is made in the image of God, because intellectual nature as such is able to become all things. The intellect, in a certain sense, is all things, is being in its totality.

67. See John Caputo, "The Nothingness of the Intellect in Meister Eckhart's *Parisian Questions,*" *Thomist* 39 (1975): 85–115.

68. *Nolite timere eos, qui corpus occidunt:* Pfeiffer Sermon 56, 180; Quint Sermon 26, 271; W II (56), 80. In the same sermon he goes on to say, "I alone bring all creatures out of their reason into my reason, so that they are one with me (*daz sie in mir eine sint*)" (Pfeiffer Sermon 56, 181; W II [56], 82).

truly, for Eckhart, is to know them in their principle and source, that is, to know them in God *as* God. Eckhart is drawing, here, on the traditional Neoplatonic doctrine of "remaining," "procession," and "reversion." This doctrine is meant to express the (causal) relationship between the different principles involved in emanation. An effect is said to remain in its cause insofar as it maintains an element of identity or "sameness" with the cause. It proceeds insofar as it undergoes a separation or manifests some distinction from its cause.[69] Finally, the effect is said to revert toward its cause in its striving to rectify the separation, and draw back together into a unity. "Intellect," Proclus writes, "everywhere holds the revertive rank, elevating and drawing back together with itself the whole multitude attached to it." It strives after "communion and connection with its cause," and this is "accomplished through similarity."[70] Hence, the perfection of the effect (intellect) depends on the extent to which it is like or is able to liken itself to its originating cause.

Hence the receptive and unitive capacities of the intellect are essentially connected: "Because the soul has the potentiality of knowing all things, it never rests until it comes to the first image where all things are one. There it rests, there in God . . . for whatever is in God *is* God."[71] Thus if the manifest, creative God is figured as a sphere emanating infinitely outwards, the human intellect may be viewed as an inverse, infinitely contracting, sphere which channels all things back into an absolutely unified center.[72]

69. Proclus for example writes: "In so far, then, as an effect has an element of identity with its cause, it remains in it, but in so far as it is other, it proceeds from it" (*Elements of Theology* 34.23–25; cited by Gersh, *Iamblichus to Eriugena,* 46).

70. Proclus (*In Parm.* 686.32–4), cited by Gersh, *Iamblichus to Eriugena,* 83.

71. Predigt 3 (DW I, 55; *TP,* 246).

72. Wackernagel makes this association of the divine spark in the human soul, its intellectual nature, with the center of the infinite intellectual sphere which is God: "Seule l'étincelle, c'est-à-dire la 'syndérèse', qui est au fond l'intériorité absolue de la créature douée d'intellect, peut être dite image du centre de la sphère infinie de l'intelligence divine: dans sa plus grande perfection, 'l'image' constitue en effet le 'quelque chose' d'incréé dans l'âme, au sujet duquel Maître Eckhart affirme que 'si l'homme était tout entier ainsi, il serait incréé et incréable' [Predigt 12; DW I, 198], affirmation qu'on lui a reproché au procès de Cologne. La tournure hypothétique indique pourtant bien que l'âme est certes créée, et que s'il y a en elle quelque chose d'incréé, ce quelque chose n'est pas propre à l'âme, mais constitue véritablement 'l'image du Dieu incréé'" (Wackernagel, *Ymagine Denudari,* 131; see also 181).

It should be noted that an analogous structure is operative, for Eckhart, in the perfecting of the will as well as the intellect. To the extent that the will is able to empty itself and become utterly receptive to God's love, and to the extent that it functions as a unitive power in loving all things in God, that is, indiscriminately and without a why, it too is able to become a vessel for divine loving, just as the intellect may become a vessel for divine knowing.[73] Indeed, the perfection of the soul, for Eckhart, entails a complete transformation of the whole soul, of its distinct powers of will and intellect, into a single unified image of God in God. "The eye in which I see God is the same eye in which God sees me. My eye and God's eye are one eye and one seeing, one knowing and one loving."[74]

~

The soul that would be transformed in God, says Eckhart, must free itself completely from all intellectual images of, and willful attachments to, creaturely things. Eckhart describes this emptying of the self of whatever is *not* God as a process of detachment. Such detachment is the precondition for what Eckhart describes as "the birth of the Word in the soul," that is, the divinization of the soul, or filiation. It is a process in which the soul must lose its own image (be "entbildet") and be transformed ("überbildet") into the image of God alone. This is to be born "in God and from God,"[75] to be "denuded of one's own images and to be transformed by images into God" (propria ymagine denudari et in deum per ymaginem transformari).[76] Hence, this process of detachment from

73. For a comprehensive and extremely insightful analysis of the central role of love in Eckhart's thought in general, see Ellen Chris Fanizzi, "Subverting the *Ordo Caritatis:* Meister Eckhart's Vision of Love" (Ph.D. diss., Boston College, 2000). In this context, in particular, see the section entitled "Beyond Knowledge and Love, *Unum est necessarium,*" 327–50.

74. Predigt 12: *Qui audit me* (DW I, 201; *TP,* 270).

75. *The Book of Divine Consolation* (DW V, 11; *EE,* 211). See also DW V, 208–9.

76. Gabriel Théry, "Édition critique des pièces relatives au procès d'Eckhart contenues dans le manuscrit 33b de la Bibliothèque de Soest," *Archives d'histoire littéraire et doctrinale du moyen âge* 1 (1926): 159. See also Predigt 40: *'blîbet in mir!'* Eckhart cites Augustine on love as a power and principle of unity with God: "'What a man loves, a man is. If he loves a stone, he is a stone, if he loves a man, he is a man. If he loves God—now I dare say no more: if I were to say that then he is God, you might stone me. But I refer you to scripture.' And therefore, when a man accommodates himself barely to God, with love, he is un-formed, then informed and transformed in the divine uniformity wherein he is one with God" (DW II, 278; W II [63], 119–20).

all particular images culminates in the soul's transformation into a divine image ("götlich bilde"),[77] into the "child of God," indeed, "into the same image" by which Christ is the Son of God.[78]

Eckhart describes this mystical union of the soul and Christ Logos as the simultaneous speaking and hearing of the Eternal Word of God. It is in and through the same divine Word that God is made manifest in creation and the soul returns to unity with God:

> As God speaks into the soul, the soul and he are one. . . . The more that we ascend in our understanding, the more are we one in him. Therefore the Father speaks the Son always, in unity, and pours out in him all created things. They are all called to return into whence they have flowed out. All their life and their blessing is a calling and a hastening back to him from whom they have issued.[79]

In order to "hear" the eternal Wisdom of God, however, the soul must rest, perfectly detached, in the still center of its being.

> Three things hinder us from hearing the eternal Word. The first is corporeality, the second multiplicity, the third temporality. If a person had passed beyond these three things, he would live in eternity, in the spirit, in oneness, and in the vast solitude; and there he would hear the eternal Word.[80]

The overcoming of corporeality means overcoming not only the limitations of our own embodied sensual existence, but also our ties to external things in general. These ties are constituted not only by our possessive attachments to and desire for particular things, but also by our "knowledge" of things external to us through the senses and also through reason. The former sort of knowing depends on sensible images and the

77. *Of the Nobleman* (DW V, 112, 21; *EE,* 242).

78. *Comm. Jn.* n. 119 (LW III, 104). Eckhart's doctrine of the birth of the Word in the soul was one of his most controversial teachings, and several versions of it were cited in the papal Bull which condemned twenty-six articles taken from his writings as heretical or as dangerous. Bernard McGinn points out that although the birth of Christ in the believer's soul was a theme considered suspect in the thirteenth century, it has very ancient and well-established roots in the history of Christian spirituality. "The notion that Christ is born in the faithful heart through baptism has deep roots in the Greek fathers, and from the time of Gregory of Nyssa the birth of Christ in the believer was also used as a way to express the mystical union of the soul and the Logos" ("Theological Introduction," in *EE,* 50).

79. Predigt 53: *Misit dominus manum suam* (DW II, 536–37; *EE,* 205).

80. Predigt 12: *Qui audit me* (DW I, 192–93; *TP,* 267).

latter on concepts.[81] Both forms of knowledge limit the soul's capacity to "hear the eternal Word," which remains always ineffable and inexpressible. In the tradition of negative or apophatic theology, Eckhart denies that God can be grasped in a positive cognitive manner: "[T]he brightness of the divine nature is beyond words. God is a word, a word unspoken."[82] And again, "In scripture, God is called by many names. I say that whoever perceives something in God and attaches thereby some name to him, that is not God. God is above names and above nature."[83]

The second thing that hinders us from hearing the Eternal Word, says Eckhart, is multiplicity. To the extent that the object of our will is some particular thing in distinction from something else, our love is divided, scattered, and imperfect.[84]

> For he that loves one thing more than another loves a creature among creatures and does not love one God in all things and all things in God; for in One there is not more or less. This is what the Lord significantly says: 'He that loves . . . more . . . is not worthy of me.' For God is One in whom there is no number, no more or less.[85]

The "perfect man" loves all things as God loves, without distinction, and loves them in God.[86]

Further, conceptual distinctions do not apply to the divine nature as they do to the plurality of created beings. God cannot be "named" this or that, for God is Absolute Unity, and as such utterly indistinct. Eckhart elaborates: "We must understand that the term 'one' is the same as 'indistinct' [i.e. not-to-be-distinguished, not separate], for all distinct things are two or more, but all indistinct things are one."[87] Thus what distinguishes

81. Predigt 76: *Videte qualem caritatem* (DW III, 316; *TP*, 327).

82. Predigt 53: *Misit dominus manum suam* (DW II, 529; *EE*, 203).

83. Ibid. (DW II, 533; *EE*, 204).

84. For Eckhart authentic loving is done only with an undivided heart. The heart that seeks God must itself be one and undivided. It must become an image of the divine One which it loves. See Sermo XXX (LW IV, 271–81) and Sermo XL (LW IV, 335–45).

85. Daniels, "Rechtfertigungsschrift," 33; translated in *Meister Eckhart: A Modern Translation*, trans. Raymond Blakney (New York: Harper and Row, 1941), 271.

86. "And among creatures [God] does not love one more than another: for as each is wide enough to receive, in the same measure He pours Himself into it. . . . God loves all creatures equally and fills them with His being. And thus too, we should pour forth ourselves in love over all creatures" (DW III, 294–95; W II [88], 279–80).

87. *Comm. Wis.* n. 144 (LW II, 482; *EE*, 34).

God as *one,* or Absolute Unity, from the plurality of things is God's indistinguishability. Paradoxically God is both distinct and indistinct. In Sermo IV.1 Eckhart writes that "God is most indistinct in himself according to his nature, in that he is truly and properly one and completely distinct from other things."[88] Bernard McGinn very insightfully points out that in this double play of identity and difference Eckhart was after "a way of speaking about God as simultaneously totally immanent to creatures as their real existence and *by that very fact* absolutely transcendent to them as *esse simpliciter* or *esse absolutum.*"[89]

This notion of God as not-to-be-distinguished is another way of articulating God's infinite nature: a surpassing of all limited (and delimited) being, not as something absolutely cut off from finite nature, but rather as a "beyond" which is infused throughout as its ground. The true in-finite or un-limited is *one* through and through. It must encompass the finite within itself, and so surpass it. Thus Eckhart notes that the term *unum* "sounds negative but is really affirmative; it is the negation of negation, which is the purest affirmation and the fullness of the term affirmed."[90] In other words, the negation of the negation is not again mere affirmation (of a this or a that), but, like the "hyper-" of Pseudo-Dionysius, an unspeakably rich beyond, it is an absolute fullness in emptiness.

The limitations of temporality is the third and last thing that hinders the seeker of God from hearing his eternal Word. Even the smallest segment of time, the "now," writes Eckhart in Predigt 69, though neither a piece of time nor a part of time (in the same way, presumably, that a point is neither a piece nor a constituent "part" of a line), must be overcome. For "it is certainly a taste of time and a point of time and a boundary of time." The now marks and divides. It differentiates between this and that, just as the attachment to a particular place does. One errs in seeking God in the "here" and "now." "Everything that touches time or the taste of time must completely disappear. . . . [Similarly for space,] the place on which I stand is very small. Yet however small it may be, it has to disappear if one is to

88. Sermo IV.1 (LW IV, 28; *EE,* 42).
89. *EE,* 34.
90. *Comm. Wis.* n. 147 (LW II, 485; *EE,* 34).

see God."[91] In Predigt 10 Eckhart writes in a similar vein that "everything temporal is far from God and alien to him. In considering time, even if one takes it in the smallest amount, in a now, it is still time and exists in itself. As long as one has time and place, number, multiplicity, and amount, things are not right with him and God is far from him and alien."[92]

As the Being of all beings, God dwells in all that is insofar as each thing *is,* but in nothing insofar as it is *this* being in its particularity. God is not in time, not in division, not in anything continuous or quantitative. God is nowhere where there is a "more" or a "less," a difference of degree or limitation of any kind. God is infinite unity, and as such, the negation of all negation. Thus, Eckhart concludes, "insofar as someone understands and loves temporal things, insofar as he is divided in himself, insofar as he is attached to continuous quantity and corporeal imagination, insofar as there is a more or less for him, God does not dwell in him."[93] The detached soul, on the other hand, like God, is equally present everywhere and nowhere.[94] Having earthly attachments nowhere, such a soul loves and lives without distinction, without a why, responding to all that is in equanimity.[95]

> Heaven is at all points equidistant from earth. Likewise the soul should be equally distant from all earthly things, no nearer to the one than to the other. Where the noble soul is, she must maintain an equal distance from all earthly things, from hope, from joy and from sorrow: whatever it is, she must rise superior to it.[96]

This detachment works toward a formal coalescence of being "one in One," a true reflection or image of the divine unity.[97] In the "Councils on Discernment" Eckhart writes of the perfectly detached man, "no one can hinder this man, for he intends and seeks and takes delight in nothing but

91. Predigt 69: *Modicum et iam non videbitis me* (DW III, 170; *TP,* 313).

92. Predigt 10: *In diebus suis placuit deo* (DW I, 169; *TP,* 264).

93. *Comm. Jn.* n. 208 (LW III, 175–76), my translation.

94. Ibid. n. 210 (LW III, 178).

95. On living and loving "without a why" and its connection to loving without a medium see Fanizzi, "Subverting the *Ordo Caritatis,*" 295–300 and 308–27.

96. Predigt 68: *Scitote, quia prope est regnum dei* (DW III, 147; W II [69], 167).

97. See Bernard McGinn, "Meister Eckhart on God as Absolute Unity," in *Neoplatonism and Christian Thought,* ed. Dominic J. O'Meara (Albany: SUNY Press, 1982), 128–39.

God, for God has become one with the man in all his intention. And so, just as no multiplicity can disturb God, nothing can disturb or fragment this man, for he is one in that One where all multiplicity is one and is one un-multiplicity."[98] Such a soul then becomes like a still pool of water, or perfect mirror,[99] undisturbed and even, a perfectly reflecting image of "one in One."

THE INFINITY OF THE HUMAN SOUL

Eckhart recognizes that as a creature each human being finds him or herself rooted in space and time. He holds, however, that there is a power in the soul, the intellect, which is able to think beyond this imbeddedness in the here and now.[100] Just as all things are equally close to God, so too, they are equally close to the soul. For the mind is not limited by the perspective imposed by the body's temporal and spatial location. "Jerusalem is as near my soul as the ground I stand on now. Yes, in holy truth! Whatever is a thousand miles further off than Jerusalem is as close to my soul as my own body is."[101] I may find myself physically present here and now, but in my mind I can think of a place as distant as you like and beyond, and I can think of a time a hundred years from now or yesterday afternoon. There is no limit to the mind's ability to think beyond the limitations of a given perspective. Indeed recognizing a perspective *as* limiting is already to view it from beyond those limits. To recognize a perspective *as* a perspective is to recognize it against the cognitive background of a-perspectival understanding. More broadly, to recognize a limit *as* a limit is to think it against the background of infinity.[102]

98. *Councils on Discernment,* Council 6, "Of detachment and of the possession of God" (DW V, 202; *EE,* 252).

99. The image in the mirror is a traditional metaphor frequently employed by Eckhart, and the process of *Entbildung* should be understood in this context as one in which the quality of the mirror is perfected. See Wackernagel, *Ymagine Denudari,* 130, especially n. 415; and Haas, *Sermo mysticus,* 227–29.

100. See, for example Predigt 69 cited above. Mahnke notes that the assertion that reason transcends spatiality was cited as heretical in the first list of condemned propositions but defended by Eckhart. He held that the omnipresence of reason is true by virtue of the fact that "reason disregards the here and now" (Mahnke, *Unendliche Sphäre,* 155). See Théry, I, 179 and 201.

101. Predigt 42: *Adolescens, tibi dico: surge* (DW II, 305; W II [80], 236).

102. On the "principle of perspective" see Harries, *Infinity and Perspective,* 43 and 149.

Although we are limited by our embodied existence to a perspectival perception of the world, our minds have the capacity to transcend beyond this perspectival sensate knowledge, to "knowledge in the principle," to a vision of reality beyond the distortion of spatial and temporal perspectives. This potentially infinite capacity of human self-transcendence amounts to the ability to think of reality from the "perspective" of the center of an infinite sphere.[103] All places and times are equally close to me. As a disembodied thinker, the "center" of my cognitive activity is thus equally everywhere and its limits nowhere. To view reality beyond the limitations of perspective is to "see" it *from* infinity, as it were.

For Eckhart this overcoming of the limitations of space and time is only a step on the way to the overcoming of all limiting determinations, which blind us to the ultimate unity of all beings in their divine source. Karsten Harries has pointed out, however, that this reflection on perspective can be put to a quite different use:

> The idea of the pure "I," to which all things are equally close or distant, can be uncovered and made the measure of what our senses present to us. Measured by this idea, these presentations, limited as they are by their ties to perspective, will have to appear deficient. To overcome this deficiency, we have to try to redescribe the world in such a way that all those aspects which presuppose the particular point of view assigned to us by our body drop out. Only by liberating ourselves from the limitations imposed on us by our location here and now can we progress towards a more adequate grasp of what is.[104]

Thus these same reflections on perspective and on the human capacity for self-transcendence actually serve as the foundation for the ideal of objectivity which was to govern the new science. This is, however, a direction which Eckhart's meditations never took.

Eckhart would have us push well beyond an "objective" vision of the world. For him it is not simply our embeddedness in the "here and now" which thwarts our access to ultimate reality but also our attachment to the negativity of "this and that," the tendency to seek for ultimate reality in *determinate* existence. True perception of reality comes for Eckhart when

103. On Eckhart's conception of the infinity of the human soul, and its capacity for self-transcendence see Harries, *Infinity and Perspective,* 260–183.

104. Harries, "Infinite Sphere," 11.

we are able to move beyond the outer manifestation of determinate entities toward the common ground of all that is in God. Again, the intellect is understood here as an inverse, infinitely contracting, sphere which channels all things back into an absolute unity. This means turning inward into the ground of my soul, to discover there coincidence with the divine center of the infinite sphere: "When I am united with That wherein all things are existent whether past, present or future, they are all equally near and equally one; they are all in God and all in *me*."[105] The soul which reaches back into unity with the divine principle soars aloft and stands "gazing into this richness of God's: there there is breadth without breadth, expanseless expanse, and there the soul knows all things, and knows them perfectly."[106]

From the infinite unity of God, all things are recognized in their ultimate reality as "God in God": "Because the soul has the potentiality of knowing all things, it never rests until it comes to the first image where all things are one. There it rests, there in God. . . . [God] is a pure abiding within himself, where there is no this or that; for whatever is in God *is* God."[107] Thus perfect knowledge of all things consists in knowledge of the infinite unity of all things. Even when Eckhart mentions the divine archetypes of all created things in God, his emphasis is not on the image character of the divine Ideas, but rather on their ultimate identity with God. Thus the blade of grass, the milk cow, and the human soul are all "God in God."[108]

Hence, in the soul's return to the generative God, "morning knowl-

105. Predigt 65: *Deus caritas est* (DW III, 102; W I [5], 52). Vladimir Lossky describes this coincidence as follows: "Vus *ex parte Dei,* tous les points dans la sphère finie, celle de l'univers créé, coïncident avec le centre de la sphère infinie qui est Dieu. Il y aura donc autant de centres personnels et 'uniques', réunissant dans leur unité les *omnia* de la périphérie créée, qu'il y a d'êtres faits à l'image de Dieu, susceptibles de trouver le point d'identité avec le Centre absolu en pénétrant par leur *intelligere* dans la sphère intellectuelle infinie. Cette sphère sans circonférence, sans extériorité créée, est l'Omni-unité divine, l'identité de toutes choses avec l'Un dans la région de la transcendance intériorisée, plus 'intime' à chacun que son être-propre, non-identique, de créature" (Lossky, *Théologie négative,* 172–73).

106. Predigt 38: *In illo tempore missus est angelus Gabriel* (DW II, 232; W I [29], 216–17).

107. Predigt 3: *Nunc scio vere* (DW I, 55, 2ff.; *TP,* 246).

108. See Mahnke, *Unendliche Sphäre,* 33 and 105 n. 4; and Haas, *Sermo mysticus,* 236–37.

edge" (knowing the creatures as God in God) replaces "evening knowledge" (knowing creatures in themselves):[109]

We ought also to know that those who know God alone also know along with him created things; for knowledge is a light of the soul, and all men naturally long for knowledge. . . . The authorities say that when one knows creatures in themselves, that is called an "evening knowledge," and then we see created things in images of various distinctions; but when one knows created things in God, that is called and is a "morning knowledge," and then we can see created things without distinction and transformed from every form and made unlike every likeness in the One that is God himself.[110]

Here we witness the paradoxical character of the perfection of the image. The language of image-exemplar suggests a process of approximation in which the image may be a better or worse reflection of its exemplar. As long as the image is grasped in its distinctive difference from the exemplar, however, it is understood in the mode of "evening knowledge." This form of knowing operates through the conceptual mediation of difference (i.e. it grasps its object as X and so *not* Y). Such knowing is always haunted by the gap between image and exemplar. It is merely approximate knowing. When an image is grasped in its essence, as not-other than its exemplar, "as God in God," the language of image-exemplar becomes superfluous. A perfect image is indistinguishable from its exemplar.[111] This is "transformed" or "morning" knowledge, knowledge of all things in the principle of infinite unity.

The soul's drive toward perfection, toward union with God, is thus played out in the passing over of human intellectual nature from evening knowledge into morning knowledge. The human soul, Eckhart holds, has an unlimited and innate will to know which urges the intellect on its search for the ultimate ground and principle of all that is.[112] "I am a knower." "Before all else I am a knower." "I naturally and preeminently desire

109. On the distinction between morning and evening knowledge, see Augustine, *De Genesi ad litt.* IV, cc. 22–24; and *De civitate Dei* XI, c. 7.

110. *Of the Nobleman* (DW V, 116; *EE,* 244–45).

111. "Image and image are so completely one and joined together that one cannot comprehend any distinction between them. . . . I say further: God in his omnipotence cannot understand any distinction between them, for they are born together and die together" (Predigt 69 [DW III, 176–77; *TP,* 314]).

112. LW III, 348.

knowledge. . . . What I will, that I seek, and knowledge comes first." "The very nature and life of man, as man, is to know and be a knower."[113] This will to knowledge is unlimited and remains unrestricted unless it becomes entangled by a determinate interest in something below the level of unrestricted or infinite knowing *in* the principle itself, i.e. a knowledge of "God in God."

Thus, for Eckhart we must leave behind evening knowledge, which grasps creatures in their difference from the divine exemplar. The goal of all knowledge is the collapse of image and imaged, to know as God "knows," where there is no difference between thought and object. Once again, in retrospect, we can see in this understanding of human nature as an unlimited will toward knowledge, the foundation for the modern ideal of infinite progress in science, understood as the drive toward a more and more objective, increasingly adequate picture of the world. For Eckhart, however, the end goal of this drive toward knowledge is not a better and better understanding of the multiplicity of things in their particularity, but rather an understanding of things as unified in their ground, where the distinction between "what is" and "what is thought" disappears.

It is for this reason that he sees no essential connection between "evening knowledge" and "morning knowledge." They stand in stark opposition to each other as difference to identity, as the finite (determinate) to the absolute unity of the infinite. Something needs to be added to Eckhart's account here, if "evening knowledge" is to be transformed into the modern pursuit of progressively more objective knowledge of *this* concrete world. What is needed is something like the notion of a regulative ideal guiding this unending progress. Such an ideal would have to share in the natures of both evening and morning knowledge, that is, it would have to have the concrete determinacy of the "evening" realm of difference, but in the "morning" aspect of infinite unity or identity. The "best" description would thus function as the ideal completion and goal of all relatively "better" descriptions. As we shall see, Nicholas of Cusa will forge this essential connection between the realm of evening knowledge

113. DW I, 52ff.; LW II, 353; DW III, 173ff.; LW III, 117. See Kelly, *Eckhart on Divine Knowledge*, 55.

and that of morning knowledge by relating the "privative" infinity of the human soul to the absolute infinity of the divine incarnate in the world.

This is a move Eckhart is not at all prepared to make, despite his understanding of the infinite nature of the human soul, its unlimited desire for knowledge, and its infinite capacity for self-transcendence. Indeed, the direction of Eckhart's teaching and writing is consistently aimed at moving the soul away from its dispersion in, and attachment to, the created world.[114] Hence Eckhart's transference of the divine attribute of infinity to the human soul should not be confused with later Renaissance and early modern conceptions of the dignity and worth of the individual as such, valued precisely *for* its characteristic difference and unique expression or reflection of the whole universe of which it is a part. The tenor and direction of Eckhart's thought, here, stands in stark contrast to the interest in, and focus on, the infinite richness of individual being found in Cusanus and the subsequent tradition that links Bruno to Leibniz to Kant. Eckhart's overriding interest is in absolute Being not determinate beings, in unity not diversity, in identity not difference. He writes, for example:

> I used to wonder (it is many years ago) whether I should be asked why one blade of grass is so unlike another; and as it happened, I *was* asked why they are so different. Then I said it is more marvelous that all blades of grass are so much alike. One master says that the blades of grass are all different owing to the superfluity of the goodness of God, which he pours out superabundantly into all creatures to reveal His majesty the more. So I said, it is more wonderful how much the grass-blades are alike, explaining that just as all angels are one in their original pure nature, so all blades of grass are one in their original pure nature, and there all things are one.[115]

For Eckhart the final goal of all intellectual, volitional, and spiritual striving is the general overcoming of *all* individual particularities and oppositions. Further, in pursuing the ultimate perfection of the soul, its utter

114. See Mahnke, *Unendliche Sphäre,* 156. He rightly underscores that for Eckhart, the more general a form of being, the nobler it is. Thus more noble than perception, which only animals have, is vegetative life which extends also to plants, and the most noble of all is the bare being which all creatures have in common. Indeed the most noble is the Godhead itself, which is nothing other than all-encompassing being *(esse purum et plenum),* which is purified from the totality of special and individual particularizations.

115. Predigt 22: *Ave, gratia plena* (DW I, 519; W II [53], 64). See Mahnke, *Unendliche Sphäre,* 155–56.

detachment from *all* things, a person must free himself even from his conception of and will toward God. Thus Eckhart boldly asserts that "the noblest and the ultimate thing that a person can forsake is that he forsakes God for God's sake."[116] Such a person refuses to make recourse to or take rest in the divine qualities of wisdom, or truth, or goodness. In seeking to unite with its ultimate ground, the intellect "is not satisfied with goodness or with wisdom or with truth or with God himself. In good truth, it is as little satisfied with God as with a stone or a tree. It never rests, it bursts into the ground from which goodness and truth come forth and perceives it [God's being] *in principio,* in the beginning, where goodness and truth are going out, before it acquires any name, before it bursts forth."[117]

This breaking through or penetration of the soul into the divine ground that is the Godhead beyond God constitutes the final return, drawing the soul back into that ultimate unity, the ground of the divine *bullitio* or emanation of the three Persons of the Trinity. Thus the return to the source mirrors the procession from the source. The soul passes first through all created things to the place of "divine repose," and finally breaks through to the "God beyond God," to the ineffable source of God himself, and all things in God.

That is why I say that if a man will turn away from himself and from all created things, by so much will you be made one and blessed in the spark in the soul, which has never touched either time or place. This spark rejects all created things, and wants nothing but its naked God, as he is in himself. It is not content with the Father or the Son or the Holy Spirit, or with the three Persons so far as each of them persists in his properties. I say truly that this light is not content with the divine nature's generative or fruitful qualities. I will say more, surprising though this is. I speak in all truth, truth that is eternal and enduring, that this same light is not content with the simple divine essence in its repose, as it neither gives nor receives; but it wants to know the source of this essence, it wants to go into the simple ground, into the quiet desert, into which distinction never gazed, not the Father, nor the Son, nor the Holy Spirit. In the innermost part, where no one dwells, there is contentment for that light, and there it is more inward than it can be to itself, for this ground is a simple silence, in itself immovable, and by this immovability all things are moved, all life is received by those who in themselves have rational being.[118]

116. Predigt 12: *Qui audit me* (DW I, 196; *TP,* 268).
117. Predigt 69: *Modicum et iam non videbitis me* (DW III, 179; *TP,* 315).
118. Predigt 48: *Ein meister sprichet* (DW II, 419–21; *EE,* 198).

The soul breaks forth into the innermost ground of the divine nature, into "the quiet desert" where it at last comes to hear the eternal silence of the "unspoken Word." The soul becomes one in One, united in this "simple silence," the utter stillness and immovability by which all things are moved and from which all life flows. The unending pursuit of the divine thus finally comes to rest in infinite unity.

It is important to note that in this union of the soul with its ultimate ground, in which it becomes wholly one in One, the soul becomes in truth the image of God. As such, it too is revealed in its core as an utter stillness or immobility, from which all the fruits of its human nature flow forth. Thus, the dialectic of transcendence and immanence found in the nature of the divine is reflected in human being proper. This is the sense of Eckhart's distinction between the inner and outer man in his treatise *On Detachment.* The outer man must be seen to be grounded in and flow forth from the being of the inner man. Eckhart uses, by way of analogy, the image of a door opening on a hinge. The planks of the door correspond to the outer man and the hinge to the inner man. As the door opens and shuts the planks are moved backwards and forwards, but the hinge remains immovable in one place.[119] Further the unmoved hinge is the ground of the moving door. Thus the outer man is not something wholly exterior to the internal man, which is to be somehow cast off. It is, rather, the outward manifestation of the inward man, and it is through the outward man that the fruits of all inner perfection flow forth into the world. Thus detachment is *not* world-flight; it is not a running away from things and people, a turning solitary and going apart from the world. It consists rather of an inward solitude, an inward turn into the still ground of all things. Such a turn is a "letting" which allows the divine to manifest itself in all activities under all circumstances.

119. *On Detachment* (DW V, 422; *EE,* 291). See also *Councils on Discernment* (Council 23): "[A person] ought not to flee or deny or suspect his own inwardness. He should learn to work in it and with it and from it, so that he can transform inwardness into activity and bring his activities into his inwardness" (DW V, 291; *EE,* 280).

[11]

The Speculative Interpretation of the Infinite Sphere in Nicholas of Cusa's On Learned Ignorance

With Nicholas of Cusa begins a new chapter in the history of the metaphor of the infinite sphere.[120] Here for the first time the metaphor is transferred from God to the world, and the infinitization of the cosmos, which was tentatively begun with Meister Eckhart's intensive infinitization of the being of each created thing, is carried much further in the Cusan's speculative cosmology.[121] Now the universe *as such* is described as an infinite sphere. This cosmological application of the infinite sphere

120. For a general study of the infinite in the thought of Nicholas of Cusa see Mariano Alvarez-Gómez, *Die Verborgene Gegenwart des Unendlichen bei Nikolaus von Kues* (Munich and Salzburg: Verlag Anton Pustet, 1968).

121. For more general studies on the relationship between Meister Eckhart and Nicholas of Cusa and their place in the German mystical tradition in general see Herbert Wackerzapp, *Einfluß Meister Eckharts;* Rudolf Haubst, "Nikolaus von Kues als Interpret und Verteidiger Meister Eckharts," in *Freiheit und Gelassenheit: Meister Eckhart Heute,* ed. Udo Kern (Munich: Kaiser, 1980), 75–96; Donald F. Duclow, "Nicholas of Cusa in the Margins of Meister Eckhart: Codex Cusanus 21," in *Nicholas of Cusa in Search of God and Wisdom,* ed. Gerald Christianson and Thomas M. Izbicki (Leiden: Brill, 1991), 57–69; Josef Koch, "Meister Eckharts Weiterwirken im Deutsch-Niederländischen Raum im 14. und 15. Jahrhundert," in *La mystique rhénane: Colloque de Strasbourg, 1961* (Paris: Presses Universitaires de France, 1963), 133–56; F. W. Wentzlaff-Eggebert, *Deutsche Mystic Zwischen Mittelalter und Neuzeit* (Tübingen: Verlag J. C. B. Mohr, 1947). See also Cusanus' defense of Eckhart in his *Apologia Doctae Ignorantiae,* translated by

metaphor marks a decisive shift away from the traditional medieval world picture and articulates for Cusanus both the extensive and intensive infinity of the universe. With this shift in the application of the metaphor comes a correspondent shift in value. The cosmos and all of its individual parts begin to take on a value and nobility in themselves, as worthy objects of admiration and investigation. Interest in the richness and complexity of the newly infinite cosmos is viewed no longer as a purely negative dispersal in multiplicity which must be overcome if one is to find rest in divine unity, but rather as an impetus to pursue the spur or track of the divine infinite in the unending hunt for knowledge.[122] Thus the cosmological and ontological consequences of the Cusan's infinitization of the universe are, as we shall see, tied to corresponding shifts in his anthropology and epistemology.

THE DIVINE INFINITE OR MAXIMUM

The first book of *De docta ignorantia* (1440) is devoted to a consideration of the absolute infinity of God. Immediately the attempt to describe infinite unity, the absolute Maximum, runs up against the paradox that all our concepts are limited and limiting. Concepts are used to distinguish between things. If something is "this," it is not "that." Yet the unqualifiedly Maximum is neither this nor that; it is unlimited and all-embracing unity, "infinite Oneness" which precedes all opposition, indeed, a oneness in which opposites coincide. The impossibility of adequately

Jasper Hopkins in *Nicholas of Cusa's Debate with John Wenck: A Translation and an Appraisal of "De Ignota Litteratura" and "Apologia Doctae Ignorantiae"* (Minneapolis: Arthur J. Banning Press, 1988), 57–59.

122. Compare with Blumenberg's analysis of the rehabilitation of theoretical curiosity at the end of the Middle Ages, from the Christian (in particular Augustinian) suspicion that it distracted the believer from care of the soul, in his overall reading of the emergence of modernity in Part III of the *Legitimacy*. As we have seen, Blumenberg views Cusanus' doctrine of "learned ignorance" as a proto-modern gesture toward "method" in that it constitutes a commitment to reflect on the surpassability of the state of knowledge at any given time. The "trace of God in the world" becomes a track to be pursued in a never-ending hunt for wisdom. Yet in his analysis, Blumenberg fails to consider the way in which the modern notion of progress is grounded in an understanding of nature as a law-like and yet inexhaustible field of investigation directing thought toward an objectivity that is never entirely to be attained. And it is here, as we shall see, that the *intensive* infinitization of the cosmos plays such a crucial role.

"naming" God is not due simply to an intrinsic limitation of language but is rooted, for Cusanus, in reason's inability to conceptualize the unity of contradictories.

> [J]ust as God transcends all understanding, so, a fortiori, [He transcends] every name. Indeed, through a movement of reason, which is much lower than the intellect, names are bestowed for distinguishing between things. But since reason cannot leap beyond contradictories: as regards the movement of reason, there is not a name to which another [name] is not opposed. Therefore, as regards the movement of reason: plurality or multiplicity is opposed to oneness.[123]

But absolute Maximality must be thought of as "Oneness to which neither otherness nor plurality nor multiplicity is opposed."[124] Thus in order to "think" infinite unity, we must move to negate the limitations inherent in whatever concepts we use to describe it. If we describe the Maximum as "oneness" we must at once deny the opposition to plurality and multiplicity which is implied by the name. The same will hold true for any description of the divine infinite. "And so the theology of negation is so necessary for the theology of affirmation," writes Cusanus, "that without it God would not be worshipped as the infinite God but, rather, as a [determinate, finite] creature."[125]

By denying the possibility of arriving at an adequate name or concept for God, Cusanus places himself in the tradition of negative theology. Any positive affirmation of God must fall infinitely short of the nature of absolute Maximality, which is unlimited by any particular determination. Yet there is a new tone to his doctrine of "*learned* ignorance." Although the perfect name for God is only, and can only be, the infinite reality which *is* God, Cusanus underscores the fact that there *are* better or worse names for God, better or worse affirmations or denials. "For example it is truer that God is not stone than that He is not life or intelligence; and [it

123. *De Docta Ignorantia* I, 24 (76), translated by Jasper Hopkins in *Nicholas of Cusa on Learned Ignorance: A Translation and an Appraisal of "De Docta Ignorantia"* (Minneapolis: Arthur J. Banning Press, 1985), 80. References to this translation will hereafter be designatied by "*DI*" followed by the book number, chapter number, section number, and page number of the translation.

124. *DI* I, 24 (76), 80.

125. *DI* I, 26 (86), 84.

is truer that He] is not drunkenness than that He is not virtue." Similarly, "the affirmation which states that God is intelligence and life is truer than [the affirmation that He is] earth or stone or body."[126] Learned ignorance is not a skeptical state which suspends all judgments concerning the divine nature on the grounds that God is absolutely unknowable. It is not a doctrine which teaches that the highest knowledge of divine things to which we can attain is a recognition of our own ignorance, to know that we do not know anything.[127] Rather, Cusanus holds that by reflecting on the limitations of our power of conceptualization, that is, by becoming learned about our ignorance, we can actually *approach* knowledge of the absolute Maximum. Indeed the adequacy of our knowledge of God approaches the truth of the divine Maximum "according to the degree of our instruction in ignorance."[128]

The tradition of negative theology has long recognized that the negation of our affirmations of God are to be understood not as the simple nullification of the conceptual work done by the affirmation, but rather, as a sort of springboard which pushes thought beyond the limitation of determinate understanding to an intuition of the absolute. When we affirm that God is not this or that, we point to that which lies beyond this or that. What is novel in Cusanus' work in *On Learned Ignorance* is his focus on the *connection* between our approximate conceptualizations of the divine infinite and the reality which is its measure. Cusanus is interested in the way in which our conceptions of the unqualified Maximum may be better or worse, and the way in which the absolute infinite itself is the measure of their adequacy. In Eckhartian terms we may say that he focuses on the problem of the relation between "evening knowledge" and "morning knowledge," and the way in which the former may approximate (though never arrive at) the latter,

126. *DI* I, 26 (89), 85.

127. Cusanus has sometimes been viewed as a skeptic. See, for example, Richard H. Popkin's *The History of Skepticism from Erasmus to Spinoza* (Berkeley: University of California Press, 1979), xvi, 83, and 198. This view represents a serious misreading, however, of the aim and tenor of Cusanus' doctrine of learned ignorance, which finds its deepest roots neither in the tradition of Academic nor in Pyrrhonian skepticism but rather in that of negative theology.

128. *DI* I, 26 (89), 85.

In Chapter One of Book One, Cusanus explains how it is that knowing is not-knowing. All knowledge is arrived at by means of a comparison of what is unknown and uncertain with what is known and certain. "Hence, the infinite, qua infinite, is unknown; for it escapes all comparative relation."[129] This is "self-evident" since "there is no comparative relation between the infinite and the finite."[130] Where there are comparative degrees of greatness, we do not arrive at the unqualifiedly Maximum. Anything which is not the unqualifiedly Maximum can be greater still and is, as such, finite. The absolute Maximum, however, does not admit of more or less. It does not stand in a comparative relation with anything. It is the ultimate superlative. Nevertheless, although we will never be able to *arrive* at knowledge of the divine infinite,[131] our comparative knowledge may indeed *approach* the absolute Maximum. While Cusanus emphasizes the fact that the gap between the finite and the infinite can never be closed by relative increases in the realm of the finite—anything finite, no matter how great, remains infinitely distant from the absolute infinite—he nevertheless holds that within the realm of finite knowledge a given description may be better or worse. And it is the absolute infinite ("infinite truth") which is the measure for this comparative relation. Hence the *absolute* infinite is the measure for the *privative* infinity of unending approach to it.

CUSANUS' USE OF MATHEMATICAL METAPHORS

While the absolute Maximum or infinite transcends reason's attempts to grasp it, to define it, i.e. to delimit it, our recognition that the infinite cannot be captured by means of finite images or concepts already implies that the human intellect is somehow tied to the infinite, that there is a background awareness or intuition of the infinite which operates at the limits of rational thought. For Cusanus, reason finds itself in the paradox-

129. *DI* I, 1 (3), 50.

130. *DI* I, 3 (9), 52.

131. "And in harmony with this [verdict] Rabbi Solomon states that all the wise agreed that the sciences do not apprehend the Creator. Only He Himself apprehends what He is; our apprehension of Him is a defective approximation of his apprehension" (*DI* I, 16 [44], 67).

ical position of being unable to grasp the infinite, but still compelled to "think" it at the absolute limit of all thought.[132] It is precisely our awareness of the *way* in which absolute infinity inevitably overruns the limitations of our attempts to conceptualize it, which throws into relief this background intuition of it.

Our experience of counting demonstrates the way in which our intuition of the absolutely infinite informs this simple operation. No matter how far I count, I can always keep going. For every finite "n" I can posit an "n plus 1," and be no nearer an end at 10,000,000 than I was at 10. I can (in principle) keep counting indefinitely. For Cusanus the indefinitely extended is intelligible as such only against the background of the absolutely infinite. That is, I can recognize an unending series as *essentially* unending only if I have in mind a measure of completeness by virtue of which the series presents itself as "the *always* outstanding."[133] Without this background intuition of the absolutely infinite, I might assume that there *is* a "greatest" number. The fact that I recognize the surpassability of any number, no matter how large, means that I am regarding it in the light of an intuition of absolute Maximality. Or, to put it another way, I can apprehend something as merely comparatively great (i.e. as actually or potentially surpassable) only because I have a background awareness of what it is to be superlative, or absolutely great.[134]

132. In this sense Cusanus' conception of the absolute infinite functions on analogy to a Kantian idea of reason.

133. For a more detailed analysis of Cusanus' metaphorical use of the number series see my paper "How Can the Infinite Be the Measure for the Finite? Three Mathematical Metaphors from *De docta ignorantia*" given at the American Cusanus Society's sixth centenary international conference, "Nicholas of Cusa: 1401–2001," at The Catholic University of America, October 6, 2001.

134. It is interesting to note that it is precisely this insight which forms the basis of Descartes' proof for the existence of God in the third Meditation. The simple awareness of our own finitude and imperfection, the awareness that there is always something missing or still outstanding, presupposes a background notion of the infinite, as perfect plenitude, as positive whole: "For how could I understand that I doubted or desired—that is, lacked something—and that I was not wholly perfect, unless there were in me some idea of a more perfect being which enabled me to recognize my own defects by comparison." Or again at the beginning of the fourth Meditation: "[W]hen I consider the fact that I have doubts or that I am a thing that is incomplete and dependent, then there arises in me a clear and distinct idea of a being who is independent and complete, that is, an idea of God" (Descartes, *The Philosophical Writings of Descartes,* 2:31, 37).

FIGURE 1

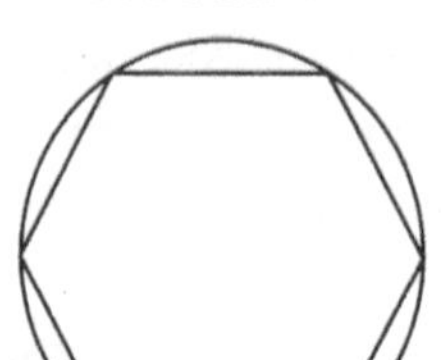

Thus Cusanus understands number (or the number series) as the unfolding of unity, where the maximum and minimum coincide (absolute unity coincides with unified infinity).[135] An example which Cusanus uses at the very beginning (and again at the end) of *On Learned Ignorance* illustrates this relationship extremely well. We can use a many-sided polygon (Figure 1) to approximate the circumference of a circle in which it is inscribed. The greater the number of sides the more accurate the approximation. As the number of sides goes to infinity, the polygon finds coincidence with the circle. To return to the terminology used in Part Two, we may say that the "privative infinity" (of unending increase) finds its measure and completion in "absolute" (all-inclusive) infinity.[136] Indeed, Cusanus prefers the example of the inscribed polygon over that of counting, because it thematizes so clearly—indeed visually—the way in which the superlative (or absolute infinite) serves as measure for the merely comparatively great.

As indicated by the examples of the inscribed polygon and the nature of counting early on in the first book of *On Learned Ignorance,* Cusanus has a marked preference for mathematical metaphors when describing the absolute Maximum (i.e. God as Infinite Unity). He explains this preference in Chapter Eleven by pointing out that "when we conduct an inquiry on the basis of an image, it is necessary that there be no doubt regarding the image, by means of whose symbolical comparative relation we are investigating what is unknown."[137] Mathematical signs—because they are more abstract than sensible things and not subject to change—are the most fixed and certain symbols we have at our disposal. Cusanus

135. Karsten Harries describes this paradoxical position of reason as follows: "[O]ur reason, although bound to the finite, operates against the background of an intuition of the infinite. Counting is a case in point. Cusanus understands number as unfolded unity. This metaphor of an unfolding of unity demands something like a distinction between form and a field in which this form can operate, between *peras* and *apeiron*. The former will never conquer the latter: no matter how far I count, I can always go on" (Harries, "Infinite Sphere," 8).

136. Note that Cusanus distinguishes between the two as the "privative" (unbounded) and the "negative" (absolute) infinite. *DI* II, 1 (97), 90.

137. *DI* I, 11 (31), 61.

thus concludes that "since the pathway for approaching divine matters is opened to us only through symbols," mathematical signs are the most suitable of all signs "because of their incorruptible certainty."[138]

He immediately grants that no image or symbol (not even mathematical symbols) can capture the nature of the unqualifiedly Maximum, "which cannot be any of the things which we either know or conceive." Hence, "when we set out to investigate the Maximum symbolically, we must leap beyond simple likeness."[139] We can do this by constructing an exploding image or metaphor (like that of the infinite sphere, for example) which propels us beyond the realm of the finite. We begin, explains Cusanus, by considering finite mathematical figures, their characteristics and relations. Next we must move beyond their representation in the imagination as finite figures, and apply their characteristics and relations (in a transformed way) to "corresponding infinite mathematical figures." Finally, we must move beyond figures and images altogether by considering these relations as they apply to the simple Infinite as such. Thus the divine Infinite may be approached in thought by considering the characteristics of an infinite line, triangle, circle, or sphere, and by recognizing that such infinite figures would all coincide with each other at infinity.

From the Qualitatively Finite to the Absolutely Infinite

Cusanus begins by considering the relation between a circle and its straight-line tangent (see Figure 2). As the length of the radius of the circle increases, its circumference approaches coincidence with the straight-line tangent, i.e. the greater the circle the smaller its curvature in relation to the straight-line tangent. Thus Cusanus speculates: at the limit, "at infinity" as we might say, the greatest circle is "minima curva" or "maxima recta," i.e. the infinite circle is a straight

FIGURE 2

138. *DI* I, 11 (32), 62. See also *De possest* I, 179 b; *De mathematica perfectione* II B, 101 a; and *Complementum theologicum* II B, 92 b. Cusanus holds that the certainty of mathematical knowledge is due to the fact that it is produced by the creative power of the human mind, an image of the divine. See, e.g., *De beryllo* 32.

139. *DI* I, 12 (33), 62.

line.[140] Next he considers the characteristics of an "infinite" triangle: it will be one infinite line which is concomitantly three lines and it will have only one infinite angle which is concomitantly three angles. It won't be composed of sides and angles, "rather, the infinite line and the [infinite] angle are one and the same thing, so that the line is the angle, because the triangle is the line."[141] Thus, once again, the infinite triangle *is* an infinite line.

FIGURE 3

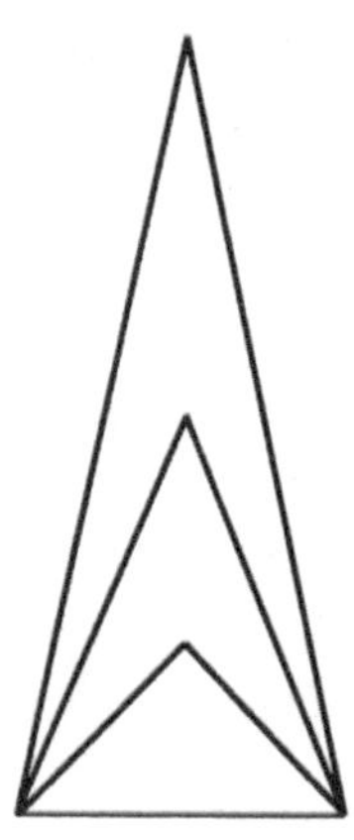

To help conceptualize this unimaginable triangle, he asks us to move in thought from the idea of a "quantitative" triangle to that of a "non-quantitative" triangle. For any quantitative triangle the sum of its angles adds up to 180 degrees; also, the larger any one angle, the smaller the other two. Further, the sum of the length of any two sides of a triangle is always greater than the length of the remaining side, though this sum decreases and approaches the length of the third side when the angle that is formed by those two sides itself increases. Cusanus invites us to imagine a tall isosceles triangle in which the narrow angle at its apex gradually increases in size while the length of its base remains constant (see Figure 3). As the angle at the apex of the triangle increases, the two angles at its base decrease and the two sides that define the apex shorten as its altitude gradually collapses toward the base.

Now, in the case of a "quantitative" triangle the apex angle may *approach* 180 degrees and the length of the sum of the two sides that define

140. *DI* I, 13 (35), 63. Note that, when the mathematical formula for curvature is applied to the case of a circle (this case, in fact, serves as the motivating example for the definition of curvature), the curvature goes to zero as the radius goes to infinity. On the basis of this motivating relation, the radius of curvature is defined (for a general curve) as the reciprocal of the curvature at a given point. (I have O. Bradley Bassler to thank for this piece of mathematical information.)

Although Cusanus does not mention it, it should be noted that the problem of infinity appears in the case of the smallest as well as the largest. Even in the case of a finite circle, the difference between the straight line tangent and the circle becomes infinitely small as one zooms in, closer and closer to their point of coincidence.

141. *DI* I, 14 (37), 65.

it may *approach* the length of the base, but these limits cannot be reached without the dissolution of the triangle itself. Nevertheless, Cusanus holds, we can hypothesize that these limits *are* reached while the triangle remains nonetheless a triangle—though now, clearly a "non-quantitative" triangle, which has been resolved into a simple line.[142] The one line is simultaneously all three sides and all three angles. At the limit, when the altitude of the triangle reaches zero, the two sides that had defined the apex of the triangle come into coincidence with the base line of the triangle. The three lines become one line. The angle at the apex of the triangle "maximizes" to 180 degrees, and so comes into coincidence with the base line. Each of the two angles at the base, in turn, "minimizes" to zero degrees, and so also comes into coincidence with the base line. At the limit, the maximum (apex) angle coincides with the minimum (base) angles, and all three coinciding angles themselves coincide with the base line of the triangle. The one line is simultaneously all three lines and all three angles of the "non-quantitative" triangle. "Hence," Cusanus concludes, "by means of this hypothesis, which cannot hold true for quantitative things, you can be helped in ascending to nonquantitative things; that which is impossible for quantitative things, you see to be altogether necessary for nonquantitative things. Hereby it is evident that an infinite line is a maximum triangle."[143]

The non-quantitative triangle helps us to "think" the maximum triangle, precisely because it allows us to visualize the approach to a limit in which opposites coincide. This also helps us to understand how Cusanus is conceiving of an "infinite" geometrical figure. Notice that the infinite triangle is *not* thought here as an indefinitely large triangle. Cusanus does not ask us to imagine a finite triangle, and then imagine doubling the length of the sides, and then doubling them again, and so on. Such incremental increase could never lead to a "maximal" triangle, in Cusanus' sense. An infinite triangle is not an indefinitely "large" triangle. It is neither great nor small. It has no quantity.

It is worth taking a moment, in this context, to consider another exam-

142. *DI* I, 14 (38–39), 65.
143. *DI* I, 14 (39), 65.

ple that Cusanus did *not* use. When we try to make the move from considering the finite non-quantitative triangle (that is at the same time a finite line segment) to the thought of an "infinite" triangle (that is at the same time an "infinite" line), we may be tempted to think of this "infinite line" as a line that is indefinitely extended in two directions. But if that were what Cusanus had had in mind, he could have constructed a quite different example to help us think the coincidence of lines and angles in the infinite triangle. Consider the following example, which he might have used but did not. Imagine a tall, pointy isosceles triangle whose apex angle increases, as do the lengths of the base and the sides, as the altitude diminishes. The angle at the apex maximizes to 180 degrees and the two angles at the base minimize to zero degrees. All the while, the three lines increase in length until the top two lines collapse onto the base, which is now indefinitely extended in both directions. At the limit, all three angles and all three lines resolve into one indefinitely extended line. No doubt Cusanus would have rejected this particular example as very misleading, because, although it does help us to think the coincidence of lines and angles, it nevertheless encourages us to think of the infinite line as indefinitely extended, rather than as a complete, indivisible, non-quantitative whole.

Cusanus returns to the idea of an infinite line later in Book I. His immediate concern, in the examples of the maximum triangle and the maximum circle, is to illustrate the principle of the coincidence of opposites in the infinite. *At their limit,* the characteristics of the maximum circle and the maximum triangle collapse into identity with characteristics which would describe their contrariety in the realm of quantitatively finite figures. Curvature coincides with rectitude, (tri-)angularity with non-angularity (linearity). Thus we approach the notion of an infinite "triangle" or "circle" at the limit in which the finite image finally explodes and circle and triangle disappear. As long as the figures remain quantitatively finite, contrary qualities remain in opposition. (Indeed it is the contrariety of the qualities that defines the figures—curvature and angularity are essential, defining characteristics of circles and triangles.) No matter how much we increase the length of the radius of the circle or the angle at the apex of the triangle—so long as they remain quantitatively *finite*—we still have a circle or a triangle, and we still have the opposition between curvature and rectitude, angularity and non-angularity. This quantity may be increased indefinitely and yet figure and opposition still remain. When we "think" of the circle and triangle as infinite, or as no longer quantitative, however, the figure vanishes and the contrariety disappears. For Cusanus, the trick is in experiencing the way in which this coincidence occurs at the limit, the limit approached but never reached by quantitative increase. That is, the key lies in experiencing the relation between the privative infinite and the absolute infinite *in the limit concept.*

It is significant that these are all examples in which the indefinite increase in one aspect of the figure occurs concomitantly with an indefinite decrease in another. In the case of the circle, the radius increases to infinity while the curvature decreases to nothing. (The radius maximizes as the curvature minimizes.) In the case of the triangle, as the angle at the apex increases maximally, the other two angles minimize and the altitude of the triangle decreases to nothing. The paradigmatic example of the polygon inscribed in a circle discussed earlier displays this same structure in an even more transparent way. While the number of sides of the polygon approaches infinity and the polygon resolves into identity with the circle, the area between polygon and circle diminishes to nothing.

In other words, in all three cases we are asked to imagine an indefinitely extended progressive approach to a given limit.[144] The indefinite increase of a given quantity (radius, angle, sides) results in the progressive minimization of another quantity (curvature, altitude, area). It is because of this simultaneous maximization and minimization that we can experience the *approach* to a limit, and thus intellectually "think" the coincidence of opposites in the infinite (curvature and rectitude, or angularity

144. Note that in the case of the circle a *fixed* tangent is used to gauge the decrease in curvature (i.e. as the arch approaches coincidence with the tangent). In the case of the triangle the length of the base of the triangle remains constant as the altitude decreases, i.e. as the apex of the triangle approaches the base. In the case of the inscribed polygon the circle is the constant, fixed finite reference toward which the polygon approaches. In order for us to visualize the approach to a limit, there must be a *fixed* reference *toward* which qualities/quantities converge.

and linearity). If all we had was a figural maximization without a corresponding minimization (e.g. an equilateral triangle whose sides expanded to infinity), we would experience the "limiting case" only as the dissolution of the triangle itself (an "infinite triangle" could not actually *be* a triangle any more than an "infinite circle" could *be* a circle—there could be no bounding periphery in either case). We would not, however, experience a convergence to a limit, and thus the *coincidence* of contrary qualities.

By reflecting on the characteristics and relations of these infinite mathematical figures, Cusanus holds, we may begin to intuit something of the nature of absolute or divine infinity itself. That is, we may use the insights won in our speculative consideration of these infinite mathematical figures in order to "think" (or intuit) symbolically the infinite, all-inclusive unity of the absolute Maximum in which all opposites coincide. This divine infinity can be comprehended "incomprehensively" only *at the limit* of all thought. Thus, for example, when we think of the characteristics of an infinite triangle, we approach in thought the three-in-oneness of the divine Trinity:

> [A]n infinite triangle cannot be composed of a plurality of lines, even though it is the greatest and truest triangle. . . . And because it is the truest triangle—something which it cannot be without three lines—it will be necessary that the one infinite line be three lines and that the three lines be one most simple line. And similarly regarding the angles, for there will be only one infinite angle; and this angle is three angles, and the three angles are one angle. Nor will this maximum triangle be composed of sides and angles; rather, the infinite line and [infinite] angle are one and the same thing, so that the line is the angle, because the triangle is the line.[145]

Thus, by reflecting on the linear oneness of a maximal, or infinite, triangle, we approach, "in learned ignorance," an intuition of the Trinity. "For we see that we do not find first one angle and then another and then still another, as in the case of finite triangles; for there cannot be numerically different angles in the oneness of an incomposite triangle. Rather, one thing exists trinely without numerical multiplication."[146] Thus the "gen-

145. *DI* I, 14 (37), 65. See especially *DI* I, 19–20.
146. *DI* I, 19 (57), 73. See also I, 20 (62).

eration" of the three Persons of the Trinity is not an imaging of three distinct persons, but rather (as in Eckhart) the production of the self-same: Oneness, Equality-of-Oneness, and the Union of Oneness and Equality-of-Oneness, "as if we were to speak of [one and] the same thing as *this, it, the same.*"[147]

If the vanishing image of an infinite triangle brings us closer to the thought of the Trinity, that of an infinite circle helps bring us to an intuition of the infinite unity of God, which encompasses all things and from which all things unfold.[148] Cusanus begins his discussion of this metaphor in a fairly traditional vein. "A circle," he writes, "is a perfect figure of oneness and simplicity." He quickly adds, however, that "this oneness is infinite," so that only an infinite circle begins to approach symbolically (albeit always inadequately) the absolute unity of the divine. The infinite circle further figures God's eternity:

> The Maximum's most one duration is so great that in its duration the past is not other than the future, and the future is not other than the present; rather, they are the most one duration, or eternity, without beginning and end. For in the Maximum the beginning is so great that even the end is—in the Maximum—the beginning.[149]

For Cusanus, God's eternity is an infinite unity, a positive infinity which enfolds the world's temporality. The unfolding of the world's temporality is characterized by duration, by an extended ordering of past, present, and future.

Cusanus' description of eternity—"the most one duration" in which "even the end . . . is the beginning"—is structurally parallel to his description of the "infinite" or maximal number. The maximum "number" could never be arrived at by counting, by ascending an indefinitely extended, ordered continuum. A "maximum" number, greater than any positable number, would be infinite and so embrace all plurality and de-

147. *DI* I, 8 (25), 59. Cusanus borrows this characterization of the Trinity from Augustine, who had described God the Father as unity *(unitas)*, the son as Equality *(aequalitas)*, and the Holy Spirit as the connection of both *(concordia, connexio)* (*De doctrina christiana* I, 5). It was the Cusan, however, who first used the geometric image of an infinite triangle to symbolize the Trinity. See Mahnke, *Unendliche Sphäre*, 183.

148. See II. 3.

149. *DI* I, 21 (63), 75 and 76.

grees of comparatively greater and lesser in absolute unity. The maximal "number" would coincide with the minimum "number," i.e. unity or oneness. Indeed, absolute unity or oneness cannot be thought of as number at all. It is, rather, the beginning and end of all number.[150] Similarly, maximal "duration," eternity, is not properly speaking duration at all. It is the infinite unity of all times, past, present, and future. Once again, it is the absolutely infinite which enfolds the privative infinity of extended multiplicity.

The image of the infinite circle figures this relationship between God's absolute infinity and the privative infinity of the universe:

> You see that because the center is infinite, the whole of the Maximum is present most perfectly within everything as the Simple and the Indivisible; moreover, it is outside of every being—surrounding all things, because the circumference is infinite, and penetrating all things, because the diameter is infinite.[151]

The infinite circle is a simple and indivisible totality. Its "infinite circumference" signifies the notion of the all-embracing and its "infinite center" the notion of intensive concentration. It is significant to note that (in contrast to Eckhart) Cusanus includes the "infinite diameter" in his characterization of the infinite circle (and later also of the infinite sphere). It is the diameter that joins center and circumference. Indeed, in an infinite circle, the diameter may be conceptually identified with both circumference and center. The "infinite diameter" spans the entire area between the greatest and the smallest circle (i.e. circumference and center) and in so delineating this area, observes Cusanus, acts itself as a kind of circumference. It may also be thought of as a kind of center, or middle, as that which lies between the limits.[152] It is not incidental that Cusanus gives equal weight here to the diameter—that which lies between and links center and circumference. Indeed it is indicative of his more general tendency to link the transcendent and immanent dimensions of the divine by developing the notion of intensive infinity. And, as we shall see, this move is

150. *DI* I, 5 (13–14), 54–55. Cusanus assumes the traditional Greek notion that one is not itself a number, but is the principle or ground of all number.

151. *DI* I, 21 (64), 76.

152. See Mahnke, *Unendliche Sphäre,* 85.

reflected in the systematic centrality of his Christology and its singular importance in both his epistemology and his ontology.

The last and most fitting geometric symbol Cusanus uses to describe God in the first book of *On Learned Ignorance* is that of the infinite sphere. What was said about the center, circumference, and diameter of the infinite circle may be said of the infinite sphere as well. Further, the infinite sphere is the final actuality of all the potential contained in the center—the full actuality of all length, width, and depth. It actually contains every possible spatial figure within itself. In this way the infinite sphere represents the most divine characteristic: it is in the infinite actuality of the divine that all possibility is realized and perfected.

> Therefore, all actual existence has from the Maximum whatever actuality it possesses; and all existence exists actually insofar as it exists actually in the Infinite. Hence, the Maximum is the Form of forms and the Form of being, or maximum actual Being.[153]

Here, as Mahnke notes, Cusanus moves beyond Plotinus' doctrine of originary unity. Infinite multiplicity is contained in *actuality* in the infinite unity, not just in potentiality, because in absolute infinity the opposition between potentiality and actuality is overcome.[154]

Cusanus makes a point of clarifying that the divine Maximum actually *is* whatever is possible, since in the Maximum possibility and actuality coincide. In the case of what is nonmaximal, possibility is never identical with actuality but must be actualized *from* that possibility. In order to illustrate his point he uses the example of the generation of a triangle (sector ABC) from the rotation of a finite line segment (AB). Here the finite line may be said to be potentially (but not actually) a triangle. In contrast an infinite line actually *is* an infinite triangle. It is not a triangle in the way in which we say a finite line is

FIGURE 4

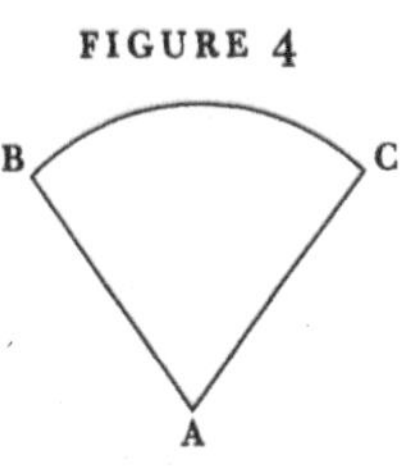

153. *DI* I, 23 (70), 78.

154. Mahnke, *Unendliche Sphäre,* 86. See also *De possest.* The title of this work is a term coined by Cusanus to describe this particular coincidence of opposites in God, who is perfect actuality and possibility at the same time. In the divine Infinite, what *can be* and what *is* are indistinguishable. Only God is actually what he can be *(possest).* See also *De venatione sapientiae,* 13.

potentially a triangle (i.e. that a triangle can be generated *from* it); rather, it is *actually* an infinite triangle identical to the infinite line itself.[155]

Finally, Cusanus notes: "Since the Maximum is like a maximum sphere . . . it is the one most simple and most congruent measure of the whole universe and of all existing things in the universe." This is so because "God is the one most simple Essence *(ratio)* of the whole world, or universe."[156] How are we to understand this assertion that God is the measure and essence of all that is? How can the Infinite be the measure and form of something finite?

The Absolute Infinite as Measure of the Finite

The answer to this question penetrates to the heart of the Cusan's ontology. In the Absolute Maximum, he explains, everything *is* the Absolute Maximum and the Maximum is each thing in such a way that it is all of them together and none of them in particular. In order to elucidate this paradox Cusanus once again has recourse to a mathematical metaphor. God's infinite unity is the essence and measure of all essences (the Form of all forms, the Being of all beings) in the same way that an infinite line is the measure and essence of all finite lines.

> A finite line is divisible, and an infinite line is indivisible; for the infinite, in which the maximum coincides with the minimum, has no parts. However, a finite line is not divisible to the point that it is no longer a line, because in the case of magnitude we do not arrive at a minimum than which there cannot be a lesser. . . . Hence, a finite line is indivisible in its essence [*ratio*]; a line of one foot is not less a line than is a line of one cubit. It follows, then, that an infinite line is the essence of a finite line. Similarly, the unqualifiedly Maximum is the Essence of all things. But the essence is the measure. Hence, Aristotle rightly says in the *Metaphysics* that the first is the measure [*metrum et mensura*] of all things because it is the Essence of all things.[157]

A finite line has a determinate length, say two feet. It can be divided in half (into two one-foot lines), in quarters, etc. An infinite line on the other hand is indivisible and cannot be thought of in terms of magnitude at all.

155. *DI* I, 16 (42), 67.

156. *DI* I, 23 (72), 79. Hopkins notes that at *DI* I, 17 (49:5) the Maximum is said to be *ratio infinita,* just as at I, 16 (45:17–18) it is called *infinita essentia* (p. 191 n. 120).

157. *DI* I, 17 (47), 68–9. See Aristotle *Metaphysics* 10.1.1052b20–24.

Nor is it to be thought of as a line extended indefinitely in two directions as we often tend to think of the "number line" extending in both directions from the origin—here the difference in length between one unit and two units from the origin remains, insofar as the entire number line is the additive sum of all its units. This is not at all what Cusanus has in mind when he speaks of an "infinite line," for the infinite is not a sum total of the finite parts. It *has* no (finite) parts.[158] It is an absolutely unified totality, pure continuity with the integrity and simplicity of a single point. Here again, the maximum (line) coincides with the minimum.[159]

Now, a finite line of determinate length, while divisible, nevertheless exhibits something of the character of pure continuity as such. That is, it "is not divisible to the point that it is no longer a line." No matter how small the divisions are made, the integrity of its linear continuity remains intact. Its linear continuity cannot be reduced to discrete atomic parts. That is, in its essence, even the finite line is impartible. Thus, he underscores that "a line of one foot is not less a line than a line of one cubit." Both exhibit the same quality of linear continuity, the integrity of their respective magnitudes. The fact that all finite lines are "divisible" *ad infinitum* is simply a result of the more fundamental "infinity" exhibited in the nature of continuity itself: the unified totality that makes any continuum *continuous* and not discrete. It is this "absolute" infinity that makes the "privative" infinity of unending division possible in the first place.[160]

Cusanus thus holds that an infinite line is the essence of *all* lines. This

158. Or if we speak of the "parts" of the infinite, then it is in a completely different sense, for the parts of the infinite are themselves infinite and convertible with the whole. See, for example, *DI* I, 15 (40), 66; and *DI* I, 16 (46), 68.

159. Cusanus clearly says that "in an infinite line one foot is not shorter than two feet, so it is not the case that an infinite line exceeds the length of one foot more than it exceeds the length of two feet" (*DI* I, 16 [46], 68). Indeed, he emphasizes that "in an infinite line a line of two feet and a line of three feet do not differ" (*DI* I, 17 [48], 69). Both, he explains, are "convertible" with the entire infinite line. In the language of modern mathematics we would describe this "convertibility" as a one-to-one correspondence between each and every point on the one-foot line with each and every point on the infinite line, and similarly for the two-foot line, or any finite line segment.

160. For a more detailed analysis of Cusanus' analysis of the division of the continuum, and the manner in which the infinite line serves as measure for all finite lines, see my paper "Three Mathematical Metaphors" given at The Catholic University of America, October 6, 2001.

essence "is one and equal in each and every line,"[161] and it is what makes for the linear continuity of all lines no matter how long or short. The difference between a line of two feet and a line of three feet is not due to a difference in their essence, he says, but rather results "from an accident, because the lines do not participate equally in the essence. Hence, there is only one essence of all lines, and it is participated in in different ways."[162]

What does it mean to say that different entities participate differently in the same essence? In the line example we may say that all lines have the same essence in that they are all continuously extended. They all have linear integrity. Their difference is a difference in length or magnitude. This variation in length, in the gradation of magnitude, answers Cusanus, is due to their unequal participation in the one infinite essence.

> [A] finite straight line, insofar as it is straight, does not admit of more and less. But because [it is] finite, one [straight] line is—through a difference of participation in the infinite line—longer or shorter in relation to another; no two [finite lines] are ever found to be equal.[163]

Similarly, the difference between determinate entities in the world is due to the degree of participation a given finite entity is capable of. Reality, explains Cusanus, is constituted by a whole hierarchy or range of degrees of perfection among the entities of the world.

The Universe as Image of the Absolute Maximum

When the infinite oneness of the Divine is "unfolded" in creation, the result is a totality of finite beings, each utterly unique, and each participating in the one Infinite Essence. To illustrate this idea, consider the following example, which I take to be very much in the spirit of Cusanus' own mathematical metaphors: consider the generation of innumerable finite lines from the motion of a single point. Imagine a point moved indefinitely in a straight line. At each (infinitesimal) stage along the way a line of finite length, of a unique and determinate magnitude, is generated.

161. *DI* I, 17 (48), 69.
162. Ibid.
163. *DI* I, 18 (53), 71.

No two lines are precisely equal. The infinite richness contained in the potentiality of the point is unfolded in a potentially unending number of finite lines, each with its own distinct magnitude. But no single line segment, no matter its length, could ever exhaust the infinite richness of the point. Cusanus himself uses the analogy of the generation of numbers from the number one, which "enfolds" all numbers, and which coincides with the maximum number.[164]

The infinite unity of God is unfolded in the multifarious variety and multiplicity of entities in the world. Now, although the different entities participate to differing degrees in Maximum Oneness, or the divine infinite, it is by virtue of the fact that they *do* participate that each created being must be understood as a "finite infinity."

> For the Infinite Form is received only finitely, so that every created thing is, as it were, a finite infinity or a created god, so that it exists in the best way in which this can best occur. [Everything is] as if the Creator had said, "Let it be made," and as if because a God (who is eternity itself) could not be made, there was made that which could be made: viz., something as much like God as possible.[165]

The universe, for Cusanus, is thus an image (albeit a necessarily imperfect image) of the absolute Maximum. There can only be one absolute Maximum. The created universe, however, is as much like the absolute Maximum as possible. It is the expression of divine unity unfolded in the realm of plurality. Cusanus accordingly describes the universe as a "contracted" or "concrete" maximum *(maximum contractum seu concretum)*. Because the concrete world receives from the absolute Maximum everything it is—just as a mirror image owes its existence to the face which it

164. *DI* I, 18 (52), 71.

165. *DI* II, 2 (104), 93. Blumenberg, it seems, willfully misreads this passage as voluntaristic. See Blumenberg, *Legitimacy*, 563. Louis Dupré ("Nature and Grace in Nicholas of Cusa's Mystical Philosophy," 155) has pointed out that, in general, Blumenberg misinterprets Cusanus' declaration that possibility is created by God no less than actuality as a reaffirmation of the nominalist conception of God's *potentia absoluta* with its voluntaristic consequences. On the contrary, Dupré insists, possibility for Cusanus "does not precede actuality as a well-defined vacuum . . . *within* which God may choose to create whatever he pleases. Possibility emerges from the divine Being simultaneously with actuality. Hence Cusanus's universe actualizes all its possibilities." In this context see Peter J. Casarella, "Nicholas of Cusa and the Power of the Possible," *American Catholic Philosophical Quarterly* 64 (1990): 7–34.

mirrors[166]—everything which can be said of the absolute Maximum, can also be said of the contracted maximum, though of course not in an absolute sense. That is, the universe imitates the absolute greatness of God in a concrete and limited fashion. The absolute oneness of God is expressed in the unity of the many; divine eternity is spelled out in temporal succession; absolute simplicity is imaged as the totality of a compound; perfect identity is expressed as the equality of the different, etc.[167] Creation is thus understood by Cusanus in general as the imaging of absolute infinity in the "contracted infinity" of the universe.[168]

THE EXTENSIVE INFINITIZATION OF THE COSMOS

Cusanus understands the universe to be "infinite" in a twofold sense: both extensively (spatially unbounded) and intensively (infinitely rich in each part). It is his denial of the spatial finitude of the cosmos in the first sense, and his rejection of traditional medieval cosmology in particular, which in large part have earned him the reputation as a radical forerunner of modern cosmology, as a speculative thinker ahead of his time.[169] This

166. This analogy is misleading however, insofar as a mirror image of a face depends not only on the face, but also on the existence of the mirror: "[F]or it is not the case that as a mirror is a mirror before it receives the image of a face, so created being exists prior to derivative [participating] being; for created being *is* derivative being" (*DI* II, 2 [102–3], 92). See also the related passage at II, 3 (111), 96.

167. See, for example, *DI* II, 4 (114), 97; and II, 3 (106), 94.

168. *DI* II, 4 (114), 96.

169. Mahnke, for example, holds that Cusanus' use of the infinite sphere metaphor to describe the universe was a scientific insight of the greatest significance. He writes: "Aus dem Geiste der mathematischen Mystik wird hier nämlich die moderne, exakte Kosmologie geboren, oder wenigstens eine für sie grundlegende Erkenntnis: die der unendlichen, mittelpunktlosen Ausdehnung der Sternenwelt" (Mahnke, *Unendliche Sphäre,* 86). Koyré notes that already Giordano Bruno, Kepler, and Descartes had viewed Nicholas of Cusa as just such a radical forerunner of the modern cosmology. Koyré, in contrast to Mahnke, however, holds the view that it is a mistake to view Cusanus as a forerunner of Copernicus, since his conception of the cosmos "is not based upon a criticism of contemporary astronomical or cosmological theories, and does not lead, at least in his own thinking, to a revolution in science." Still he admits that Cusanus' bold speculations went "far beyond anything Copernicus ever dared to think of" (Koyré, *Closed World,* 8).

Harries, on the other hand, makes a convincing argument in his article "Infinite Sphere,"

section will be devoted to a discussion of this aspect of his cosmological speculation. While Cusanus is best known for his extensive infinitization of the cosmos, I will emphasize in what follows that this move goes hand in hand with his view that the universe also exhibits an *intensive* infinity in each of its parts, and that it is the way in which he develops this latter insight which heralds a radically modern conception of reality on the one hand and of human knowledge on the other.

Cusanus underscores the fact that, properly speaking, only God is infinite, that is, infinite in an absolute sense. The universe, he insists, is infinite only in a privative sense.[170] If we consider its material and spatial aspect, this means that the created cosmos cannot be conceived of as physically bounded by anything else. It is privatively infinite in the sense that it *lacks* limits in which it can be enclosed. It is the nature of the world to overrun any boundaries I might posit for it. Thus the universe is an epiphany of the divine Infinite, a "contracted" image of God. It is infinite unity "unfolded" in diversity and multiplicity, endlessly spread out in space and time.[171]

Cusanus' Critique of Aristotelian Prime Matter

In true Platonic fashion, Cusanus holds that the world produced by the creator is the most perfect world possible,[172] and that its imperfection arises from the limitations of matter, though of course matter in this case is

that the new world view of the sixteenth century, often assumed to be the *result* of the Copernican revolution and the new science, in fact has its foundation in an earlier shift in human self- and world-understanding, and that the Copernican revolution itself was first of all made possible by the new perceptual and intellectual possibilities opened up by late medieval mystical and speculative reflection on the nature of infinity and perspective.

170. "[O]nly the absolutely Maximum is negatively infinite. Hence, it alone is whatever there can at all possibly be. But since the universe encompasses all the things which are not God, it cannot be negatively infinite, although it is unbounded and thus privatively infinite. And in this respect it is neither finite nor infinite. For it cannot be greater than it is" (*DI* II, 1 [97], 90).

171. "[A]lthough [the universe] is maximally one, its oneness is contracted through plurality, just as its infinity [is contracted] through finitude, its simplicity through composition, its eternity through succession, its necessity through possibility, and so on—as if Absolute Necessity communicated itself without any intermingling and yet necessity were contractedly restricted in something opposed to it" (*DI* II, 4 [114], 97).

172. See e.g. Plato's *Timaeus* 29e ff., and Plotinus' *Enneads* 2.9.17.

not conceived of as a preexisting sub-stratum, but rather as "possibility-of-being":

> Hence although God is infinite and therefore had the power to create the world as infinite, nevertheless because the possibility was, necessarily, contracted and was not at all absolute or infinite aptitude, the world—in accordance with the possibility of being—was not able to be actually infinite or greater or to exist in any other way [than it does].[173]

Here Cusanus radically departs from the Aristotelian conception of (prime) matter as absolute possibility, as pure potentiality able to take on a potentially infinite variety of forms.

An Aristotelian would, of course, deny that such unformed matter could be conceived of as having actual physical existence. While matter may be conceived of independently from form as such "pure possibility," it nonetheless never exists independently of form. Cusanus, however, holds that even such a conceptual distinction is nonsensical and that it misconstrues the very nature of matter as such. All possibility, including all material possibility, is (by definition) contracted,[174] i.e. is the possibility of being *this* or *that*. Here Cusanus develops the idea already hinted at in the *Timaeus*, that there are traces of the forms already present in the possibility or matter of the cosmos. Matter, for Cusanus, is not merely formlessness and lack but exhibits as well a certain "aptitude" (for taking on form). This aptitude, he insists, is not absolute, or "infinite," as the Aristotelians had held, but contracted.[175]

> [U]nless the possibility of things were contracted, there could not be a reason for things but everything would happen by chance, as Epicurus falsely maintained. That this world sprang forth rationally from possibility was necessarily due to the fact that the possibility had an aptitude only for being this world. Therefore, the possibility's aptitude was contracted and not absolute.[176]

He goes on to explain that the earth, sun, indeed all created things were "latently present in matter," present "in terms of a certain contracted pos-

173. *DI* II, 8 (139), 106–7.

174. Only god is Absolute possibility that coincides with Absolute actuality. DI *II*, 8 (136), 106.

175. *DI* II, 8 (135 & 137), 105–6.

176. *DI* II, 8 (138), 106.

sibility."[177] Wherever we encounter possibility in the world it will already be limited and determined, "contracted" in a particular way.

In his earlier discussion of the Aristotelian understanding of matter, he points out that to a certain extent "the Peripatetics" recognized the fact that forms lie present in matter as possibilities to be actualized. He gives the example of a carpenter attempting to carve a chest from stone. His inability to do so is not due to his ineptitude as a carpenter to give proper form to the material, but rather due to the material itself. Wood makes a good chest. Stone does not.[178] An Aristotelian, no doubt, would claim that *this* level of material recalcitrance is due to the fact that wood and stone are already materials with a certain form (and could be further analyzed in terms of their elemental composition). When considering matter as such, however, they do not hesitate to *conceive* of it as altogether independent of form, and so designate it as "absolute possibility." It is precisely for this reason that they understand it to have an unlimited aptitude for taking on any and all possible forms, and so describe it as "boundless" or "infinite."

Cusanus categorically rejects this conception of prime or pure matter. The possibility that is constitutive of the universe, he holds, is necessarily contracted. Potency and actuality are mutually implicating terms, and all things exist to a relatively greater or lesser degree of potency or actuality. Nothing in the universe exists in absolute potency (or is ever fully actualized). All created things are always to some extent actual and to some extent potential. The two modes of being are always present in any entity whatsoever. One cannot exist without the other: ". . . the actuality is contracted through the possibility, so that it does not at all exist except in the possibility. And the possibility does not at all exist unless it is contracted through the actuality."[179]

177. Ibid.

178. "For the fact that from stone a chest cannot be made by a craftsman is a defect in the material. But the fact that someone other than the craftsman cannot make a chest from wood is a defect in the agent. Therefore, both matter and an efficient cause are required. Hence, in a certain way, forms are in matter as possibilities, and they are brought to actuality in conformity with an efficient cause" (*DI* II, 8 [135], 105).

179. *DI* II, 8 (137), 106.

For this reason it would be nonsensical, for Cusanus, to conceive of the matter of the universe as absolute possibility. Matter, for him, is always already contracted, always already limited in some way so as to be predisposed to certain forms. This amounts to saying that even the material aspect of reality must be understood as intelligible, as rational.

And so it is that Nicholas of Cusa denies the kind of infinity which Aristotle had claimed was proper to matter (infinite aptitude), but asserts (where Aristotle had denied) the physical (i.e. spatial) *boundlessness* of the world. Cusanus can agree with Aristotle that matter is not actually extendable to infinity, because he distinguishes between the absolutely infinite and the indefinite or boundless. Just as Cusanus rejects the notion of absolute potency on the grounds that (other than God) there can be no absolute minimum in the world, so too, he asserts the boundlessness of the cosmos on the grounds that (other than God) there can be no absolute Maximum which would serve to limit it. Although the world is not infinite properly speaking, it cannot for this reason be conceived of as finite, because it lacks (maximum) boundaries within which it is enclosed. The following passage may thus be read as an implicit critique of Aristotle's failure to make this critical distinction between the finite, the absolutely infinite, and the "privatively" infinite:

> [A]lthough with respect to God's infinite power, which is unlimitable, the universe could have been greater: nevertheless since the possibility-of-being, or matter, which is not actually extendable unto infinity, opposes, the universe cannot be greater. And so, [the universe is] unbounded; for it is not the case that anything actually greater than it, in relation to which it would be bounded, is positable. And so, [it is] privatively infinite.[180]

Almost exactly two centuries later, Descartes will defend his view that the universe is *not* finite and bounded, but *indefinitely* extended (i.e. privatively infinite), by pointing out that after all "the Cardinal of Cusa and several other Divines have supposed the world to be infinite, without ever being reproached by the Church; on the contrary, it is believed that to make His works appear very great is to honor God."[181]

180. *DI* II, 1 (97), 90.

181. René Descartes, "Lettre à Chanut," June 6, 1647, *Oeuvres,* ed. Adam Tannery, vol. 5, p. 50 sq., Paris, 1903. Cited by Koyré, *Closed World,* 6.

Perspective and the Destruction of the Aristotelian Cosmos

Much has been made of the destructive effect Cusanus' transference of the infinite sphere metaphor to the created world had on medieval cosmology, and rightly so. In the second book of *On Learned Ignorance* Cusanus' cosmological speculations led him to deny the finitude of the cosmos and its enclosure in a system of perfect crystalline spheres, to deny the traditional distinction between the celestial and the terrestrial realms, and to assert the relativity of motion.[182]

Nicholas of Cusa begins Chapter Eleven of Book Two (innocuously entitled "Corollaries regarding motion") by denying that there is a fixed center to the universe, a still point about which the heavenly spheres revolve. This would imply an absolute minimum with regard to motion, an inadmissible supposition since no concrete entity can exhibit either absolute maximality or absolute minimality of any kind. Thus the earth cannot lie at the dead center of the cosmos. In the same way, if there is no fixed center to the world-machine, there can be no bounding circumference, for any circumference is defined by its equidistance from some fixed center. Cusanus thus stands Aristotle's argument for the finitude of the world on its head:

> Hence, the world does not have a [fixed] circumference. For if it had a [fixed] center, it would also have a [fixed] circumference; and hence it would also have its own beginning and end within itself, and it would be bounded in relation to something else, and beyond the world there would be both something else and space *(locus)*. But all these [consequences] are false. Therefore, since it is not possible for the world to be enclosed between a physical center and [a physical] circumference, the world—of which God is the center and the circumference—is not understood. And although the world is not infinite, it cannot be conceived as finite, because it lacks boundaries within which it is enclosed.[183]

The world is not enclosed between a physical center and a physical circumference. The earth does not lie at the center of the world nor does the sphere of the fixed stars define its circumference.[184]

182. See for example Mahnke, *Unendliche Sphäre*, 88–99, and Koyré, *Closed World*, 5–24.
183. *DI* II, 11 (156), 114.
184. "Moreover, in the sky there are not fixed and immovable poles—although the heaven of

Cusanus goes on to deny the existence of any true or exact sphere in the material world, for not only can there be no exact center to the cosmos as a whole, there can be no precise center of any of the heavenly spheres or heavenly bodies. Thus the earth has no exact center nor does the sun nor Venus nor any of the heavenly spheres including the "eighth sphere" of the fixed stars. Again, without an exact center there is no precise equidistance anywhere in the physical universe, and so all these bodies merely *approximate* spherical form. Still, Cusanus holds on to enough of the traditional picture of the cosmos to assert that all these spheroids move in *approximately* circular paths around an imprecise and constantly shifting axis, and that the earth comes closer than any of the other heavenly bodies to being at the *approximate* center of the heavenly spheres.

Much has been made of the fact that from the non-existence of a still center to the universe, he concludes that all heavenly bodies, including the earth, must be in motion. This assertion that the earth moves, however, does not imply an anticipation of the Copernican theory that the earth actually rotates around the sun. Although Cusanus does assert that the earth, too, must have its own proper motion, he seems to have in mind a circular orbit very near to the (indeterminate) center of the heavenly spheres. He states explicitly that the earth is moved less than the moon, and the moon less than Venus or Mercury, and these less than the sun, etc.[185] That is, he maintains the traditional order of the planets, sun,

fixed stars appears to describe by its motion circles of progressively different sizes. . . . Therefore, in the eighth sphere there is not a star which describes, through its revolution, a maximum circle. (For the star would have to be equidistant from the poles, which do not exist)" (*DI* II, 11 [158], 115).

185. *DI* II, 11 (159–60), 116. Mahnke presents a detailed interpretation of a later manuscript (1445), written five years after *De docta ignorantia,* which describes the motions of the earth, sun, and fixed stars in more detail (Mahnke, *Unendliche Sphäre,* 91–97). The end result of his lengthy exposition is that while Cusanus is able to explain the daily appearance of the motions of the sun and the fixed stars, he is unable to work out adequately their annual motions, and he does not discuss the planetary motions at all. Nor does he explain the appearance of the motions of the sun and the stars by referring to the composition of the three real motions of the earth in the way Copernicus does. Rather he attributes two, slower motions to the earth, and he attributes the appearance of the motion of the sun and stars primarily to the faster motion of their heavenly spheres. In this he maintains a geocentric world view, and refers all of the heavenly motions to the earth as the fixed center of the whole coordinate system, since, according to him, it lies closest to the center of the system of spheres and exhibits the least motion.

moon, and stars, although he holds that none of their orbits are precise or ever repeated in exactly the same way twice.[186]

While certainly curious, this irregular, imprecise view of the world system still assumes a fairly traditional picture of the structure and organization of the heavenly bodies. Cusanus does not stop here, however. He goes on in what follows to undermine even this irregular version of the traditional world system by reflecting on the phenomenon of perspectival appearance. He asks the reader to share a simple thought experiment. Imagine standing on the north pole of the eighth sphere. From that perspective, he points out, the earth would appear to be at the zenith of the cosmos. In contrast, if someone else were standing on the earth directly below the north pole of the eighth sphere, it would appear to him that the pole is at the zenith. Wherever one was, in fact, one would believe oneself to be at the center of the cosmos. Therefore, Cusanus insists, the reader who truly wants to understand the motion and structure of the universe correctly must leave behind his geo-centrist preconceptions and recognize that what appear to us to be the center and poles of the world-machine are in fact merely conjectural reference points, determined relative to whatever position we happen to occupy in the cosmos.

Thus, if someone were on the sun, he would take the sun to be the center of the world and would fix a set of poles in relation to himself. If he were on the earth he would fix a set of coordinates relative to an earth-centered cosmos, if on Mars a set relative to a Mars-centered cosmos, and so on.[187]

Mahnke concludes that, from an astronomical point of view it is obvious that Nicholas of Cusa is no forerunner of Copernicus. In fact, if one were to consider the precision of his explanation from the point of view of a geocentric system of spheres, his explanation would lag *far* behind that of Ptolemy, and from the perspective of a heliocentric cosmos even further behind that of Aristarchus of Samos (with whom Cusanus was not familiar) and his predecessors among the Pythagoreans and Platonists.

Mahnke notes, however, that Cusanus was not attempting to put forward a new and precise astronomical theory in this hurriedly thrown together manuscript. Indeed, as Mahnke points out, he was convinced that human reason is simply unable to attain to more than imprecise conjectures in this area of knowledge. He holds that a precise knowledge of the cosmos, because of the deviations of physical reality from the world of mathematical ideas, is not in fact possible. See *DI* II, 11 (159), 115; compare with *De coniecturis* I, 2 and 13.

186. *DI* II, 11 (160), 116.

187. *DI* II, 12 (162), 117.

Therefore, if . . . you want truly to understand something about the motion of the universe, you must merge the center and the poles, aiding yourself as best you can by your imagination. . . . Thereupon you will see—through the intellect, to which only learned ignorance is of help—that the world and its motion and shape cannot be apprehended. For [the world] will appear as a wheel in a wheel and a sphere in a sphere—having its center and circumference *nowhere,* as was stated.[188]

It is in this passage that Nicholas of Cusa comes the closest to declaring explicitly that the universe has the form of an infinite sphere. Clearly he does not intend an image, here, of a finite series of imbedded (though imprecise) spheres. He explodes this world picture when he asks the reader to imaginatively *merge* the "center" and "poles" generated by perspectival appearance, so that what was thought of as the pole becomes the center of another possible sphere. Its pole in turn could become the center of some further sphere, and so on. Such radical de-centering clearly invokes the image of a privatively infinite sphere, i.e. one whose center and circumference are *nowhere* to be found.

It has been suggested that, given Cusanus' conception of the universe as an image of the divine Infinite—a concrete likeness of God unfolded in the diversity and multiplicity of space and time—it is not surprising that he finds the metaphor of the infinite sphere singularly appropriate in describing not only God's existence but also the physical "shape" of the universe itself. Indeed, insofar as it is a sensible, spatial image, the infinite sphere would seem to be a more fitting representation of the cosmos than of God.[189] Notice, however, that when Cusanus uses the image of the infinite sphere here to describe the physical dimensions of the world, he shifts the metaphor in a subtle but significant way. The world is not represented as a sphere with its "center everywhere and its circumference nowhere," or as a sphere with its "center and circumference everywhere." Rather, it is described as a sphere with its center and circumference *nowhere.* The image given here is not one of infinite plenitude but rather of unending vacuousness. Such a privatively infinite sphere is strangely hollow, bereft of place, of significance, and of definition. It is an image of homogeneous, absolute orientationless space.[190]

188. *DI* II, 11 (161), 116, my emphasis.

189. See Mahnke, *Unendliche Sphäre,* 87; and Harries, "Infinite Sphere," 8.

190. For a discussion of the varying intonations given to the infinite sphere metaphor over

For Cusanus, however, this image of the universe as a privatively infinite sphere is not the last word. While it is indeed nonsensical to speak of a *physical* center or circumference in an indefinitely extended universe, the world—as an epiphany of the divine Infinite—finds its *metaphysical* center and circumference in God. Only God is precisely equidistant to all things, because God alone is "Infinite Equality," the Essence of all that is. "Hence, the world-machine will have its center everywhere and its circumference nowhere, so to speak; for God, who is everywhere and nowhere, is its circumference and center."[191] From a physical point of view, the center and circumference of the universe are nowhere to be found. From a metaphysical (or ontological) perspective, however, the cosmos has its center and circumference in God, who is the Being and Essence of all things. Thus, throughout the text, Cusanus blends the two perspectives, as in the above passage, in order to arrive at his own peculiar cosmology.[192] It is this infusion of the presence of the divine Infinite throughout the unbounded cosmos which loans an *intensive* infinity to the structure of the being of all things. We will discuss this intensive infinitization of the cosmos at greater length in the next section (see below, p. 219).

Perspective and the Dignity of the Omnipresent "Center"

A major consequence of Cusanus' assertion of the infinity of the universe is his rejection of the Aristotelian distinction between the sub- and

time, see Jorge Luis Borges, "The Fearful Sphere of Pascal," in *Labyrinths, Selected Stories and Other Writings* (New York: New Directions Publishing Company, 1964), 189–92, and Harries' correction of Borges' historical sketch in his own essay "Infinite Sphere," 5–6. Harries underscores the fact that Cusanus' cosmological use of the infinite sphere metaphor reveals a transformed conception of space which anticipates the objective, homogeneous, undifferentiated space of the new cosmology: "space is now understood as an infinite, homogeneous continuum, the Aristotelian conception of space as essentially tied to bodies is denied—the transcendence of the intellect over the body [that is, the ability to recognize a given perspective *as* a perspective] mirrors itself in the transcendence of space over bodies" (Harries, "Infinite Sphere," 15). See also chapters 2 and 3 on Nicholas of Cusa in Harries, *Infinity and Perspective,* 22–63.

191. *DI* II, 12 (162), 117.

192. See for example *DI* II, 11 (157), 115: "Therefore, He who is the center of the world, viz., the Blessed God, is also the center of the earth, of all the spheres, and all things in the world. Likewise, He is the infinite circumference of all things." And also II, 11 (159), 115: "Therefore, the poles of the spheres coincide with the center, so that the center is not anything except the pole, because the Blessed God [is the center and the pole]."

superlunar realms of the cosmos, that is, of the hierarchy of world regions, which fundamentally distinguishes the "lower," corruptible realm of the earthly from the "higher," incorruptible, noble realm of the heavens. In a centerless, imprecise universe such an absolute distinction cannot be maintained. Though the earth seems to be more centrally located, it is also (from this perspective) closer to the conjectural pole of the cosmos. One can no longer hold that the earth is the lowest and meanest and most humble body in the cosmos. It, too, must be recognized as a "noble star" which has its own light and warmth and exerts its own influence on all the other stars. It is not a dark body devoid of light in contrast to the other stars as had traditionally been maintained. If seen from far enough away, Cusanus speculates, it too would appear as a bright star, just as the sun in turn possesses a dark, earthy center beneath its fiery periphery.

By admitting the earth to the ranks of the noble stars, Cusanus in fact does away with Aristotle's absolute distinction between terrestrial and celestial matter. The sun and moon, for example, are described in terms of the same "terrestrial" elements (earth, air, fire, and water) as our earth. Further, Cusanus asserts, we have no reason to suppose that change and decay occur only on the earth and not in fact throughout the universe. And he adds that, in any case, the phenomenon of decay should not be understood as complete annihilation, but rather only as the dissolution of a given body's component parts and their subsequent reunification into something else. This process, he suggests, may well occur in the whole of the universe in a similar manner: "For since there is one universal world and since there are causal relations between all the individual stars, it cannot be evident to us that anything is altogether corruptible."[193]

All heavenly bodies, including the earth, he asserts, are members of equal worth and dignity in an infinitely rich and diverse organic totality.[194] All members of the cosmos (like parts of a body) contribute to the perfec-

193. *DI* II, 12 (172), 120.

194. While the discussion so far has focused on the way in which Cusanus' extensive infinitization of the cosmos led him to assert the nobility and dignity of the earth, it should be noted that this consequence derives with equal (if not greater) force from his intensive infinitization of the cosmos.

tion of the whole, simply by conserving and perfecting their own natures. They are inextricably linked together in a reciprocal relation of influence and communion with each other.

Therefore, the earth is a noble star which has a light and a heat and an influence that are distinct and different from [that of] all other stars. . . . And each star communicates its light and influence to the others, though it does not aim to do so, since all stars gleam and are moved only in order to exist in the best way [they can]; and as a consequence thereof a sharing arises (just as light shines of its own nature and not in order that I may see, yet, as a consequence, a sharing occurs when I use light for the purpose of seeing). Similarly, Blessed God created all things in such a way that when each thing desires to conserve its own existence as a divine work, it conserves it in communion with others.[195]

Cusanus also takes issue with the view that the inhabitants of the earth are inferior due to their "low" position in the cosmos.[196] He assumes (given the principle of plenitude) that the other stars are indeed inhabited by other beings, but holds that, though different, they are not of a more noble or perfect nature than the inhabitants of the earth.[197] Indeed, he writes, "with regard to the intellectual natures a nobler and more perfect nature cannot, it seems, be given . . . than the intellectual nature which dwells here on earth and in its own region."[198] We will have more to say about his high regard for the human intellect in what follows.

Human beings, he asserts, do not yearn for another nature but yearn only to be perfected in the one they were given by their creator. And this is true of all other creatures, which rest in their own natures and strive only toward their own perfection. Everything in the universe has its own singular nature; "each thing is one and is perfect in the way it can be,"[199] though

195. *DI* II, 12 (166), 118.

196. Koyré remarks that this is a rather curious argument in favor of the relative perfection of the earth. "Thus, being convinced that the world is not only unlimited but also everywhere populated, Nicholas of Cusa tells us that no conclusion as to the imperfection of the earth can be drawn from the alleged imperfection of its inhabitants, a conclusion that nobody, as far as I know, ever made, at least not in his time" (Koyré, *Closed World,* 22).

197. "[N]atures of different nobility proceed from [God] and inhabit each region (lest so many places in the heavens and on the stars be empty and lest only the earth . . . be inhabited)" (*DI* II, 12 [169], 119).

198. *DI* II, 12 (169), 119.

199. *DI* III, 1 (189), 128.

of course, within any given species, an entire range of perfections will be articulated. When considering human beings, for instance, it is clear that at any given time some individuals will be found to be more perfect and excellent in certain respects than others. Solomon for example excelled all others in wisdom, Absalom in beauty, and Sampson in strength.

Cusanus astutely observes, however, that because of the different "religions, sects, and regions" in the world, this difference of orientation will inevitably give rise "to different judgements of comparison (so that what is praiseworthy according to one [religion, sect, or region] is reprehensible according to another)." Further, given the fact that there are people scattered throughout the world entirely unknown to us, we have no way of knowing (even according to the standards of our own native land) "who is more excellent than the others in the world."[200] And it is indeed these standards that we inevitably use in making such judgments of comparison. For, from a cultural perspective he emphasizes, we are subject to the same sort of centrist illusion that leads us to believe that the earth lies in the center of the cosmos. Just as we experience the earth as the center of the cosmos, so too, we are naturally inclined to a certain degree of "provincialism" in regard to our own native land. It is home and center for us, a place unlike all others.[201] In fact, Cusanus concludes, God makes ingenious use of our tendency to experience the world from a centrist perspective:

> God produced this state of affairs in order that each individual, although admiring the others, would be content with himself, with his native land (so that his birthplace alone would seem most pleasant to him), with the customs of his domain, with his lan-

200. Ibid.

201. Cusanus himself is a case in point. As Karl Jaspers remarks in his introduction to "Nicholas of Cusa," in *The Great Philosophers,* vol. 2, trans. Ralph Manheim (New York: Harcourt, Brace and Jovanovich, 1966), 117: "Cusanus was a German who became a European at an early date; yet though his life was centered in Rome, he did not forget his origins. In his native Cusa he left a memorial to himself, upon which he lavished most of the income he gained from his position: he founded a home for the aged with extensive living quarters and farm buildings, a church, and considerable land holdings." . . .

"In his testamentary dispositions the Cardinal directed that he be buried in S. Pietro in Vincoli, the church in Rome attached to his cardinalcy, where his tomb with an impressive portrait engraved in stone can be seen today. His heart was transferred in a casket to the church of his foundation in Cusa."

guage, and so on, so that to the extent possible there would be unity and peace, without envy.[202]

Insofar as we ourselves are the "center" (a center we take with us wherever we are) of our own experience of the world, we will inevitably find ourselves subject to the perspectival illusion of believing our center to be *the* center of the world. And yet we are not completely trapped in this illusion. Insofar as we are able to recognize a perspective *as* a perspective, we have already moved beyond its limitations, at least in thought. This is an insight Cusanus may well owe to Meister Eckhart; it is certainly one he applies with remarkable results both in his attitude toward world religions and cultures and in his reinterpretation of the structure of the cosmos.

It is also the foundation of his reflections on the relativity of motion, reflections which, once again, show him to be a thinker far ahead of his time. When discussing the motion of the world-machine he writes:

> [S]ince we can discern motion only in relation to something fixed, viz., either poles or centers, and since we presuppose these [poles or centers] when we measure motions, we find that as we go about conjecturing, we err with regard to all [measurements]. And we are surprised when we do not find that the stars are in the right position according to the rules of measurement of the ancients, for we suppose that the ancients rightly conceived of centers and poles and measures.[203]

202. *DI* III, 1 (189), 128. It should be noted that while Cusanus shows a remarkable degree of ecclesiastical and cultural tolerance—no doubt due to his reflection on the perspectival nature of our experience—he is certainly not a "cultural relativist" in any absolute sense. He *does* think that certain standards and opinions are better than others, and that certain religions and belief systems (Christianity, of course, at the forefront) come closer to the truth than others, though none attain to the perfect truth about the divine. See especially *DI* III, 8 (229), and III, 9 (238).

See also, for example, *De pace fidei,* a dialogue which takes the form of a conversation in Heaven around the throne of God. The interlocutors are God, the Logos, Peter, Paul, and representatives of seventeen nations—a Greek, an Italian, an Arab, a Hindu, a Chaldaean, a Jew, a Scythian, a Frenchman, a Persian, a Syrian, a Spaniard, a Turk, a German, a Tartar, an Armenian, a Bohemian, and an Englishman. In the dialogue a perpetual peace is envisioned. Religious wars will cease when all of mankind becomes aware, that for all the variety of rituals, there is only one religion, the common worship of the one true God.

On the extent to which Cusanus truly advocates religious tolerance, and the extent to which he only recognized his own Christian faith in the outwardly alien manifestations of the faith of others, see Karl Jaspers' discussion in "Nicholas of Cusa," 227–28.

203. *DI* II, 11 (159), 115.

Cusanus holds that the ancients were unable to recognize the boundless, centerless, and imprecise nature of the cosmos because they "lacked learned ignorance," which in this case would certainly have led them to the principle of perspective. By applying this principle, Cusanus writes, it would have become evident that the earth does indeed move even though we do not perceive this to be the case. For we are able to perceive motion only by comparing it with something we take as fixed.[204]

He illustrates his point with a simple example.[205] Just as passengers on a ship far from the shore are unable to determine anything about the motion of the ship without reference to the stationary shore, so the inhabitants of the earth are in no position to determine anything about the earth's motion. They naively assume that the earth is a stationary body and assume that it is the still center of all heavenly motion, but if they inhabited some other star, they would draw the same conclusion, for they would again appear to be located at the fixed center of the cosmos. Thus, it appears to everyone as though they themselves occupied the unmoving center of the world, and that everything else moves in relation to it. In reality, however, the universe (as an infinite sphere) has no fixed circumference or center of motion, and there is no point of complete rest. Rather, everything is in endless motion relative to everything else, and so no absolute knowledge of the motion and structure of the universe is possible.

By reflecting in this way on the ultimate relativity of all motion, Cusanus in fact thinks far beyond Copernicus. For although Copernicus had to reflect on the relativity of the apparent motion of the sun and stars in order to propose his new system, he only replaces the assumption of one fixed center (the earth) with a new one (the sun). When thought through to its logical conclusion (and it is not clear to what extent Cusanus himself was able to do this consistently), this principle of perspectival relativity has a destructive effect on geo- and helio-centrisms alike, indeed, on any attempt to define a fixed center to the universe.

204. *DI* II, 12 (162), 116–17.
205. *DI* II, 12 (162), 117.

THE INTENSIVE INFINITIZATION OF THE COSMOS

As we have seen, when Nicholas of Cusa transfers the metaphor of the infinite sphere from God to the world, he has in mind a curious blending of extensive and intensive infinity. The cosmological application of the metaphor not only marks a decisive shift away from the traditional medieval world picture, it also heralds a correspondent shift in value. The cosmos and all of its individual parts begin to take on a value and nobility in themselves.[206] Every created thing is a concrete image of the divine Infinite[207] and so must be understood as a "finite infinity or a created god."

Wherefore, we infer that every created thing *qua* created thing is perfect—even if it seems less perfect in comparison with some other [created thing]. For the most gracious God imparts being to all things, in the manner in which being can be received.[208]

We recall that Cusanus holds God to be the Being and the "one infinite Form" of all created things. Like Eckhart, Cusanus understands the infinite Oneness of God to be Absolute undifferentiated Being. The being of a creature, on the other hand, is purely "derivative being." It has its being wholly from God.[209] "If you consider things in their independence from God, they are nothing. . . . If you consider a thing as it is in

206. This experience of the nobility and value of the created cosmos as a whole had, of course, already been articulated to a large extent by the naturalism of the twelfth-century Neoplatonic School of Chartres. In this context, one thinks in particular of Bernardus Silvestris's *Cosmographia,* in which Nature is presented as the mediating element between God and the world. See especially Brian Stock's helpful study, *Myth and Science in the Twelfth Century* (Princeton: Princeton University Press, 1972). Still, Cusanus' emphasis on the perfection and nobility of each individual being in its infinite richness and particularity is something quite new.

207. There are clear echoes here of John Scottus Eriugena, for whom all creatures are theophanies or appearances of God. Like Eckhart, however, the momentum of Eriugena's thought is overwhelmingly directed toward the Neoplatonic return of all creatures to God. On the relation between Eriugena and Nicholas of Cusa see Werner Beierwaltes, "Cusanus and Eriugena," *Dionysius* 13 (1989): 115–52, and Dermot Moran, "Pantheism from John Scottus Eriugena to Nicholas of Cusa," *American Catholic Philosophical Quarterly* 64 (winter, 1990): 131–52.

208. *DI* II, 2 (104), 93.

209. "Absolute Maximality is Absolute Being through which all things are that which they are" (*DI* I, 2 [6], 51). See also I, 25 (85), 83.

God, it *is* God and Oneness."[210] Thus God is "Infinite Oneness," the enfolding *(complicatio)* of all things without differentiation. In their Quiddity all things exist in the Infinite Oneness which is God.

The creation of the universe may be thought of as the unfolding *(explicatio)*[211] of this infinite Oneness into differentiation and multiplicity. It is the same divine Being and Form that is imparted to all things in creation. Indeed, Cusanus writes, "creating seems to be not other than God's being all things."[212] For a creature to exist is for it to participate in the same divine Being. Its differentiation from other creatures, as noted in analogy to the infinite line, is not due to a difference in essence, but to a difference in participation: "[T]he one, infinite Form is participated in different ways by different created things."[213]

Cusanus is, of course, using the traditional Platonic language of participation in order to describe the relationship between God and the world, where "participation" means to partake in an Idea, to be informed by it, to be an image of it. Again, following in the tradition of Neoplatonism, Cusanus understands the world to be an image of the divine One, or God. But like Eckhart he radically transforms his conception of God and of the world, when he conceives of the divine One as infinite. And again like Eckhart, he emphasizes that it is an infinite God who is present whole and entire in each and every part of creation. Thus, Cusanus is quick to stress the fact that the universe of created things is not only a likeness of the divine simply by virtue of being an endless plurality of creatures spread out in space, time, and possibility—as though the likeness were only to be found in them all collectively as a group. Rather, each individual creature must itself also be recognized as an image of infinite Oneness unfolded or concretized as *this* particular creature.

210. *DI* II, 3 (110), 95. In the divine Infinite "all things are incompositely enfolded in simplicity of Oneness, where there is neither anything which is other nor anything which is different, where a man does not differ from a lion, and the sky does not differ from the earth. . . . In the Maximum they are most truly the Maximum, not in accordance with their finitude; rather [they are] Maximum Oneness in an enfolded way" (*DI* I, 24 [77], 80).

211. See Thomas P. McTighe, "The Meaning of the Couple, Complicatio-Explicatio in the Philosophy of Nicholas of Cusa," *Proceedings of the American Catholic Philosophical Association* 32 (1958): 206–14.

212. *DI* II, 2 (101), 91.

213. *DI* II, 2 (103), 92.

Cusanus, however, develops this conception of the intensive infinity *of each being* in a way that moves beyond the Neoplatonic universalism so characteristic of Eckhart's thought. Cusanus, in contrast to Eckhart, holds that the divine infinite is present in each created thing through the mediation of the universe.[214] By this he does not have in mind the existence of a type of Platonic "world soul," a notion which he categorically rejects.[215] The universe is *not* to be understood as an independently existing universal form, nor is it simply the name which we give to the collection of all existing things.[216] The universe is a contracted image of God, but it has its existence only in the existence of individual entities.[217] Unlike the absolute Maximum (God) it does not exist independently of the plurality in which it is present, for it does not exist without contraction. Hence, the universe has existence only *as* contracted in individuals. The oneness of the universe, explains Cusanus, is contracted in each particular through three grades of "universal oneness" (the categories, the genera, and the species). None exist as actual apart from particulars. This does not mean that they are "mere rational entities" (abstractions of thought). They *do* exist in particulars *as* these particulars. "Accordingly, just as humanity is neither Socrates nor Plato but in Socrates is Socrates and in Plato is Plato, so is the universe in relation to all things."[218] Only individuals actually exist. But they exist as the contraction of a species, of a genera, and of the categories—that is, they exist only as contractions of the threefold oneness of the universe.[219]

Now the *absolute* Quiddity of a thing is God himself. Thus the absolute Quiddity of the sun is the same as the absolute Quiddity of the moon: it is absolute Being, Infinite Form, without plurality or difference. The *contracted* quiddity of a thing, however, is nothing other than the thing itself, as a unique expression of the universe contracted to *this* par-

214. *DI* II, 4 (116) and 5 (117).

215. *DI* II, 9 (150).

216. *DI* II, 5 (117).

217. Thus Cusanus would agree with Ockham that only individual beings really exist, but he would disagree that universals are merely thought entities.

218. *DI* II, 4 (115), 97.

219. See also *DI* III, 1 (184), 126: "Genera exist only contractedly in species, and species exist only in individuals, which alone exist actually."

ticular thing. Thus the contracted quiddity of the sun *is* other than the contracted quiddity of the moon. This is because the universe, as the image of God, is the contracted quiddity of *all* things and is contracted in a different way in each and every thing. "Hence, although the universe is neither the sun nor the moon, nevertheless in the sun it is the sun and in the moon it is the moon."[220]

Thus God and the universe may both be said to be "present" in all things, but in two different senses. God is in everything without distinction as the absolute Being and Essence *(entitas et quidditas absoluta)* of all things, which is identical in everything. The universe, which is the unfolded image of the divine Infinite, is present in each thing *as* each thing. This leads Cusanus to assert the principle of solidarity: the presence of each thing in each thing *(quodlibet in quolibet).*[221]

> From Book One it is evident that God is in all things in such a way that all things are in Him; and it is now evident [from II, 4] that God is in all things through the mediation of the universe, as it were. Hence it is evident that all is in all and each is in each.[222]

The universe is ontologically prior to the plurality of things in the sense that it is the contraction of *all things* to the actual existence of this particular thing.[223] Since each particular thing cannot actually be all things, it is a reflection of the whole world in a limited, concrete form. Each actually existing thing is thus a concrete and unique representation of the whole universe.

Whereas in Eckhart this principle of solidarity only served to underscore the ultimate unity of all things in God, for Cusanus it presents an opportunity for reflecting on the nature of the universe as such. It is an articulation of the notion that each created thing is a unique contraction of the whole, and is as such a "finite infinity." It is a being of irreplaceable value, perfect, says Cusanus, each in its own way.

220. *DI* II, 4 (115), 97.

221. Eckhart, we recall, had already held a version of this principle of solidarity, but for him it was grounded only in the presence of God's absolute Being in all things.

222. *DI* II, 5 (117), 98.

223. "For in each created thing the universe is this created thing; and each thing receives all things in such a way that in a given thing all things are, contractedly, this thing" (*DI* II, 5 [117], 98).

Eckhart had already concluded from the ubiquity of the center of the divine sphere that the infinity of God must be present in every individual. But he intended only the One Infinite principle of all Being, which man could see reflected in all things, while individual differences were attributed to their finitude and imperfection. Not so for Cusanus, who sees in the unending multiplicity of individual natures the reflection of the infinity of the universe. Indeed, he locates their highest and most divine perfection precisely in the way in which each individual entity is an utterly unique contraction or reflection of the whole universe.

Whereas Eckhart had emphasized God's immanence in every part of creation as a way of focusing on the divine Origin and Goal of all things, Cusanus becomes interested in the mechanics of this omnipresence, in the means. Eckhart is interested in the fact *that* God is present in creation. Cusanus is interested in the *way* in which God is present in creation, i.e. via the (privatively) infinite universe. To put it another way, Eckhart focuses on God as center and circumference of the world (Beginning and End); Cusanus is fascinated with the divine Diameter which penetrates all things, the Middle which links all things.[224] This orientation will lead Cusanus, as we shall see, to focus on the incarnate divinity of Christ. First, however, let us consider the consequences of Cusanus' intensive infinitization of the world for his theory of knowledge.

THE INTENSIVE INFINITE AND THE PROBLEM OF KNOWLEDGE

The *intensive* infinitization of the world raises new problems for traditional theories of knowledge. A gap is opened up between the infinite richness of the world and the ability of the human intellect to comprehend

224. "You see that because the center is infinite, the whole of the Maximum is present most perfectly within everything as the Simple and the Indivisible; moreover, it is outside of every being—surrounding all things, because the circumference is infinite, and penetrating all things, because the diameter is infinite. It is the Beginning of all things, because it is the center; it is the End of all things, because it is the circumference; it is the Middle of all things, because it is the diameter. It is the efficient Cause, since it is the center; it is the formal Cause, since it is the diameter; it is the final Cause, since it is the circumference. It bestows being, for it is the center; it regulates being, for it is the diameter; it conserves being, for it is the circumference" (*DI* I, 21 [64], 76).

this infinity by means of finite rational constructs. All human knowledge, Cusanus holds, is arrived at by means of comparison. Concepts are the vehicle of comparison by which similarities and differences between things are expressed. "All names are bestowed on the basis of a oneness of conception [ratio] through which one thing is distinguished from another."[225] That is to say, we distinguish between things when we identify them with names: "This is a rose." "That is an oak tree." We may further describe this particular rose in such detail that it is distinguished from all other roses. We may describe it "in accordance with generic, specific, spatial, causal and temporal agreement and difference among similar things,"[226] but our description could never exhaust the particularity of *this* rose, since by nature all concepts apply to a multitude of "similar" things without ever being able to name the uniqueness of a particular thing. Just as the only adequate name for God *is* God, so too, the perfect or "proper name" for this rose would have to be nothing other than this rose itself.

No two finite things, Cusanus underscores, are exactly alike. Each individual is infinitely rich in its particularity, each is a "finite infinity," and as such an utterly unique contraction of the whole universe. Thus precise knowledge—not only of the divine Maximum, but of any given finite thing as well—is a human impossibility. While the divine Infinite is unknowable because it does not stand in a comparative relation with anything else, a finite particular is equally unknowable because there is no end to the comparisons which can be made. We will always find degrees of equality or similarity between two things, for any given thing is precisely equal only to itself. Cusanus holds that it is obvious that "we cannot find two or more things which are so similar and equal that they could not be progressively more similar *ad infinitum.*"[227] As a result, all knowledge which is gleaned by comparing similarities among things is at best approximate, and all concepts which identify things according to these similarities must be understood as approximations, for "the measure and the measured—however equal they are—will always remain different."[228]

225. *DI* I, 24 (74), 79–80.
226. *DI* I, 3 (9), 52.
227. Ibid.
228. Ibid.

Therefore, it is not the case that by means of likenesses a finite intellect can precisely attain the truth about things. For truth is not something more or something less but is something indivisible. Whatever is not truth cannot measure truth precisely. . . . Hence, the intellect, which is not truth, never comprehends truth so precisely that truth cannot be comprehended infinitely more precisely.[229]

Cusanus makes an analogy here between the attempt of a finite intellect to attain the truth about things by means of concepts and comparisons and the attempt to "square the circle," i.e. to approximate the circumference of a circle by an inscribed polygon.[230] "The more angles the inscribed polygon has the more similar it is to the circle. However, even if the number of its angles is increased *ad infinitum,* the polygon never becomes equal [to the circle] unless it is resolved into an identity with the circle."[231] The polygon remains infinitely distinct from the circle as long as it has (a finite number of) sides, i.e. as long as it remains a polygon and is not resolved into identity with the circle. "A non-circle [cannot measure] a circle, whose being," Cusanus writes, "is something indivisible."[232] The circumference of the circle is "indivisible," i.e. homogeneous throughout, whereas a polygon is composed of a series of distinct angles and sides. It is only "at the limit" as the number of sides actually "goes to infinity," as we would say, that the polygon is finally resolved into identity with the circle. Similarly, absolute truth must be thought of as the identity of concept and thing, where the thought of something at the same time constitutes its being or its existence. Thus perfect or "infinite" knowledge is creative knowledge, in which word and thing coincide. Such divine knowledge of the "thisness" of things in the world is not possible for a finite intellect. Here Cusanus relinquishes the traditional understanding of the proper

229. *DI* I, 3 (10), 52.

230. In the strictest sense, the traditional problem of squaring the circle involves producing with straightedge and compass a square whose area equals the area of a given circle. However, the problem eventually became associated with attempts to calculate the area of a circle by more general means—hence the term "quadrature" which was associated with this procedure. For a technical account of the development of these procedures, see C. H. Edwards, *The Historical Development of the Calculus* (New York: Springer Verlag, 1979). See also Margaret E. Baron, *The Origins of the Infinitesimal Calculus* (Oxford and New York: Pergamon, 1969).

231. *DI* I, 3 (10), 52.

232. Ibid.

human theoretical attitude as *theoria,* in which the essential and determinate form of the world appeared to the contemplative gaze of the beholder.

Hence, regarding truth, it is evident that we do not know anything other than the following: viz., that we know truth not to be precisely comprehensible as it is. For truth may be likened unto the most absolute necessity (which cannot be either something more or something less than it is), and our intellect may be likened unto possibility. Therefore, the quiddity of things, which is the truth of beings, is unattainable in its purity; though it is sought by all philosophers, it is found by no one as it is. And the more deeply we are instructed in this ignorance, *the closer we approach to truth.*[233]

It is essential to underscore that learned ignorance here is not a simple act of resignation in the face our inability to attain to absolute truth about the natural world (as for example in nominalism), but rather a way of *approaching* truth by means of approximations which may indeed be considered better or worse, just as an inscribed polygon with a thousand sides better approximates the circle than one with only a hundred sides. And just as, finally, it is the circle itself which is the measure of the degree of adequacy of my always inadequate approximations, so too it is the individual being in its infinitely rich particularity which remains the elusive measure of my attempts to grasp its being.

Again, this insistence on our inability to know anything exhaustively may seem to be a negative result, but it does not have the same kind of negative status as a purely skeptical position. In fact it is not a skeptical argument at all. Rather, it forms the basis for an understanding of the project of knowledge acquisition as itself unbounded. And it opens up the possibility for a new methodology for acquiring knowledge about the world via conjectures, via model building.[234] Just as God is the creative

233. *DI* I, 3 (10), 52–53, my emphasis.

234. On Cusanus' theory of conjecture see Josef Koch, *Die Ars coniecturalis des Nikolaus von Kues,* vol. 4 of *Arbeitsgemeinschaft für Forschung des Landes Nordrhein-Westfalen, Geisteswissenschaften* (Cologne: Westdeutscher Verlag, 1956); Wilhelm Dupré, "Absolute Truth and Conjectural Insights," in *Nicholas of Cusa on Christ and the Church,* ed. Gerald Christianson and Thomas Izbicki (Leiden: Brill, 1996), 323–38; and Clyde Lee Miller, "Nicholas of Cusa's 'On Conjectures' *(De coniecturis),*" in *Nicholas of Cusa in Search of God and Wisdom,* ed. Gerald Christianson and Thomas M. Izbicki (Leiden: Brill, 1991), 119–40, and "Perception, Conjecture, and Dialectic in Nicholas of Cusa," *American Catholic Philosophical Quarterly* 64 (1990): 35–54. See also Hans Blumenberg's introduction to *Nikolaus von Cues, Die Kunst der Vermutung: Auswahl aus den Schriften* (Bremen: Carl Schünemann Verlag, 1957).

center of all that is, so man is the center and creator of a limitless conceptual region, which "mirrors" (more or less adequately) the world unfolded in God's creative Word.[235] It is precisely because of the mind's creative power that Cusanus describes man as a "second god,"[236] reflecting God's absolute infinity, albeit in the form of the unending capacity for progress. For Cusanus the individual's deviation from universal uniformity is no longer seen as a deficiency stemming from the finitude of created being. It is, rather, to be seen as a sign of the individual's effective power, which is a divine gift and the aspect of humanity which is most godlike. That is, Cusanus locates the most valuable and most divine aspect of the individual human being precisely in his or her particular independence of action.[237] Whereas Eckhart had held that the perfection of human nature and its transformation into a true image of God could be brought about only by a complete emptying of the soul's *own* images *(Entbildung)*, for Cusanus this transformation is accomplished only by virtue of the fact that the human being is a living, creative image of the divine, not a passive reflection of the identical exemplar.[238]

235. "It must be the case that surmises originate from our minds, even as the real world originates from Infinite divine Reason. For when, as best it can, the human mind (which is a lofty likeness of God) partakes of the fruitfulness of the Creating Nature, it produces from itself, qua image of the Omnipotent Form, rational entities, [which are made] in the likeness of real entities. Consequently, the human mind is the form of a surmised [rational] world, just as the divine Mind is the Form of the real world. Therefore, just as that Absolute Divine Being is all that which there is [essentially] in each existing thing, so too the oneness of the human mind is the being of its own surmises" (*De coniecturis* I, 1 [5], translated by Jasper Hopkins in *Nicholas of Cusa: Metaphysical Specualtions,* vol. 2 [Minneapolis: Arthur J. Banning Press, 200], 150–51). See also *De coniecturis* II, 13–14; *De ludo globi* II; *De beryllo,* chapters 6 and 17–18.

236. See *De beryllo,* chapter 5 and *De coniecturis* II, 14. See also *Idiota de mente,* chapters 2, 4, and 7.

237. "And when I thus rest in the silence of contemplation, you, Lord, answer me within my heart, saying: 'Be yours and I too will be yours!' O Lord, the Sweetness of every delight, you have placed within my freedom that I be my own if I am willing. Hence, unless I am my own, you are not mine, for you would constrain my freedom since you cannot be mine unless I also am mine. And since you have placed this in my freedom, you do not constrain me, but you wait for me to choose to be my own" (*De visione dei,* chapter 7; in *Nicholas of Cusa: Selected Spiritual Writings,* ed. and trans. H. Lawrence Bond, The Classics of Western Spirituality [New York: Paulist Press, 1997], 247).

238. I would have to agree with Mahnke in his evaluation of this aspect of the Cusan's

CHRIST AS LIMIT CONCEPT AND MEASURE

The notion of unending "progress" demands the correlative idea of a proper measure of that progress. Indeed, how could progress be grasped as real progress and not simply as unending novelty, if there were not postulated the idea of an end goal, a telos, guiding and measuring a given stage along the way as better or worse? And yet if this progress is truly conceived of as "unending," such a measure would have to remain just out of reach, an unattainable (if guiding) telos. The paradox into which we stumble here—that the proper measure of the adequacy of knowledge must itself be simultaneously available and unavailable to the human knower—is as old as philosophical reflection on the problem of knowledge acquisition itself. Responses to the problem have ranged from Plato's theory of recollection, to Leibniz' notion of infinite analysis, to Kant's introduction of the "Ideas" of reason, to Heidegger's notion of the hermeneutic circle.

If one were to write a history of this epistemological paradox, a new chapter would begin with the introduction of infinity into the equation. How can finite, discursive concepts even begin to do justice to an infinite object of knowledge? The solution to the problem, as Cusanus recognized, must somehow involve relating two orders of infinity: the privative infinity of the unending to the absolute infinity of the complete. What is needed is a limit concept in which the two orders meet.

Cusanus attempts to think this limit with the help of the Christian dogma of the "God-man," the mediator Jesus Christ. Once the problem of relating these two orders of infinity arises, its solution in terms of the Word of God (the Second Person of the Trinity) is quite obvious for a thinker immersed in the logos-literature of Christian Neoplatonism. The creative Word of God must be thought in terms of the identity of concept

---

thought as most profoundly moving beyond his predecessors: "An dieser Stelle geht der Kusaner am weitesten über seine Vorgänger hinaus, indem er gerade in der *besonderen Selbsttätigkeit* der menschlichen Individuen ihr wertvollstes und unverkennbar göttlichstes Erbe findet. Nicht die möglichst genaue passive Widerspiegelung des identischen Urbildes, sondern die *eigentümliche* Nachbildung und *aktive* Neuschöpfung ist die höhere Leistung" (Mahnke, *Unendliche Sphäre,* 102).

and thing; and this identity in turn constitutes the absolute notion of truth as perfect correspondence.[239] Hence, if we are to properly understand the radical innovations of Cusanus' epistemology and anthropology, we must attend, with some care, to his Christology.

It would be a gross mistake to view Book Three of *On Learned Ignorance*—as many readers of Cusanus, including Blumenberg, have done—as merely an exposition in speculative terms of Cusanus' dogmatic religious beliefs (in the Incarnation, the virgin birth, the death and resurrection of Christ, the last judgment, the authority of the Church, etc.). It is, of course, speculative theology in this sense, but Cusanus the *believer* is not so easily separated from Cusanus the *philosopher,* who addresses the epistemological problem of the immanent infinite while meditating on the "mysteries" of the Christian faith. Indeed, for him they are inseparable paradoxes.

The "Individual Maximum" as Limit

Cusanus begins Book Three by reminding us that "all things are distinguished from one another by degrees, so that no thing coincides with another."[240] No two things have the same degree of contraction, and any given thing will be comparatively greater or lesser than any other thing in any given respect. Further, no one individual of a given species could ever attain the limit of its species with regard to a given perfection, for an even greater example could always be posited.[241] There is always (or could be) a faster runner, a wiser ruler, etc. Thus the universe (which exists only as contracted in individuals differing in degrees of perfection) does not exhaust the infinite, absolute power of God. The universe does not reach the limit of Absolute Maximality; genera do not reach the limit of the universe; species do not reach the limit of their genera; and individual things do not reach the limit of their species. All things are what they are in the

239. Note that it is this very reflection on the identity of a thing and its perfect definition which led Cusanus in *De li non aliud* to designate God as precisely that definitional "Not Other" by whose measure we can say, "The sky is not other than the sky," or, "This rose is not other than this rose." See Karsten Harries, "Problems of the Infinite: Cusanus and Descartes," *American Catholic Philosophical Quarterly* 64 (1990): 89–110.

240. *DI* III, 1 (182), 125.

241. *DI* III, 1 (183–85).

best way possible for them, and all things find their existence *between* a maximum and a minimum.[242] "Hence, there is nothing in the universe which does not enjoy a certain singularity that cannot be found in any other thing, so that no thing excels all others in all respects or [excels] different things in equal measure."[243]

If a maximum *were* contracted to a species,[244] Cusanus speculates, it would actually embrace all of the perfections which would be possible for that species—it would *be* a maximum, or infinite, individual, since a greater could not be posited. The idea is analogous to that of an infinite number, or a polygon with an infinite number of sides. Of course, for a number to *be* a number, or a polygon to *be* a polygon, is for it to exist in the "in-between" of comparison. There is always an n+1, always a polygon with one more side. The very notion of an infinite number or a polygon with an infinite number of sides is oxymoronic. And yet, as we see with the example of the polygon inscribed in a circle, we can think of a polygon with an infinite number of sides: it is precisely the *limit* at which circle and polygon coincide, as the number of sides is increased "to infinity." While we recognize that this progressive increase can go on *ad infinitum*, the "goal," as it were, of this unending progression is the circle, or the infinite as complete unity. The impossible coincidence of unending increase and complete infinity is conjectured here at the limit of thought.

Jesus Christ (the God-man) is, for Nicholas of Cusa, just such a limit concept. A (*non*-maximal) individual of a given species (like an n-sided polygon) exists in the in-between of comparison to others (actual or possible).

> Hence, if any positable thing were the contracted maximum individual of some species, such an individual thing would have to be the fulness of that genus and

242. *DI* III, 1 (185).

243. *DI* III, 1 (188), 127.

244. Cusanus does not assert that there actually *is* such a maximum individual and that this individual is Jesus Christ until chapter four of Book Three: "In sure faith and by such considerations as the foregoing, we have now been led to the place that without any hesitancy at all we firmly hold the aforesaid to be most true" (*DI* III, 4 [203], 133). While speculation may lead us to the thought of such a maximum individual as limit concept, the actual positing of such an ideal limit is a matter of faith.

> species. . . . It would enfold in itself the entire perfection of the [given contraction]. And it would be—above all comparative relation—perfectly equal to each given thing [of that species], so that it would not be too great [a measure] for anything nor too small [a measure] for anything but would enfold in its own fullness the perfections of all the things [of that species].[245]

The gradation of every possible degree of perfection would be enfolded in the maximum individual, just as the series of all possible polygons is enfolded in the limit of an infinitely-sided polygon.

When we reflect on the difference between a very large number or a many sided polygon and an "infinite" number or an "infinitely-sided" (maximum) polygon, we begin to see why only the latter pair, and not the former, may be thought of as adequate "measures" of all possible numbers or polygons. Any number "n" is larger than some numbers and smaller than others (and similarly for any "n-sided" polygon). But when "n" goes to infinity, it transcends the hierarchy of comparison altogether. The limit, Cusanus speculates, embraces the entire series—not as the totality of each discrete "n" but rather as simultaneously all of them together and none of them in particular. An infinitely-sided polygon, for example is no longer a polygon at all—at the limit, it has attained coincidence or identity with the circle. It embraces the whole series of n-sided polygons precisely by being a non-sided polygon, a circle.

Thus we may say that the entire series of n-sided polygons is enfolded in the infinitely-sided polygon/circle, which is the measure of each n-sided polygon in the series. It is their measure in two senses: in an obvious sense, it is the telos of their progression as a series, but it is also the standard by which each one in the series is seen to be comparatively greater or lesser. It is in this latter sense that we may say that the superlative is the measure for the intelligibility of the comparative; it is the measure of their "betweeness" (their existence between maximal- and minimal-sidedness). Again, note that it is not the circle *qua* circle that is the measure of the n-sided polygons, but rather, the circle *qua* infinite-sided (maximum) polygon.

Nicholas of Cusa thus finds in the notion of a maximal limit a very

245. *DI* III, 2 (191), 129.

profound way to conceptualize the generative relationship between the One and the many. How is multiplicity "enfolded" in unity? time in eternity? motion in rest? In short, how is the creation enfolded in the creator? Cusanus' traditional response—"Through the generative Word of God"—resonates with a new meaning when we recognize that Christ is conceived of as the limit or coincidence of the privative and the absolute infinite.

For centuries thinkers in the tradition of Neoplatonism had conceived of the essential connection between the One and the many in terms of "enfolding" and "unfolding": The One enfolds the many in that all things are in the One without distinction. The One unfolds all things and through that unfolding the One is *in* all things. Meister Eckhart developed the notion of the One as infinite Unity, enfolding all things without distinction, and creation as the unfolding of that infinite Unity in such a way that the one Infinite is present in all things. Nicholas of Cusa took this notion of the immanence of the infinite in the universe to imply that the universe itself must be understood to be (not absolutely but) privatively infinite. It was then by reflecting on the relationship between these two orders of infinity (absolute and privative)—as a variant of the problem of the One and the many—that Cusanus developed the limit concept as their connecting moment. The absolute Infinite (God as Maximum/Minimum) enfolds the privative infinite (the universe, or contracted maximum). The privative infinite exists only as unfolded in a (comparative) series of finite individuals. The limit of this series is the coincidence of the absolute and the contracted maximum, of the superlative and the comparative. It is this coincidence in a "maximum individual" which is the hinge of enfolding and unfolding.

The question immediately arises, if such a maximum individual were indeed thinkable, what kind of individual would it be? It would, Cusanus reasons, have to belong to a species that reflected the whole range of possible concrete existence. A mollusk would not do. Although it concretely exhibits sensible, bodily nature, it lacks intellectual nature. Similarly, a purely intellectual being, without bodily existence, fails to concretize sensible nature. Only in the case of human beings are both intellectual and sensible nature present concretely in the species, so that human nature embraces both the highest and the lowest form of concrete existence. In this sense the human species may be thought of as a microcosm, or a small world, and it is thus the appropriate species vehicle for union with the divine Maximum.[246]

Now the "maximum individual" is a maximal human being, and so cannot be conceived of as either purely contracted (because it actually attains to all the perfections of its species) or as absolutely maximal (because it is the maximum *of* a species). It must be thought of as simultaneously absolute *and* contracted, just as the infinitely-sided polygon must be thought of as simultaneously polygon *and* circle. The concept of the "hypostatic union" of human and divine nature in Jesus Christ, is thus a limit concept. It is the union or coincidence of the Second Person of the Trinity with the perfect microcosm which is maximal humanity.[247] As such it is the hinge of divine enfolding and unfolding.

In Him [Christ] the least, the greatest, and the in-between things of the nature that is united to Absolute Maximality would so coincide that He would be the perfection of all things and all, qua contracted, would find rest in Him as their own perfection. The measure of this man would also be the measure of an angel and of each thing; for through union with Absolute [Maximality], which is the Absolute Being of all things, He would be the universal contracted being of each creature. Through Him all things would receive the beginning and the end of their contraction, so that through Him who is the contracted maximum [individual] all things would go forth from the Absolute Maximum into contracted being and would return unto the Absolute [Maximum] through this same Medium—[in other words,] through [Him who is] the Beginning of their emanation and the End [i.e. the Goal] of their return, as it were.[248]

246. "Now, human nature is that [nature] which, though created a little lower than the angels, is elevated above all the [other] words of God; it enfolds intellectual and sensible nature and encloses all things within itself, so that the ancients were right in calling it a microcosm, or a small world. Hence, human nature is that [nature] which, if it were elevated unto a union with Maximality, would be the fulness of all the perfections of each and every thing, so that in humanity all things would attain the supreme gradation" (*DI* III, 3 [198], 131).

247. This "hypostatic union" of God and man, Cusanus emphasizes, occurs "in the fulness of time." See *DI* III, 3 (202), 133; III, 4 (203), 133; III, 5 (211–14), 136–37. This phrase signifies that "twinkling of the eye" which itself functions as limit concept for the coincidence of time and eternity.

248. *DI* III, 3 (199), 131–32.

Christ as "Equality-of being-all-things"[249] is thus the principle of generation *and* of ontological determinacy. The maximum individual, the God-man, is the bridge between undifferentiated (infinite) unity and the concrete universe of things. He is the union of "Equality of Oneness" and concrete microcosm. "Through [the maximum individual] all things, qua existing, would be from Him who exists absolutely [i.e. divinity]; and, qua contracted, they would be from Him to whom contraction is supremely united [i.e. maximum humanity]."[250] That is, the cause of the contraction of things, their determination toward this or that, must be accounted for by a principle of ontological determinacy at the heart of the infinite unity which enfolds this diversity. Christ, the God-man, or maximum individual, fulfills this function. He is "Equality-of-being-all-things" in two senses simultaneously. As the Second Person of the Trinity, he is "Equality of Oneness" (the absolute enfolding of all things in the divine); as maximal human being (microcosm), he is the concrete enfolding of all creatable things as distinct. Hence, Cusanus repeats his formula that "God is in all things in such a way that all things are in God," but this time from the point of view of Christ as the Medium of this immanence.

How then, is Christ's mediation to be distinguished from that of the universe (as contracted maximum)? Why does Cusanus need the Mediation of Christ here? Bruno, we recall (see pp. 99–101 and 140–41), did away with this "position" in his system of self- and world-interpretation. Cusanus, however, recognizes the need for a principle of ontological determinacy, which relates the absolute infinity of God with the privative infinity of the universe. The universe, for Cusanus, is the concrete *unfolding* of everything absolutely *enfolded* in God. What is needed in order to conceptualize the moment of transition from absolute unity to concrete

249. *DI* III, 3 (200), 132. See also I, 24 (80), 81–82: "[T]he Son is called Son because He is Equality of Oneness, or of Being, or of existing. Hence, from the fact that God was eternally able to create things—even had He not created them—it is evident [that] He is called Son in relation to these things. For He is Son because He is Equality of being [these] things; things could not exist beyond or short of Equality. Thus, He is Son because He is Equality of being of the things which God was able to make, even had He not been going to make them . . . for the Father to beget the Son was [for Him] to create all things in the Word."

250. *DI* III, 3 (202), 132.

multiplicity (and vice versa) is a limit concept in which the two coincide. Christ is this hinge at the heart of divine unfolding and enfolding, the limit in which the privative infinity of the universe coincides with the Absolute infinity of God.

The Divine Logos as Intellectual Measure

It is by reflecting on the coincidence of these two orders of infinity by means of such a limit concept that Cusanus arrives at a genuinely modern solution to the problem of finding an epistemological measure for human knowledge in the newly infinite universe. In order to clarify the way in which Christ enfolds all creatable things, Cusanus turns to a consideration of intellectual nature:

> For since the intellect of Jesus is most perfect and exists in complete actuality, it can be personally subsumed only in the divine intellect, which alone is actually all things. For in all human beings the [respective] intellect is potentially all things; it gradually progresses from potentiality to actuality, so that the greater it [actually] is, the lesser it is in potentiality. But the maximum intellect, since it is the *limit of the potentiality of every intellectual nature* and exists in complete actuality, cannot at all exist without being intellect in such a way that it is also God, who is all in all.[251]

By way of illustration, Cusanus returns to the metaphor of the inscribed polygon, which he had used at the very beginning of Book One to describe the relationship between the (human) intellect and truth. Now the polygon figures human (intellectual) nature and the circle divine (intellectual) nature. Christ is thought of as the limit in which the two coincide. While the human intellect is potentially all things (in thought), the divine intellect is actually all things (as their very Being). Christ is here conceived of as the perfect coincidence of thought and Being, or absolute truth.

Once again, Cusanus takes a traditional formula ("In the Word of God, thought and Being coincide") and explores the dynamics of this coincidence by focusing on the idea of the convergence of two absolutely disparate orders "at infinity," *at a limit.* By focusing on this dynamic, Cusanus actually rethinks the nature of the human intellect. He begins with the traditional view of the human intellect as "potentially all things." He

251. *DI* III, 4 (206), 135, my emphasis.

goes further, however, by reflecting on the fact that what is in potential *can* be actualized, and may be conceived of *as* actualized. Thus he adds that the human intellect "gradually progresses from potentiality to actuality, so that the greater it [actually] is, the lesser it is in potency." The telos of this gradual progression is complete and actual knowledge of all things. Its limit is the coincidence of human and divine knowledge in the "maximum intellect" of Christ. Hence coincidence with divine knowledge is understood to be the goal and maximal limit of human knowledge, a goal toward which human knowledge must be seen to be progressing, though a goal which can never actually be attained. It is a strictly *regulative* ideal. To think the goal, however, of perfect knowing, is to think the limit. It is to see the *measure* of the privative infinity in which human knowing finds its existence in the absolute Infinity that is its (end) determination.

The ideal of maximal knowledge, as the defining measure and limit of human knowing, finds articulation in the reappearance of the (infinite) sphere metaphor in Chapter Eight of Book Three. Here Cusanus asserts, "Christ is the center and the circumference of intellectual nature."[252] Cusanus' use of the sphere metaphor to describe Christ is reminiscent of Eckhart's references to God as an "infinite *intellectual* sphere." In Cusanus, however, the image is used specifically to describe intellectual existence in general. The image evoked is one of myriad intellectual spheres radiating from each intellectual being; or, more properly, *one* (infinite) intellectual sphere with its center in every rational soul.

It is systematically crucial, as we have seen, that Cusanus identifies this intellectual sphere with Christ (the God-man) and not simply with God, as Eckhart had. It is by recognizing *Christ* as the center and measure of human (intellectual) nature that the humanity in any given individual may be brought to perfection and union with the divine. That the intellect should function as the locus of this mystical union with the divinity should not be surprising. Cusanus follows Eckhart (and indeed much of the ancient and medieval tradition quite generally) in seeing in the intellect something divine and eternal.[253]

252. *DI* III, 8 (232), 144.

253. "For a man is his own intellect. In the intellect the perceptual contractedness is some-

Humanity was created in the image of God, and that image is found in the highest part of the human soul, namely, in the intellect. Indeed, for Eckhart, the human soul is produced through the very same image—son of God—by which Christ is Son. We recall that Eckhart is not always careful to make explicit the distinction between Christ and the human soul as divine images since, more often than not, he is speaking from the standpoint of the mystical union of image and imaged. Cusanus, on the other hand is very consistent in making this distinction. Indeed, he has systematic reasons for doing so.

If we are to understand the dynamics of this mystical union of image and imaged (of human and divine), we need to think in terms of Christ as the maximal *limit* of humanity, which finds coincidence with the Word of God. Thus, whereas Eckhart has the tendency to focus on a sort of "cosmic Christ"—either as the divine Logos of creation or as the "birth of the Word in the soul" as an eternal event, occurring out of time or at any time—Cusanus has a particular interest in the *incarnate* Word of God, in Jesus Christ as God *and* man, and in his temporal as well as his eternal existence. In this the Cardinal is certainly more obviously "orthodox" than Meister Eckhart. Again, however, it should be emphasized that Cusanus' reading of Christian "Heilsgeschichte" in the last chapters of his speculative masterwork should not be glossed over as no more than a standard exposition of Church dogma.[254] Not only is this final section of *On Learned Ignorance* a theologically original articulation of foundational Christian doctrines, Cusanus' interpretation of these doctrines in terms of Christ as a maximal limit, which thinks the coincidence of two orders of infinity, proves to be of great philosophical interest as well.

how subsumed in *(suppositatur)* the intellectual nature, which exists as a certain divine, separate, abstract being, while the perceptual remains temporal and corruptible in accordance with its own nature" (*DI* III, 4 [205], 134).

"[T]he maximality of human nature's perfection is seen in what is substantial and essential [about it]—i.e., with respect to the intellect" (*DI* III, 4 [207], 135).

"The intellect is not temporal and mundane but is free of time and of the world" (*DI* III, 6 [215], 138).

254. The titles of chapters five through nine echo the Christology propounded in the Apostle's Creed.

Faith in Truth

In these interpretations, we recognize not only the proto-modern aspect of his spirituality, but also an example of the "humanist" renewal of faith in truth as the proper object and end of human intellectual striving, characteristic of so much of Renaissance thought. Indeed, like other "Renaissance Platonists" (e.g. Ficino and Pico), Cusanus tends to identify the spiritual with the intellectual journey. That is, Christ functions for Cusanus as the center of human (intellectual) existence, not simply as an "epistemological" measure, but as a spiritual measure in the broadest sense.[255]

The perfecting of human nature therefore also involves a perfection of "the immortal virtues."[256] Here again, Christ is measure and center of our spiritual and ethical life:

> Christ's one humanity will be in all men. . . . And then whoever in this life receives any one of those who are Christ's receives Christ; and what is done to one of the least of these is done to Christ. (By comparison, whoever injures Plato's hand injures Plato; and whoever harms the smallest toe harms the whole man.) And whoever rejoices in Heaven over the least one rejoices over Christ and sees in each one Jesus, through whom [he sees] Blessed God. Thus, through His son, our God will be all things in all things; and in His son and through Him each [believer] will be with God and with all things, so that [each's] joy will be full, free of all envy and deprivation.[257]

Hence, the principle of solidarity has an ethical corollary, and the immanence of Christ in every human being demands that the value and dignity of each person be recognized.

The perfecting of human nature is also an intellectual project, which involves a mystical ascent of faith. Even if reason were wholly able to govern the senses in true Platonic fashion, Cusanus says, human nature would be unable to attain the goal of its intellectual and eternal desires.[258]

255. "For Jesus . . . is the goal not only of all understanding (because He is Truth) but also of all sensing (because He is Life), and who, further, is both the goal of being (because He is Being itself) and the perfection of every creature (because He is God and man)" (*DI* III, 11 [247], 150–51).

256. *DI* III, 6 (220), 140.

257. *DI* III, 12 (256), 154.

258. While Cusanus does not consistently distinguish between reason and intellect in the first two books of *On Learned Ignorance,* in Book Three he clearly does. See *DI* III, 6 (215–17); III, 7 (226); and III, 11 (245).

Intellect must in turn govern reason "in order that the intellect may adhere—by formed faith[259] and above reason—to the Mediator, so that it can be drawn unto Glory by God the Father."[260]

It is faith, Cusanus asserts, which grounds understanding. It is the beginning of understanding and makes understanding possible. In every branch of study certain things are presupposed as first principles. They are taken on faith. "They are grasped by faith alone, and from them is elicited an understanding of the matters to be treated. For everyone who wills to ascend to learning must believe those things without which he cannot ascend."[261] The most fundamental "first principle" in any and every field of knowledge, then, which would ground the very possibility of knowing anything, would be belief in truth itself. Thus the possibility of understanding as such demands faith in Christ who is absolute Truth. It is this faith which guides the intellect, which by nature desires "most abstract truth." It is perpetually moved toward this object which "is all things, because it is God." And, "the intellect—immortal and incorruptible—is not satisfiable until it attains unto God for it is fully satisfied only by an eternal object."[262]

Faith in truth guides the unending pursuit of knowledge, which finds satisfaction only in Christ, who embraces all things in divine unity. Such knowing is beyond sensible intuition and discursive reasoning. It is beyond the opinion and doctrine of the Church, which leads with symbols. God, as infinite Unity, cannot be comprehended by finite forms, nor can

259. I.e. faith formed by love. See *DI* III, 6 (219) and III, 11 (250).

260. *DI* III, 6 (217), 139.

261. *DI* III, 11 (244), 149.

262. *DI* III, 10 (240), 148. Compare with Eckhart LW III, 348. Compare also with Marcilio Ficino's "Five Questions Concerning the Mind," translated by Josephine Burroughs in *The Renaissance Philosophy of Man,* ed. Ernst Cassirer, Paul Oskar Kristeller, and John Herman Randall, Jr. (Chicago and London: The University of Chicago Press, 1948): "Surely, the condition natural to our intellect is that it should inquire into the cause of each thing and, in turn, into the cause of the cause. For this reason the inquiry of the intellect never ceases until it finds that cause of which nothing is the cause but which is itself the cause of causes. This cause is none other than the boundless God. . . . As long as any truth or goodness is presented which has distinct gradations, no matter how many, you inquire after more by the intellect and desire further by the will. Nowhere can you rest except in boundless truth and goodness, nor find an end except in the infinite" (201).

the created things of this world, which partake of infinite Being. True (complete) knowledge is, in Eckhartian terms, "principial" knowledge. Thus, Nicholas of Cusa like Eckhart describes the mystical ascent of the person of faith to unity with God.

It is learned ignorance that leads one in the ascent of the "Mountain that is Christ." First one must turn away from the outer senses to an inner listening, hearing the voice of God in that of the prophets and saints. Then one must be prepared to leap beyond perceptible things altogether and become caught up in "simple intellectuality." "[T]he unsayable would [there] be said and the unhearable would [there] be heard—even as the invisible is there seen."[263] This mystical moment of "incomprehensible comprehension" occurs when faith reaches its maximal limit. For maximum faith coincides with minimum faith which is true knowledge, or absolute certainty.[264]

Hence, it is the power of faith that makes a human being Christlike, which transforms that person into Christ's image.[265] We are never so united with Christ, however, either in this life or in the next, that we lose our respective degrees of difference in the union.[266] Here we find a marked difference from Meister Eckhart. We recall that, for Eckhart, the ascent to union with the divine One involves the intellectual transcendence not only of the "here and now" (the perspectival distortions of space and time), but also of the illusion of "this and that" (the tendency to seek for the real in determinate existence). The mystical journey for Eckhart thus entails an absolute leave-taking from multiplicity and difference in any form. The end of this journey is thus described as a final breakthrough to the Godhead beyond even God, "into the simple ground, into the quiet

263. *DI* III, 11 (247), 150.

264. "[This maximum faith] cannot be in a pilgrim, who is still not a full attainer [of his goal], as was Jesus. However, the pilgrim must will actually to have for himself maximum faith in Christ—[to have it] to such an extent that his faith will be elevated to such a level of indubitable certainty that it will also be not at all faith but supreme certainty devoid of all doubt in any respect whatsoever. This is the mighty faith which is so maximal that it is also minimal, so that it embraces all the things which are believable with regard to Him who is Truth" (*DI* III, 11 [248–49], 151).

265. *DI* III, 11 (252–53), 152.

266. *DI* III, 12 (255).

desert into which distinction never gazed, not the Father, nor the Son, nor the Holy Spirit."[267]

While Eckhart's end goal can only be characterized as absolute rest in the infinite One, Cusanus envisions the end goal of the journey of faith to be life in Christ. Never completely subsumed in this unity, the individual retains his identity as *this* individual, so that "no one either in this life or the next can so love Christ that he would therefore be Christ and man. For all who are united with Christ (difference of degree remaining) . . . are united in the following way: they could not be more greatly united and still have their respective difference of degree remain."[268] If we consider the analogy of the inscribed polygon, we may say that "life in Christ" is a life which *approaches* the limit of coincidence with the absolute, indeed comes infinitesimally close, but is never completely resolved into identity. The life of "the Blessed" is still a human life, an eternal life of unending intellectual fulfillment:

> Now, our intellectual desire is [the desire] to live intellectually—i.e., to enter further and further into life and joy. And since that life is infinite: the blessed, still desirous, are brought further and further into it. And so they are filled—being, so to speak, thirsty ones drinking from the fount of life. And because this drinking does not pass away into a past (since it is within eternity), the blessed are ever drinking and ever filled; and yet, they have never drunk and have never been filled.[269]

The life of the blessed, united with *Christ,* is a life that finds its existence in the "Augenblick," the moment in which time and eternity meet. This is not the final satisfaction of a desire, and so a coming to rest in eternity, but rather an existence on the cusp of time and eternity, at the limit where "enjoyment does not pass away into a past, because the appetite does not fade away during the enjoyment."[270] In this moment of eternity-time, intellectual desire is continually and simultaneously satisfied and aroused.

We need not wait for a mystical experience or for "the life to come" in order to recognize that the human intellect is inextricably tied to the

267. Predigt 48: *Ein meister sprichet* (DW II, 420; *EE,* 198).
268. *DI* III, 12 (255), 154.
269. *DI* III, 12 (258), 155.
270. *DI* III, 12 (259), 155.

infinite. "Blessed is God," writes Cusanus, "who has given us an intellect which cannot be filled in the course of time. Since the intellect's desire does not come to an end, the intellect—on the basis of its temporally insatiable desire—apprehends itself as beyond corruptible time and as immortal."[271] It is precisely because of the insatiable desire of the intellect to push ever onwards in search of truth, precisely because of its fundamental nature as *privatively* infinite, that it comes to recognize its ideal measure and end in absolute infinity.

271. Ibid.

Concluding Remarks

The preceding analysis of the infinitization of the universe at the hands of Meister Eckhart and Nicholas of Cusa is not meant to stand in place of Blumenberg's provocative and often deeply insightful account of the epochal transition in the *Legitimacy*—although it certainly does aim at correcting some of the more serious distortions and gaps in his reading. The larger story of the epochal transition to modernity is far too complex to be reduced to a few moves, however significant, in any one tradition or pattern of development. Shifting the focus of Blumenberg's account of the epochal threshold from nominalism's intensification of divine transcendence to Neoplatonic intensification of divine immanence, and from a consideration of the pair Cusanus-Bruno to that of Eckhart-Cusanus, has made it possible to reexamine the character of the epochal threshold in a new light. It has thrown into relief the emergence of an entire nexus of interpretive expectations and orienting questions tied to the problem of finding a measure in the newly infinite world.

Reading Hannah Arendt—sometimes with and sometimes against Blumenberg—has helped to highlight the problem of world alienation that accompanies the modern turn to self-assertion and the concomitant loss of traditional standards and measures for human thought and action. Indeed, once *theoria* becomes hypothesis and action is spelled out in terms of world immanent self-realization, the carry-over question "What is to be the measure for human thought and action?" emerges with a new urgency. The need to respond to this question in a manner appropriate to the modern age has proved to be of central importance in the rich, varied, and continuing development of modern systems of self- and world-interpretation. And as we have seen, it has been addressed at least in part with the help of conceptual tools developed in the context of late medieval Neoplatonic reflections on the nature of infinity and on the human capacity for self-transcendence.

This capacity for self-transcendence, the ability to think beyond ourselves, beyond our imbeddedness in space and time, in *this* body, in *this* historical context, etc., is an essential part of what makes us human. It grounds our capacity to love and to reason. The scientist no less than the mystic depends on the human ability to take leave of *this* world in all of its immanence. If Blumenberg is right to characterize the modern age in terms of world immanent self-realization—and surely he is—it must be emphasized that this project would not be possible without the human capacity to transcend our finite imbeddedness in the world. It is precisely our ability to think beyond ourselves which allows us to make the distinction between appearance and reality and to recognize a given perspective *as* a perspective, to designate one description of reality as more "objective" than another. Further, the pursuit of objectivity that drives the engine of modern science is grounded in an experience of the recalcitrance of a transcendent reality, the resistance of natural phenomena to the imposition of human conjectural schemes. In the end, Blumenberg's reading of the epochal transition is limited by his assumption that modern theory relinquishes the cognitive ideal of *adaequatio.* In an important sense perfect adequacy to what is has remained the measure of theoretical accomplishment in the modern age, but it has been transformed into a regulative ideal. While we inevitably fall short of this regulative ideal, we are able to think it at the limit of thought as the measure and goal of our progress. In order to account for the emergence of *this* modern notion, that of a regulative ideal which guides potentially unending progress, we have had to look beyond the nominalist-realist controversy which Blumenberg makes his point of departure and delve deeper into the tradition of Neoplatonic mysticism and speculative philosophy.

At the end of the Middle Ages, the world presented itself as precisely what it is and nothing else. On this point both the nominalist and the mystic would agree. For both, the rose blooms "without a why." To ask *why* the world is the way it is, in all of its specificity, comes to be seen in both traditions (though for different reasons) as somehow missing the point. It simply *is.*[1] Blumenberg presents this state of affairs entirely as the result of nominalism's dismantling of High Scholasticism: the rejection of a hierarchy of rational forms mediating between God and the world. For the nominalist, the world no longer presents itself as a necessary and intelligible order, the expression in matter of pre-existent Forms in the divine Mind. Each thing is wholly and uniquely created by an omnipotent God.

Since Blumenberg reads the late medieval scene in the *Legitimacy* entirely from the perspective of the argument between nominalists and realists, it is not at all surprising that he interprets the significance and character of Cusanus' thought insofar as (and only insofar as) it may be seen to be a response to this debate. Indeed, Blumenberg depicts Cusanus as a thinker who makes a last great effort to salvage the rationality and stability of the medieval cosmos in the wake of nominalism's devastating critique of medieval Scholasticism, by attempting to forge a (finally unsuccessful) middle path between nominalism and traditional realism. By focusing on the tension between what he sees as rationalist and voluntarist elements in Cusanus' thought, however, he misses the import of the Cusan's discovery of the limit concept as the coincidence of two orders of infinity. It is here that we may see the emergence of the modern notion of a regulative ideal guiding unending progress. Blumenberg misses the crucial importance of the emergence of this idea precisely because of its origins in the tradition of Neoplatonic mysticism, a tradition which he regards as systematically akin to Gnosticism and thus fundamentally anti-modern in its emphasis on divine transcendence.[2]

In fact, as I have stressed in my reading of Eckhart and Cusanus, this

1. Ockham would say it simply is because God willed it so. Eckhart would say it simply is because it cannot *be* anything other than an expression of God's infinite Being.

2. Indeed, for Blumenberg, Neoplatonic mysticism shares this characteristic with late medieval nominalism—both are interpreted as the resurgence of ancient Gnosticism.

tradition is particularly concerned to understand the divine as simultaneously transcendent *and* immanent. Speculation focusing on the play between divine transcendence and immanence was not something new in these late medieval figures, but had been a dominant theme in Neoplatonic thought since Plotinus. Further, Blumenberg is wrong to insist that the "systematic" character of Cusanus' philosophy (the mutual interconnectedness of his speculations concerning God, the universe, and humanity) can only be understood as arising from his concern to save the substance of the medieval world through a sort of emergency consolidation of its leading themes. Thus, for example, Blumenberg writes:

> The Cusan did not formulate his concern for the continuance of the age. But the unity of his thought can be understood precisely and only on the basis of such a concern. The most definite indication of this fact lies in the "systematic" effort of his work, which no longer has the almost naive serial unity of the Scholastic texts of the Middle Ages, the commentaries on the sentences, collections of questions, and *summas*. The endeavor to hold together a threatened structure leads directly to this "systematic" consistency, unknown to the ancient world and the Middle Ages.[3]

Blumenberg is at best sloppy and at worst willfully myopic here, when he concludes that the systematic unity of Cusanus' thought is wholly unknown in the ancient and medieval world. He ignores entirely the Neoplatonic tradition with its overriding emphasis on the systematic interconnection between the One and the many. Thinkers from Plotinus and Proclus to John Scottus Eriugena and Bernardus Silvestris exhibit the same concern to interrelate their theology, cosmology, and anthropology. Blumenberg presents Cusanus' work as a last-ditch effort at consolidation, wholly uncharacteristic of the tradition he is trying to rescue. This is a serious misreading, both of the tradition from which Cusanus springs and of the motivation and tone of Cusanus' thought.[4] Cusanus is simply not invested, in this way, in "saving" the tradition of medieval Scholasti-

3. Blumenberg, *Legitimacy*, 483–84.

4. Gadamer has rightly remarked on this misreading of Cusanus: "Mir scheint, daß Blumenberg die großartige Leichtigkeit, mit der der Cusaner das gesamte Erbe des scholastischen und des antiken Denkens neu aneignet und umformt, etwas verkennt. Wenn etwas an diesen Schriften aus den Mußestunden eines viel beschäftigten Kirchenmannes wahrhaft überwältigend ist, dann ist es nicht Angestrengtheit, sondern die Leichtigkeit, mit der er alles hinsetzt, mit

cism, with its commentaries, questions, and *summas*.[5] While highly original in its details and in its conclusions and applications, the overall framework of Cusanus' thought, and certainly its systematic interconnectedness, is grounded in the long tradition of negative theology and Neoplatonic metaphysical speculation.

Again, Blumenberg paints a picture of Cusanus standing in the ruins of medieval Scholasticism, unwilling to embrace the radically anti-rationalistic character of nominalism, and attempting to construct a systematic philosophy which would intensify and unify the medieval tendencies toward *both* theocentrism and anthropocentrism.[6] This picture is provocative, but misleading. It tells the story of the epochal transition at the end of the Middle Ages from the perspective of the conflict between nominalist voluntarism and Scholastic realism. The historical narrative, however, is far more complicated.[7] Blumenberg sees the epochal threshold defined in terms of the "intensification of divine transcendence." I would agree that this is indeed a crucial element in the story of this transition, but it cannot stand alone. This transition must be understood in terms of the

---

einer fast ans Spielerische streifenden Argumentationskunst, die eine große innere Sicherheit und Überlegenheit ausstrahlt" (Gadamer, review of *Die Legitimität der Neuzeit*, 208).

5. Blumenberg himself recognizes this to a certain extent, at least in Cusanus' cosmology. See Blumenberg, *Legitimacy*, 485.

6. "The crisis-laden self-dissolution of the Middle Ages can be linked to the systematic relations in the metaphysical triangle: man, God, world. This presupposes an ambivalence in Christian theology. On the one hand, theology's theme is *anthropocentric:* The biblical God's concern, within history and beyond its eschatological invalidation, for man's salvation is transformed with the help of the received Stoic idea of *pronoia* [providence] into an idea of world government and the coordination of nature, history, and man, which is fully unfolded in the Scholastic system of pure rationality. On the other hand, there is the *theocentric* motive: the dissolution of Scholastic rationality through the exaggeration of the transcendence, sovereignty, hiddenness, fearsomeness of its God. The first motive holds the metaphysical triangle of theology, anthropology, and cosmology together; the second tears it apart. The ability of the second motive to prevail shows at the same time that the systematic consistency of the structure constituted by the first motive is insufficient, that it is superficially harmonized heterogeneity" (ibid., 484).

7. And again, Blumenberg himself seems to recognize that his reading of the epochal threshold in the *Legitimacy* is too myopically focused on nominalism, when he supplements his analysis in the *Genesis of the Copernican World* with attention to the tradition of Renaissance Humanism in order to account for the early modern renewal of faith in the human capacity for truth.

intensification of both divine transcendence *and* divine immanence—in particular if we are to understand the character of the infinitization of the universe which occurred at the end of the Middle Ages.

In order to tell *this* story, we have had to examine both the tradition of nominalism and the tradition of late medieval mysticism. Both may be viewed as in part responding to the crisis of medieval Aristotelianism (in the wake of the Condemnation of 1277), by focusing on the character of God's infinity. For the nominalist, Ockham, this infinity is spelled out in terms of God's omnipotent will. Ockham intensifies the connection between God and creature by doing away with anything which would mediate between the creative will of God and his creation. By making this connection between creator and creature completely dependent on God's infinite will, however, the created world loses its rational ground. Hence Blumenberg is quite right to underscore the fact that it was precisely this aspect of divine infinity which rendered the nominalist world radically contingent, and each thing in it utterly unique.

The radically "contingent" quality of the world, and the intensive immediacy and uniqueness of everything in it, would also be explained by Meister Eckhart, the mystic, in terms of divine infinity—not, however, in terms of the infinity of God's will, but rather in terms of the infinity of God's Being. Every created thing, for Eckhart, derives the whole of its existence from God, who in turn is understood to be present "whole and entire" in every part of creation. As we have seen, Nicholas of Cusa builds on Eckhart's intensive infinitization of the world in his metaphysics of contraction. For Cusanus, every individual is utterly unique not because it is the unmediated result of divine omnipotence as in Ockham, but rather because it represents a unique contraction of divine infinity and as such must be seen as a "finite infinity."

Hence, late medieval nominalism may be seen to contribute to the infinitization of the cosmos in an indirect way, insofar as "possible world" speculation had a destructive effect on Aristotelian cosmology and physics and opened the door for creative explorations of hypothetical alternatives. Late medieval mysticism, on the other hand, as it was developed in the speculations of Meister Eckhart and Nicholas of Cusa, led directly to the infinitization of the cosmos (both intensively and extensively). It is telling, indeed, that Blumenberg sees the crucial transition in the process of the infinitization of the universe to lie between Cusanus and Giordano Bruno and *not* between Eckhart and Cusanus.[8] Such a move would make sense if the Copernican revolution were viewed as the pivotal event in the epochal transition. This is, however, an approach that Blumenberg is careful to avoid, insofar as it would make Copernicus into an agent of transformation.

> There are no witnesses to changes of epoch. The epochal turning is an imperceptible frontier, bound to no crucial date or event. But viewed differentially, a threshold marks itself off, which can be ascertained as something either not yet arrived at or already crossed.[9]

Blumenberg views this transitional "something" as the *whole-hearted* "translation" of God's transcendent infinity to the world.[10] For Blumenberg, Cusanus is the thinker who makes this translation in a "restricted" sense and only through the mediation of the Incarnation. Bruno is the thinker who, rejecting the Incarnation as no longer thinkable, makes this translation in a complete and "exhaustive" manner.[11] Thus the world, in

8. Eckhart is mentioned only once in the entire *Legitimacy* and then only in a quotation of Friedrich Überweg, who had situated Cusanus as the "most important middle term between Eckhart and Leibniz" (Blumenberg, *Legitimacy*, 471).

9. Ibid., 469.

10. Blumenberg's tendency to equate infinity with "transcendence" leaves him consistently unable to recognize in the immanence of divine infinity in the world anything other than a "translation" of divine transcendence to the universe. Toward the beginning of his chapter on Cusanus he notes that the Cusan's "intensification of anthropology and cosmology" requires a continual coupling of "the intensification of transcendence with the intensification of immanence" (ibid., 488). In the subsequent interpretation, however, Blumenberg continually shifts attention away from the second half of this couple. The infinite sphere metaphor, for example, which was consistently used precisely to underscore the simultaneous transcendence *and* immanence of the divine, is interpreted by Blumenberg simply as a "representation of transcendence." He remarks, for instance, "It is characteristic of the Cusan's endeavor to let the world participate in the 'advances' of the comprehension and representation of transcendence that he applies the formula from what was originally a purely theological speculation to the world as well" (491). Similarly, Cusanus' use of the *complicatio-explicatio* couple to describe the relationship between creator and creation is glossed as a systematic means of "retranslating" God's transcendence to the world and mankind (482).

11. Cusanus would find Bruno's notion that the cosmos is a *fully* adequate self-reproduction

Bruno's philosophy, comes to "reoccupy" the position which Christ had held in that of Cusanus. In this way, Blumenberg is able to read the "infinitization of the world" as a process of reoccupation and *not* one of secularization.

We have seen, however, that the intradivine generation of the Second Person of the Trinity cannot be conflated with the creation of the world without losing a crucial *systematic* function: that of providing a principle of ontological determinacy which would act as measure in the face of a newly infinitized universe. That is, Cusanus' Christology serves the fundamental "assertion need" for measure. This is a need which Bruno does not yet recognize, but one which becomes more and more pressing as celebration of the world's infinity gives way to an uncanny sense of homelessness and orientationlessness in the newly infinitized universe. Cusanus, on the other hand, had already recognized the need for something like a world-immanent logos to counter the anarchic potential of homogeneous infinity. In this, he shows himself to be a more "modern" thinker than either Eckhart or Bruno. While Eckhart ultimately aimed at absorption in the transcendence of absolute infinity, and Bruno reveled in the immanence of privative infinity, Cusanus looked for a measure in the intersection of both.

Cusanus found, in a new interpretation of the traditional belief in Christ as the Incarnation of the divine, a regulative ideal that could function as a measure for human existence, both practical and theoretical. Christ is conceived of as immanent "in" every human being, as the limit and measure of human nature. Hence, on the one hand, the ethical implications of the principle of solidarity demand that the value and dignity of each person be recognized. On the other hand, the problem of knowledge in a newly infinitized world is countered by the capacity of the human intellect for unending self-transcendence, guided by the limit concept of truth as Christ-like knowledge functioning as a regulative ideal.

---

of God incoherent. For Cusanus such a thesis ignores the distinction between absolute and privative infinity. The universe cannot be a perfect image of divine infinity precisely *because* it is only privatively infinite. Bruno makes the mistake of equating totality with unity and the comparatively great with the absolutely great. But to recognize something *as* a totality, or as comparatively great, one must first have an intuition of unity and of maximality.

Blumenberg is surely correct when he identifies human self-assertion as a characteristically modern existential attitude toward the world, and he is right to identify the primary expression of that self-assertion in the extraordinary productivity and progress of modern science. The possibility of that progress, however, presupposes an understanding of nature as a law-like and yet inexhaustible field of investigation directing thought "toward an objectivity," to use Blumenberg's formulation, "that is never entirely to be reached, received or accomplished."[12] The peculiarly modern notion of such a regulative ideal, guiding the (potentially unending) progress of knowledge, finds its origins precisely in that limit concept which Cusanus took to be the intersection of two orders of infinity: the mind's unending capacity to transcend itself, and the absolute infinity of the real, which is not other than what it is.

12. Blumenberg, *Legitimacy*, 499.

Bibliography

I. HANS BLUMENBERG

A. Major Works and Works Cited

B. English Translations

II. MEISTER ECKHART AND NICHOLAS OF CUSA

A. Primary Sources

B. Translations

III. GENERAL

I. HANS BLUMENBERG

A. Major Works and Works Cited

"Beiträge zum Problem der Ursprünglichkeit der mittelalterlich-scholastischen Ontologie." Ph.D. diss., Kiel, 1947.

"Die ontologische Distanz. Eine Untersuchung über die Krisis der Phänomenologie Husserls." Habilitationsschrift, Kiel, 1950.

"Paradigmen zu einer Metaphorologie." *Archiv für Begriffsgeschichte* 6 (1960): 7–142.

Die kopernikanische Wende. Frankfurt: Suhrkamp, 1965.

Die Legitimität der Neuzeit. Frankfurt: Suhrkamp, 1966. *Die Legitimität der Neuzeit.* Revised edition. Frankfurt: Suhrkamp, 1988.

"On a Lineage of the Idea of Progress," translated by E. B. Ashton. *Social Research* 41 (1974): 5–27.

"Ernst Cassirers gedenkend." *Revue Internationale de Philosophie* 28 (1974): 456–63.

Die Genesis der kopernikanischen Welt. Frankfurt: Suhrkamp, 1975.

Arbeit am Mythos. Frankfurt: Suhrkamp, 1979.

Schiffbruch mit Zuschauer: Paradigma einer Daseinsmetapher. Frankfurt: Suhrkamp, 1979.

Die Lesbarkeit der Welt. Frankfurt: Suhrkamp, 1981.

Wirklichkeiten in denen wir leben: Aufsätze und eine Rede. Stuttgart: Reclam, 1981.

Lebenszeit und Weltzeit. Frankfurt: Suhrkamp, 1986.

Das Lachen der Thrakerin. Eine Urgeschichte der Theorie. Frankfurt: Suhrkamp, 1987.

Die Sorge geht über den Fluss. Frankfurt: Suhrkamp, 1987.

Matthäuspassion. Frankfurt: Suhrkamp, 1988.

Höhlenausgänge. Frankfurt: Suhrkamp, 1989.

Ein mögliches Selbstverständnis. Aus dem Nachlass. Stuttgart: Reclam, 1997.

Die Vollzähligkeit der Sterne. Frankfurt: Suhrkamp, 1997.

Begriffe in Geschichten. Frankfurt: Suhrkamp, 1998.

Gerade noch Klassiker. Glossen zu Fontane. Munich: Hanser, 1998.

Lebensthemen. Aus dem Nachlaß. Stuttgart: Reclam, 1998.

Goethe zum Beispiel. Frankfurt: Insel, 1999.

B. English Translations

"The Life-World and the Concept of Reality." In *Life-World and Consciousness. Essays for Aron Gurwitsch,* translated by Theodore Kisiel, edited by Lester E. Embree, 425–44. Evanston: Northwestern University Press, 1972.

"The Concept of Reality and the Possibility of the Novel." In *New Perspectives in German Literary Criticism. A Collection of Essays,* translated by David Henry Wilson, edited by Richard E. Amacher and Victor Lange, 29–48. Princeton: Princeton University Press, 1979.

The Legitimacy of the Modern Age. Translated by Robert M. Wallace. Cambridge: M.I.T. Press, 1983.

"Self-Preservation and Inertia. On the Constitution of Modern Rationality." *Contemporary German Philosophy* 3 (1983): 209–56.

Work on Myth. Translated by Robert M. Wallace. Cambridge: M.I.T. Press, 1985.

"An Anthropological Approach to the Contemporary Significance of Rhetoric." In *After Philosophy,* translated by Robert M. Wallace, edited by Kenneth Baynes, James Bohnan, and Thomas McCarthy, 427–58. Cambridge: M.I.T. Press, 1987.

The Genesis of the Copernican World. Translated by Robert M. Wallace. Cambridge: M.I.T. Press, 1987.

"Being—A MacGuffin: How to Preserve the Desire to Think," translated by David Adams. *Salmagundi* 90/91 (1991): 191–93.

"Light as Metaphor for Truth. At the Preliminary Stage of Philosophical Concept Formation." In *Modernity and the Hegemony of Vision,* edited by David Michael Levin, 30–60. Berkeley: University of California Press, 1993.

Shipwreck with Spectator: Paradigm of a Metaphor for Existence. Translated by Steven Rendall. Cambridge: M.I.T. Press, 1997.

"Does it Matter When? On Time Indifference," translated by David Adams. *Philosophy and Literature* 22 (1998): 1.

II. MEISTER ECKHART AND NICHOLAS OF CUSA

A. Primary Sources

Daniels, Augustinus. "Eine lateinische Rechtfertigungsschrift des Meister Eckhart." *Beiträge zur Geschichte der Philosophie des Mittelalters,* vol. 23, no. 5. Münster: Verlag der Aschendorffschen Verlagsbuchhandlung, 1923.

Eckhart, Meister. *Meister Eckhart: Die deutschen und lateinischen Werke: Herausgegeben im Auftrage der Deutschen Forschungsgemeinschaft.* Stuttgart: W. Kohlhammer, 1936– .

———. *Meister Eckhart.* Vol. 2 of *Deutsche Mystiker der Vierzehnten Jahrhunderts.* Edited by Franz Pfeiffer. 1857. Reprint. Göttingen: Vandenhoeck und Ruprecht, 1906.

Laurent, M.-H. "Autour du procès de Maître Eckhart. Les documents des Archives Vaticanes." *Divus Thomas* (Piacenza). Ser. III 13 (1936): 331–48, 430–47.

Nicholas of Cusa. *Opera omnia Nicolai de Cusa issu et auctoritate Academiae Litterarum Heidelbergensis.* Leibzig-Hamburg: Meiner, 1932– .

Pelster, Franz. "Ein Gutachten aus dem Eckehart-Prozess in Avignon." *Aus der Geisteswelt des Mittelalters. Festgabe Martin Grabmann* (*Beiträge zur Geschichte der Philosophie des Mittelalters* Supplement III). Münster, 1935, 1099–1124.

Théry, Gabriel. "Édition critique des pièces relatives au procès d'Eckhart contenues dans le manuscrit 33b de la Bibliothèque de Soest." *Archives d'histoire littéraire et doctrinale du moyen âge* 1 (1926): 129–268.

B. Translations

Eckhart, Meister. *Master Eckhart: Parisian Questions and Prologues.* Translated by Armand A. Maurer. Toronto: Pontifical Institute of Mediaeval Studies, 1974.

———. *Meister Eckehart: Deutsche Predigten und Traktate.* Translated by Josef Quint. Munich: Carl Hanser Verlag, 1963.

———. *Meister Eckhart: The Essential Sermons,* Commentaries, Treatises, and Defense. Translated by Edmund Colledge, O.S.A., and Bernard McGinn. The Classics of Western Spirituality. New York: Paulist Press, 1981.

———. *Meister Eckhart: A Modern Translation.* Translated by Raymond Blakney. New York: Harper and Row, 1941.

———. *Meister Eckhart: Sermons and Treatises.* 3 vols.Translated by M. O'C. Walshe. Shaftesbury, Dorset: Element Books, 1979 and 1987.

———. *Meister Eckhart: Teacher and Preacher.* Translated by Bernard McGinn, Frank Tobin, and Elvira Borgstädt. The Classics of Western Spirituality. New York: Paulist Press, 1986.

Nicholas of Cusa. *A Concise Introduction to the Philosophy of Nicholas of Cusa, with introduction, text and translation of "Trialogus de Possest,"* by Jasper Hopkins. Minneapolis: University of Minnesota Press, 1978 and 1980.

———. *A Miscellany On Nicholas of Cusa.* Edited with critical analysis and translation by Jasper Hopkins. Minneapolis: Arthur J. Banning Press, 1994.

———. *Nicholas of Cusa: The Catholic Concordance.* Edited and translated by Paul E. Sigmund. Cambridge: Cambridge University Press, 1991.

———. *Nicholas of Cusa on God as Not-other: A Translation and an Appraisal of "De Li Non Aliud,"* by Jasper Hopkins. Minneapolis: Arthur J. Banning Press, 1983.

———. *Nicholas of Cusa On Learned Ignorance: A Translation and Appraisal of "De Docta Ignorantia,"* by Jasper Hopkins. 2d. ed. Minneapolis: Arthur J. Banning Press, 1985.

———. *Nicholas of Cusa: Metaphysical Speculations. Six Latin Texts Translated into English,* by Jasper Hopkins. Minneapolis: Arthur J. Banning Press, 1998.

———. *Nicholas of Cusa: Metaphysical Speculations.* Vol. 2. Translated by Jasper Hopkins. Minneapolis: Arthur J. Banning Press, 2000.

———. *Nicholas of Cusa On Wisdom and Knowledge.* Introduced and translated by Jasper Hopkins. Minneapolis: Arthur J. Banning Press, 1996.

———. *Nicholas of Cusa: Selected Spiritual Writings.* Edited and translated by H. Lawrence Bond. The Classics of Western Spirituality. New York: Paulist Press, 1997.

———. *Nicholas of Cusa's Debate with John Wenck: A Translation and Appraisal of "De Ignota Litteratura" and "Apologia Doctae Ignorantiae,"* by Jasper Hopkins. 3d ed.Minneapolis: Arthur J. Banning Press, 1988.

———. *Nicholas of Cusa's Dialectical Mysticism: Text, Translation, and Interpretive Study of "De Visione Dei,"* by Jasper Hopkins. Minneapolis: Arthur J. Banning Press, 1985.

———. *Nicholas of Cusa's Metaphysic of Contraction.* Analysis and translation by Jasper Hopkins. Minneapolis: Arthur J. Banning Press, 1983.

———. *Nicolas de Cues: Sermons eckhartiens et dionysiens.* Introduction, translation, and commentary by Francis Bertin. Paris: Les Éditions du CERF, 1998.

———. *Nikolaus von Cues: Die Kunst der Vermutung. Auswahl aus den Schriften.* Edited with introduction by Hans Blumenberg. Bremen: Carl Schünemann Verlag, 1957.

———. *Nikolaus von Cues: Die Mathematischen Schriften.* Translated by Joseph Hofmann. Hamburg: Felix Meiner Verlag, 1952.

———. *Schriften des Nikolaus von Kues in deutscher Übersetzung im Auftrag der Heidelberger Akademie der Wissenschaften.* Leipzig-Hamburg: Meiner, 1936– .

———. *Vier Predigten im Geiste Eckharts.* Edited and translated by Joseph Koch. Heidelberg: C. Winter, 1937.

III. GENERAL

Adams, D. "Metaphors for Mankind: The Development of Hans Blumenberg's Anthropological Metaphorology." *Journal of the History of Ideas* 52 (1991): 152–66.

Adams, Marilyn McCord. *William Ockham.* 2 vols. Notre Dame: University of Notre Dame Press, 1987.

Alan of Lille. *Alain de Lille: Textes inédits.* Ed. M.-T. D'Alverny. Paris: Vrin, 1965.

———. *Alani de Insulis Opera omnia* 210 in *Patrologiae cursus completus. Series Latina.* Edited by J.-P. Migne. Paris, 1855.

Alexander of Hales. *Summa theologiae.* Edited by Quaracchi. 4 vols. Florence: Collegium S. Bonaventurae, 1924.

Alsberg, Paul. *Das Menschheitsrätsel: Versuch einer prinzipiellen Lösung.* Dresden: Sibyllen Verlag, 1922.

———. *In Quest of Man: A Biological Approach to the Problem of Man's Place in Nature.* Oxford and New York: Pergamon Press, 1970.

Alvarez-Gómez, Mariano. *Die Verborgene Gegenwart des Unendlichen bei Nikolaus von Kues.* Munich and Salzburg: Verlag Anton Pustet, 1968.

Arendt, Hannah. *The Human Condition.* Chicago: University of Chicago Press, 1958.

Aristotle. *The Complete Works of Aristotle.* Edited by Jonathan Barnes. 2 Vols. Princeton: Princeton University Press, 1984.

Armstrong, A. H. *An Introduction to Ancient Philosophy.* London: Methuen, 1947.

———. "Plotinus' Doctrine of the Infinite and Christian Thought." *Downside Review* 73 (Winter 1954–5): 47–58.

———. "Plotinus." Part 3 of *The Cambridge History of Later Greek and Early Medieval Philosophy,* edited by A. H. Armstrong. Cambridge: Cambridge University Press, 1967.

Augustine of Hippo. *St. Augustine: Tractates on the Gospel of St. John 1–10.* Translated by John W. Rettig. Fathers of the Church, Vol. 78. Washington: The Catholic University of America Press, 1988.

———. *Augustine: The City of God against the Pagans.* Translated by R. W. Dyson. Cambridge: Cambridge University Press, 1998.

———. *De civitate Dei.* Edited by B. Dombart and A. Kalb. *Corpus Christianorum, Series Latina* 47–48. Turnhout: Brepols, 1955.

———. *De doctrina christiana.* Edited by J. Martin. *Corpus Christianorum, Series Latina* 32. Turnhout: Brepols, 1982.

———. *De Genesi ad litteram.* Edited by J. Zycha. *Corpus Scriptorum Ecclesiasticorum Latinorum* 28.1. Vienna: F. Tempsky and Leipzig: G. Freytag, 1894.

Bacon, Francis. *Novum Organum with Other Parts of the Great Instauration.* Translated and edited by Peter Urbach and John Gibson. Chicago and La Salle, Ill.: Open Court, 1994.

Baeumker, Clemens. "Das pseudo-hermetische 'Buch der vierundzwanzig Meister' (Liber XXIV philosophorum): Ein Beitrag zur Geschichte des Neupythagorismus und Neuplatonismus im Mittelalter," *Studien und Charakteristiken zur Geschichte der Philosophie insbesondere des Mittelalters. Beiträge zur Geschichte der Philosophie und Theologie des Mittelalters* 25 (1928): 194–214.

Baron, Margaret E. *The Origins of the Infinitesimal Calculus.* Oxford and New York: Pergamon, 1969.

Bassler, O. Bradley. "Labyrinthus de compositione continui: The Origins of Leibniz' Solution to the Continuum Problem 1666–1672." Ph.D. diss., University of Chicago, 1995.

———. "Leibniz on the Indefinite as Infinite." *Review of Metaphysics* 51 (1998): 849–74.

———. "Theology and the Modern Age: Blumenberg's Reaction to a Baconian Frontispiece." *New German Critique* (Fall 2001).

Beck, Lewis White. *Early German Philosophy: Kant and His Predecessors.* Cambridge: Harvard University Press, 1969.

Behrenberg, Peter, and David Adams. "Bibliographie Hans Blumenberg." In *Die Kunst der Überlebens. Nachdenken über Hans Blumenberg,* edited by Franz Josef Wetz und Hermann Timm, 426–70. Frankfurt: Suhrkamp, 1999.

Beierwaltes, Werner. *Denken des Einen: Studien zur neuplatonischen Philosophie und ihrer Wirkungsgeschichte.* Frankfurt: Vittorio Klostermann, 1985.

———. "Cusanus and Eriugena." *Dionysius* 13 (1989): 115–52.

Bergson, Henri. *L'évolution créatrice.* Paris: Presses Universitaires de France, 1948.

Bernardus Silvestris. *The Cosmographia.* Translated by Winthrop Wetherbee. New York: Columbia University Press, 1973.

Bonaventure. *Opera omnia.* Edited by Quaracchi. 10 vols. Florence: Collegium S. Bonaventurae, 1882–1902.

Bond, H. Lawrence. "Nicholas of Cusa and the Reconstruction of Theology: The Centrality of Christology in the Coincidence of Opposites." In *Contemporary Reflections on the Medieval Christian Tradition. Essays in Honor of Ray C. Petry,* edited by George H. Shriver, 81–94. Durham, N.C.: Duke University Press, 1974.

Borges, Jorge Luis. "The Fearful Sphere of Pascal." In *Labyrinths, Selected Stories and Other Writings.* New York: New Directions Publishing Company, 1964.

Brendel, O. J. *Symbolism of the Sphere: A Contribution to the History of Earlier Greek Philosophy.* Leiden: Brill, 1977.

Brient, Elizabeth. "Transitions to a Modern Cosmology: Meister Eckhart and Nicholas of Cusa on the Intensive Infinite." *Journal of the History of Philosophy* 37 (1999): 575–600.

———. "Hans Blumenberg and Hannah Arendt on the 'Unworldly Worldliness' of the Modern Age." *Journal of the History of Ideas* 61 (2000): 513–30.

———. "From *Vita Contemplativa* to *Vita Activa:* Modern Instrumentalization of Theory and the Problem of Measure." *International Journal of Philosophical Studies* 9 (2001): 19–40.

———. "How Can the Infinite Be the Measure for the Finite? Three Mathematical

Metaphors from *De docta ignorantia.*" Lecture given at the American Cusanus Society's sixth centenary international conference, "Nicholas of Cusa: 1401–2001," at The Catholic University of America, October 6, 2001.

Callahan, John F. *Four Views of Time in Ancient Philosophy.* Cambridge: Harvard University Press, 1948.

Caputo, John. "The Nothingness of the Intellect in Meister Eckhart's *Parisian Questions.*" *Thomist* 39 (1975): 85–115.

Casarella, Peter J. "Nicholas of Cusa and the Power of the Possible." *American Catholic Philosophical Quarterly* 64 (1990): 7–34.

Cassirer, Ernst. *Das Erkenntnisproblem in der Philosophie und Wissenschaft der Neueren Zeit.* Vol. 1. Berlin: Verlag Bruno Cassirer, 1922.

———. *The Philosophy of Symbolic Forms.* New Haven, Conn.: Yale University Press, 1953–1957.

———. *The Individual and the Cosmos in Renaissance Philosophy.* Translated by Mario Domandi. New York and Evanston: Harper, 1963.

Chadwick, H. "Philo and the Beginnings of Christian Thought." Part 2 of *The Cambridge History of Later Greek and Early Medieval Philosophy,* edited by A. H. Armstrong. Cambridge: The Cambridge University Press, 1967.

Clagett, Marshall. *The Science of Mechanics in the Middle Ages.* Madison: University of Wisconsin Press, 1961.

Cohn, Norman Rufus Colin. *The Pursuit of the Millenium.* Revised and expanded edition. New York: Oxford University Press, 1970.

Copernicus, Nicolaus. *On the Revolutions.* Edited by Jerzy Dobrzycki. Translated by Edward Rosen. Baltimore: The Johns Hopkins University Press, 1978.

Cornford, Francis M. *Plato's Cosmology: The "Timeaus" of Plato, Translated with a Running Commentary, by Francis MacDonald Cornford.* London: Routledge, 1935. Reprint. Indianapolis and Cambridge: Hackett Publishing Compnay, 1997.

———. *Principium Sapientiae: The Origins of Greek Philosophical Thought.* Cambridge: Cambridge University Press, 1952.

D'Alverny, M.-T. "Un témoin muet des luttes doctrinales du XIIIe siècle." *Archives d'histoire doctrinale et littéraire du moyen âge* 17 (1949): 231–32.

Denifle, Heinrich. "Meister Eckharts lateinische Schriften und die Grundanschauung Seiner Lehre." *Archiv für Literatur- und Kirchengeschichte des Mittelalters* 2 (1886): 417–615.

Denifle, Heinrich, and Aemilio Chatelain, eds. *Chartularium Universitatis Parisiensis.* Volume I, 543–61. Paris, 1889–1897. Reprint. Brussels: Culture et Civilisation, 1964.

Descartes, René. "Lettre à Chanut," June 6, 1647, *Œuvres,* ed. Adam Tannery, vol. v, p. 50 sq., Paris, 1903.

———. *The Philosophical Writings of Descartes.* 3 vols. Translated by John Cottingham, Robert Stoothoff, and Dugald Murdoch. Cambridge: Cambridge University Press, 1984–91.

Dicks, D. R. *Early Greek Astronomy to Aristotle.* Ithaca: Cornell University Press, 1970.

Dijksterhuis, E. J. *The Mechanization of the World Picture.* Translated by C. Dikshoorn. Princeton: Princeton University Press, 1986.

Dodd, C. H. *The Epistle of Paul to the Romans.* New York and London: Harper and Brothers Publishers, 1932.

Duclow, Donald F. "Gregory of Nyssa and Nicholas of Cusa: Infinity, Anthropology, and the *Via Negativa.*" *Downside Review* 92 (April 1974): 102–8.

———. "Mystical Theology and the Intellect in Nicholas of Cusa." *American Catholic Philosophical Quarterly* 64 (1990): 111–29.

———. "Nicholas of Cusa in the Margins of Meister Eckhart: Codex Cusanus 21." In *Nicholas of Cusa in Search of God and Wisdom,* edited by Gerald Christianson and Thomas M. Izbicki, 57–69. Leiden: Brill, 1991.

Dupré, Louis. "Introduction and Major Works of Nicholas of Cusa." *American Catholic Philosophical Quarterly* 64 (1990): 1–6.

———. "Nature and Grace in Nicholas of Cusa's Mystical Philosophy." *American Catholic Philosophical Quarterly* 64 (1990): 153–70.

———. *Passage to Modernity: An Essay in the Hermeneutics of Nature and Culture.* New Haven: Yale University Press, 1993.

———. "The Mystical Theology of Nicholas of Cusa's *De visione Dei.*" In *Nicholas of Cusa on Christ and the Church,* edited by Gerald Christianson and Thomas M. Izbicki, 205–20. Leiden: Brill, 1996.

Dupré, Wilhelm. "Absolute Truth and Conjectural Insights." In *Nicholas of Cusa on Christ and the Church,* edited by Gerald Christianson and Thomas M. Izbicki, 323–38. Leiden: Brill, 1996.

Edwards, C. H. *The Historical Development of the Calculus.* New York: Springer Verlag, 1979.

Eslick, Leonard J. "The Material Substrate in Plato." In *The Concept of Matter in Greek and Medieval Philosophy,* edited by Ernan McMullin. Notre Dame: University of Notre Dame Press, 1965.

Fanizzi, Ellen Chris. "Subverting the *Ordo Caritatis:* Meister Eckhart's Vision of Love." Ph.D. diss., Boston College, 2000.

Ficino, Marcilio. *Quaestiones quinque de mente.* In *Opera omnia.* Basel, 1576. Translated by Josephine L. Burroughs as *Five Questions concerning the Mind.* In *The Renaissance Philosophy of Man,* edited by Ernst Cassirer, Paul Oskar Kristeller, and John Herman Randall, Jr. Chicago and London: The University of Chicago Press, 1948.

Flasch, Kurt. *Die Metaphysik des Einen bei Nikolaus von Kues: Problemgeschictliche Stellung und systematische Bedeutung.* Leiden: Brill, 1973.

———. *Nikolaus von Kues: Geschichte einer Entwicklung.* Frankfurt: Vittorio Klostermann, 1998.

Funkenstein, Amos. *Theology and the Scientific Imagination: From the Middle Ages to the Seventeenth Century.* Princeton: Princeton University Press, 1986.

Gadamer, Hans-Georg. Review of *Die Legitimität der Neuzeit* (1966), by Hans Blumenberg. *Philosophische Rundschau* 15 (1968): 201–9.

———. "Nikolaus von Kues in modernen Denken." In *Nicolo Cusano agli inizi del mondo moderno*, 39–48. Florence: Sanzoni, 1970.

———. "[Nicolaus von Cues in der Geschichte des Erkenntnisproblems] Epilog." *Mitteilungen und Forschungsbeiträge der Cusanus-Gesellschaft.* 11 (1975): 275–80.

Gandillac, Maurice de. *Nikolaus von Cues: Studien zu seiner Philosophie und philosophischen Weltanschauung.* Düsseldorf: L. Schwann, 1953.

Gaus, J. "Circulus mensurat omnia." In *Mensura, Mass, Zahl, Zahlensymbolik im Mittelalter.* Vol. 2. Edited by A. Zimmermann and G. Vuillemin-Diem. Berlin and New York: W. de Gruyter, 1984.

Gehlen, Arnold. *Der Mensch: Seine Natur und seine Stellung in der Welt.* Berlin: Duncker and Dünnhaupt, 1941.

———. *Urmensch und Spätkultur.* Bonn: Athenäum, 1956.

———. *Sozialpsychologische Probleme in der industriellen Gesellschaft.* Tübingen: Mohr, 1949. Later reissued as *Die Seele im technischen Zeitalter.* Hamburg: Rowohlt, 1957. Translated by Patricia Lipscomb as *Man in the Age of Technology.* New York: Columbia University Press, 1980.

Gersh, Steven. *From Iamblichus to Eriugena.* Leiden: E. J. Brill, 1978.

Gilson, Etienne Henry. *The Spirit of Medieval Philosophy.* Translated by A. H. C. Downes. New York: Charles Scribner's Sons, 1940.

Goldstein, Jürgen. *Nominalismus und Moderne: Zur Konstitution neuzeitlicher Subjektivität bei Hans Blumenberg und Wilhelm von Ockham.* Freiburg and Munich: Verlag Karl Alber, 1998.

Grant, Edward. *A Source Book in Medieval Science.* Cambridge: Harvard University Press, 1974.

———. "The Condemnation of 1277: God's Absolute Power and Physical Thought in the Middle Ages." *Viator* 10 (1979): 211–44.

———. *Much Ado about Nothing: Theories of Space and Vacuum from the Middle Ages to the Scientific Revolution.* Cambridge and New York: Cambridge University Press, 1981.

Guthrie, W. K. C. *A History of Greek Philosophy.* Vol. 5. Cambridge: Cambridge University Press, 1978.

Guyot, Henri. *L'Infinité Divine depuis Philon le Juif jusqu'à Plotin.* Paris: Alcan, 1906.

Haas, Alois M. *Sermo mysticus: Studien zu Theologie und Sprache der deutschen Mystik.* Freiburg, Switzerland: Universitätsverlag, 1979.

Halberstam, Michael. *Totalitarianism and the Modern Conception of Politics.* New Haven: Yale University Press, 1999.

Harries, Karsten. "The Infinite Sphere: Comments on the History of a Metaphor." *Journal of the History of Philosophy* 13 (1975): 5–15.

———. "Copernican Reflections." *Inquiry* 23 (1980): 253–69.

———. "Copernican Reflections and the Tasks of Metaphysics." *International Philosophical Quarterly* 23 (1983): 235–50.

———. "Hans Blumenberg. *Lebenzeit und Weltzeit.*" *Journal of Philosophy* 84 (1987): 516–20.

———. "The Limits of Autonomy." Unpublished lecture given March 10, 1988 at the Rice Center for Cultural Studies, Rice University, and again December 5, 1991 at the New School for Social Research.

———. "Problems of the Infinite: Cusanus and Descartes." *American Catholic Philosophical Quarterly* 64 (1990): 89–110.

———. *Infinity and Perspective.* Cambridge: M.I.T. Press, 2001.

Haubst, Rudolf. *Die Christologie des Nikolaus von Kues.* Freiburg im Breisgau: Herder, 1956.

———. "Nikolaus von Kues als Interpret und Verteidiger Meister Eckharts." In *Freiheit und Gelassenheit: Meister Eckhart Heute,* edited by Udo Kern, 75–96. Munich: Kaiser Verlag, 1980.

Hobbes, Thomas. *De cive.* Translated by Thomas Hobbes as *Man and Citizen,* edited by Bernard Gert. Garden City, New York: Doubleday, 1972.

Hof, Hans. *Scintilla animae: Eine Studie zu einem Grundbegriff in Meister Eckharts Philosophie.* Lund: Gleerup, 1952.

Hoffmann, Ernst. "Gotteschau bei Meister Eckehart und Nikolaus von Cues." In *Festschrift: Heinrich Zangger.* Vol. 2, edited by Max Huber et. al., 1033–45. Zurich: Rascher and Cie, 1935.

Hopkins, Jasper. *Nicholas of Cusa's Dialectical Mysticism: Text, Translation, and Interpretive Study of "De Visione Dei,"* 50–93. Minneapolis: Arthur J. Banning Press, 1985.

Horkheimer, Max, and Theodor Adorno. *The Dialectic of Enlightenment.* Translated by John Cumming. New York: Herder and Herder, 1972.

Hübener, Wolfgang. "Das 'gnostische Rezidiv' oder wie Hans Blumenberg der spätmittelalterlichen Theologie den Puls fühlt." In *Gnosis und Politik,* edited by J. Taubes, 37–52. Paderborn: Schöningh, 1984.

Hudry, Françoise, ed. *Liber viginti quattuor philosophorum, Corpus Christianorum Continuatio Mediaeualis,* vol. 143 Turnhout: Brepols, 1997.

Hudson, Wayne. "After Blumenberg: Historicism and Philosophical Anthropology." *History of the Human Sciences* 6, no. 4 (1993): 109–16.

Hyman, Arthur, and James J. Walsh, eds. *Philosophy in the Middle Ages.* Indianapolis: Hackett Publishing Company, 1983.

Imbach, Ruedi. *Deus est Intelligere. Das Verhältnis von Sein und Denken in seiner Bedeutung für das Gottesverständnis bei Thomas von Aquin und in den Pariser Quaestionen Meister Eckharts.* Freiburg, Switzerland: Universitätsverlag, 1976.

Ingram, David. "Blumenberg and the Philosophical Grounds of Historiography." *History and Theory* 29 (1990): 1–15.

Jaspers, Karl. "Nicholas of Cusa." In *The Great Philosophers.* Vol. 2, translated by Ralph Manheim. New York and London: Harcourt, Brace and Jovanovich, 1966.

John Damascene. *De fide orthodoxa.* Edited by Eligius M. Buytaert. St. Bonaventure, N.Y.: Franciscan Institute, 1955.

John Duns Scotus. *Opus oxoniense.* In *Opera omnia,* vol. V–X. Edited by Lucas Wadding. Paris: Laurentius Durand, 1639. Photoreprint, Hildesheim: Georg Olms, 1968.

———. *Ordinatio.* In *Opera omnia,* vol. I–VII. Edited by P. Carolo Balic. Rome: Vatican Polyglot Press, 1950–1973.

John Scottus Eriugena. *Periphyseon.* Translated by I. P. Sheldon Williams and revised by John J. O'Meara. Montreal: Éditions Bellarmin, 1987.

Jonas, Hans. *The Gnostic Religion: The Message of the Alien God and the Beginnings of Christianity.* 2d. ed., enlarged. Boston: Beacon Press, 1963.

———. *Das Prinzip Verantwortung.* Frankfurt: Suhrkamp, 1979.

Kahn, Charles. *Anaximander and the Origins of Greek Cosmology.* New York: Columbia University Press, 1960.

Kant, Immanuel. *Critique of Judgment.* Translated by J. H. Bernard. New York: Hafner Press, 1951.

Kelly, C. F. *Meister Eckhart on Divine Knowledge.* New Haven: Yale University Press, 1977.

Koch, Joseph. *Die Ars coniecturalis des Nikolaus von Kues.* Vol. 4 of *Arbeitsgemeinschaft für Forschung des Landes Nordrhein-Westfalen, Geisteswissenschaften.* Cologne: Westdeutscher Verlag, 1956.

———. "Meister Eckharts Weiterwirken im Deutsch-Niederländischen Raum im 14. und 15. Jahrhundert." In *La mystique rhénane: Colloque de Strasbourg 1961,* 133–56. Paris: Presses Universitaires de France, 1963.

———. "Nikolaus von Kues und Meister Eckhart: Randbemerkungen zu zwei in der Schrift *De coniecturis* gegebenen Problemen." *Mitteilungen und Forschengsbeiträge der Cusanus-Gesellschaft* 4 (1964): 164–73.

Koerner, Joseph Leo. "Ideas about the Thing, Not the Thing Itself: Hans Blumenberg's Style." *History of the Human Sciences* 6, no. 4 (1993): 1–10.

Kolakowski, Leszek. *Religion.* New York: Oxford University Press, 1982.

———. *Modernity on Endless Trial.* Chicago: University of Chicago Press, 1990.

Koyré, Alexandre. *From the Closed World to the Infinite Universe.* Baltimore and London: The Johns Hopkins University Press, 1957.

Kren, Claudia. "Astronomy." In *The Seven Liberal Arts in the Middle Ages,* edited by David L. Wagner. Bloomington: Indiana University Press, 1983.

Kuhn, Thomas S. *The Copernican Revolution: Planetary Astronomy in the Development of Western Thought.* Cambridge: Harvard University Press, 1957.

Largier, Niklaus. *Zeit, Zeitlichkeit, Ewigkeit: ein Aufriß der Zeitproblems bei Dietrich von Freiberg und Meister Eckhart.* Bern and New York: P. Lang, 1989.

Leibniz, G. W. *Discourse on Metaphysics and Other Essays.* Edited and translated by Daniel Garber and Roger Ariew. Indianapolis and Cambridge: Hackett Publishing Company, 1991.

Lerner, Ralph, and Muhsin Mahdi, eds. "Condemnation of 219 Propositions," translated by E. Fortin and P. O'Neill. Chap. 18 in *Medieval Political Philosophy: A Sourcebook.* New York: The Free Press of Glencoe, 1963.

Lindberg, David, C. *The Beginnings of Western Science. The European Scientific Tradition in Philosophical, Religious, and Institutional Context, 600 B.C. to A.D 1450.* Chicago: The University of Chicago Press, 1992.

Lossky, Vladimir. *Théologie négative et connaissance de Dieu chez Maître Eckhart.* Paris: Vrin, 1960.

Louth, Andrew. *The Origins of the Christian Mystical Tradition.* Oxford: Clarendon Press, 1981.

Löwith, Karl. *Meaning in History: The Theological Presuppositions of the Philosophy of History.* Chicago: The University of Chicago Press, 1949.

———. Review of Part I of *Die Legitimität der Neuzeit,* by Hans Blumenberg. *Philosophische Rundschau* 15 (1968): 195–201.

Lukács, Georg. *History and Class Consciousness.* Translated by Rodney Livingstone. Cambridge: M.I.T. Press, 1971.

Mahnke, Dietrich. *Unendliche Sphäre und Allmittelpunkt: Beiträge zur Genealogie der Mathematischen Mystik.* Halle: Max Niemeyer Verlag, 1937.

Maier, Anneliese. *Studien zur Naturphilosophie der Spätscholastik.* 5 vols. Rome: Edizioni di Storia e letteratura, 1951–1966.

Mandonnet, P. *Siger de Brabant et l'averroïsme latin au XIII*[me] *siècle.* 2d ed. Vol. 2, *Textes inédits,* 175–91. Louvain: Institut supérieur de philosophie de l'Université, 1908.

Manstetten, Reiner. *Esse est Deus. Meister Eckharts christologische Versöhnung von Philosophie und Religion und ihre Ursprünge in der Tradition des Abenlandes.* Freiburg im Breisgau and Munich: Verlag Karl Alber, 1993.

Marquard, Odo. "Laudatio auf Hans Blumenberg." *Jahrbuch der Deutschen Akademie für Sprache und Dichtung* 2 (1980): 53–56.

———. "Entlastung vom Absoluten." In *Die Kunst des Überlebens. Nachdenken über Hans Blumenberg,* edited by Franz Josef Wetz and Hermann Timm, 17–27. Frankfurt: Suhrkamp, 1999.

Maurer, Armand A. *Medieval Philosophy.* New York: Random House, 1962.

Maximus Confessor. *Ambigua.* Translated by Emmanuel Ponsoye. Paris: Editions de l'ancre, 1994.

McGinn, Bernard. "Meister Eckhart on God as Absolute Unity." In *Neoplatonism and Christian Thought,* edited by Dominic J. O'Meara. Albany: State University of New York Press, 1982.

McMullin, Ernan. "Four Senses of Potency." In *The Concept of Matter in Greek and Medieval Philosophy.* Notre Dame: University of Notre Dame Press, 1965.

McTighe, Thomas P. "The Meaning of the Couple, Complicatio-Explicatio in the Philosophy of Nicholas of Cusa." *Proceedings of the American Catholic Philosophical Association* 32 (1958): 206–14.

Migne, Jacques-Paul. *Patrologia Latina.* Paris: J.-P. Migne, 1844–64.

——. *Patrologia Graeca.* Paris: J.-P. Migne, 1866–1928.

Miller, Clyde Lee. "Perception, Conjecture, and Dialectic in Nicholas of Cusa." *American Catholic Philosophical Quarterly* 64 (1990): 35–54.

——. "Nicholas of Cusa's *On Conjectures (De coniecturis).*" In *Nicholas of Cusa in Search of God and Wisdom,* edited by Gerald Christianson and Thomas M. Izbicki, 119–40. Leiden: Brill, 1991.

——. "God's Presence: Some Cusan Proposals." In *Nicholas of Cusa on Christ and the Church,* edited by Gerald Christianson and Thomas M. Izbicki, 323–38. Leiden: Brill, 1996.

Mojsisch, Burkhard. *Meister Eckhart: Analogie, Univozität und Einheit.* Hamburg: F. Meiner, 1983.

Moran, Dermot. "Pantheism from John Scottus Eriugena to Nicholas of Cusa." *American Catholic Philosophical Quarterly* 64 (1990): 131–52.

Newton, Isaac. *The Principia: mathematical principles of natural philosophy.* Translated by I. Bernard Cohen and Anne Whitman, assisted by Julia Budenz. Berkeley: University of California Press, 1999.

Oberman, Heiko A. *The Harvest of Medieval Theology: Gabriel Biel and Late Medieval Nominalism.* Cambridge: Harvard University Press, 1963.

Osler, Margaret J. *Divine Will and the Mechanical Philosophy: Gassendi and Descartes on Contingency and Necessity in the Created World.* Cambridge: Cambridge University Press, 1994.

Palti, Elías José. "In Memoriam: Hans Blumenberg (1920–1996), An Unended Quest." *Journal of the History of Ideas* 58 (July 1997): 503–24.

Philo of Alexandria. *Philo. The Loeb Classical Library.* Vols. 1–10 translated by F. H. Colson and G. H. Whitaker. Two supplementary volumes containing the *Questions and Answers on Genesis and Exodus,* translated by R. Marcus. Cambridge: Harvard University Press, 1929–1962.

Pico della Mirandola, Giovanni Francesco. *De hominis dignitate, Heptaplus, De ente et uno, e scrittivari.* Edited by E. Garin. Florence: Vallecchi, 1942.

——. *On the Dignity of Man.* Translated by Elizabeth Livermore Forbes. In *The Renaissance Philosophy of Man,* edited by Ernst Cassirer, Paul Oskar Kristeller, and John Herman Randall, Jr. Chicago and London: University of Chicago Press, 1948.

Pippin, Robert. "Blumenberg and the Modernity Problem."*Review of Metaphysics* 40 (March 1987): 535–57. Reprinted in *Idealism as Modernism: Hegelian Variations.* Cambridge: Cambridge University Press, 1997.

——. "Modern Mythic Meaning: Blumenberg Contra Nietzsche." *History of the Human Sciences* 6, no. 4 (1993): 37–56. Reprinted in *Idealism as Modernism: Hegelian Variations.* Cambridge: Cambridge University Press, 1997.

Plato. *The Collected Dialogues.* Edited by Edith Hamilton. Princeton: Princeton University Press, 1982.

Plessner, Helmuth. *Zwischen Philosophie und Gesellschaft.* Berne: Francke, 1953.

Plotinus. *Enneads*. 7 vols. Translated by A. H. Armstrong. Loeb Classical Library. Cambridge: Harvard University Press, 1966–88.

Popkin, Richard H. *The History of Scepticism from Erasmus to Spinoza*. Berkeley: University of California Press, 1979.

Poulet, Georges. "Le symbole du cercle infini dans la littérature et la philosophie." *Revue de métaphysique et de morale* 64, no. 3 (1959): 257–75.

———. *The Metamorphoses of the Circle*. Translated by Carley Dawson and Elliott Coleman. Baltimore: The Johns Hopkins University Press, 1966.

Proclus. *The Elements of Theology*. Translated by E. R. Dodds. Oxford: Clarendon Press, 1963.

———. *Proclus' Commentary on Plato's Parmenides*. Translated by Glenn R. Morrow and John M. Dillon. Princeton: Princeton University Press, 1987.

———. *Théologie platonicienne*. Translated by H. D. Saffrey and L. G. Westerink. Paris: Les Belles Lettres, 1968.

Quint, Josef. "Einleitung." In *Meister Eckehart: Deutsche Predigten und Traktate*, edited by Josef Quint, 9–50. Munich: Hanser, 1959.

Reicke, S. "Säkularisierung," In *Die Religion in Geschichte und Gegenwart*, 3d ed. Vol. 5. Tübingen: J. C. B. Mohr, 1961.

Rorty, Richard. Review of *Legitimacy of the Modern Age*, by Hans Blumenberg. *London Review of Books* (March–April, 1983): 3–5.

Rothacker, Erich. *Zur Genealogie des menschlichen Bewußtseins*. Bonn: Bouvier, 1966.

———. *Philosophische Anthropologies*. Bonn: Bouvier, 1982.

Sambursky, S. *The Physical World of the Greeks*. Princeton: Princeton University Press, 1956.

Solmsen, Friedrich. *Aristotle's System of the Physical World*. Ithaca, New York: Cornell University Press, 1960.

Stock, Brian. *Myth and Science in the Twelfth Century*. Princeton: Princeton University Press, 1972.

Sullivan, J. W. N. *The Limitations of Science*. New York: The Viking Press, 1933.

Sweeney, Leo. *Divine Infinity in Greek and Medieval Thought*. New York: Peter Lang, 1992.

Taylor, A. E. *A Commentary on Plato's Timaeus*. Oxford: The Clarendon Press, 1928.Taylor, Charles. *Sources of the Self: The Making of the Modern Identity*. Cambridge: Harvard University Press, 1989.

Thomas Aquinas. *Opera Omnia: Iussu impensaque Leonis XIII, PM edita* (Leonine edition). Rome: Vatican Polyglot Press, 1882–.

———. *Quaestiones disputatae*. Edited by R. M. Spiazzi et al. 2 vols. 10th ed. Rome, 1964–1965.

Turner, Charles. "Liberalism and the Limits of Science: Weber and Blumenberg." *History of the Human Sciences* 6, no. 4 (1993): 57–79.

Ueda, Shizuteru. *Die Gottesgeburt in der Seele und der Durchbruch zur Gottheit: Die mystische Anthropologie Meister Eckharts und ihre Konfrontation mit der Mystik des Zen-Buddhismus.* Gütersloh: Mohn, 1965.

Vives, Juan Luis. *Fabula de homine.* In *Opera omnia.* Vol. 4, 3–8. Valentiae, 1783. Translated by Nancy Lenkeith as *A Fable about Man.* In *The Renaissance Philosophy of Man.* Edited by Ernst Cassirer, Paul Oskar Kristeller, and John Herman Randall, Jr. Chicago and London: University of Chicago Press, 1948.

Voegelin, Eric, "Philosophie der Politik in Oxford." *Philosophische Rundschau* 1 (1953/4): 23–48.

Wackernagel, Wolfgang. *Ymagine denudari: Éthique de l'image et métaphysique de l'abstraction chez Maître Eckhart.* Paris: Vrin, 1991.

Wackerzapp, Herbert. *Der Einfluss Meister Eckharts auf die ersten philosophischen Schriften des Nikolaus von Kues, 1440–1450.* Münster: Aschendorff, 1962.

Wallace, Robert M. "Progress, Secularization and Modernity: The Löwith-Blumenberg Debate." *New German Critique* 22 (Winter 1981): 63–79.

———. "Blumenberg: An Overview." *Annals of Scholarship* 5 (1987): 1–2.

———. "Hans Blumenberg on Descartes and the Modern Age." *Annals of Scholarship* 5 (1987): 37–63.

———. "Hans Blumenberg's Third Way, between Habermas and Gadamer." In *Dialectic and Narrative,* edited by T. Flynn and D. Judowitz, 185–96. Albany: State University of New York Press, 1993.

Waterlow, Sarah. *Nature, Change, and Agency in Aristotle's Physics.* Oxford: Clarendon Press, 1982.

Weeks, Andrew. *German Mysticism from Hildegard of Bingen to Ludwig Wittgenstein.* Albany: State University of New York Press, 1993.

Weizäcker, C. F. *The Relevance of Science.* New York and Evanston: Harper and Row, 1964.

Welte, Bernard. *Meister Eckhart: Gedanken zu seinen Gedanken.* Freiburg, Germany: Herder, 1979.

Wentzlaff-Eggebert, F. W. *Deutsche Mystic Zwischen Mittelalter und Neuzeit.* Tübingen: Verlag J. C. B. Mohr (Paul Siebeck), 1947.

Wetz, Franz Josef. *Hans Blumenberg zur Einführung.* Hamburg: Junius Verlag, 1993.

Wetz, Franz Josef, and Hermann Timm, eds. *Die Kunst des Überlebens: Nachdenken über Hans Blumenberg.* Frankfurt: Suhrkamp, 1999.

Wiener, Norbert. *The Human Use of Human Beings: Cybernetics and Society.* New York: Avon Books, 1967.

William of Ockham. *Opera philosophica et theologica.* Edited by Gedeon Gal et al. 17 vols. St. Bonaventure, NY: The Franciscan Institute, 1967–88.

———. *Philosophical Writings: A Selection.* Translated and edited by P. Boehner, O.F.M., and revised by Stephen F. Brown. Indianapolis and Cambridge: Hackett Publishing Company, 1990.

Wippel, J. "The Condemnations of 1270 and 1277 at Paris." *Journal of Medieval and Renaissance Studies* 7 (1977): 169–201.

Wolfson, Harry Austryn. *Religious Philosophy*. Cambridge: Cambridge University Press, 1961.

———. *Philo: Foundations of Religious Philosophy in Judaism, Christianity and Islam.* 2 vols. Cambridge: Harvard University Press, 1962.

———. *The Philosophy of the Church Fathers.* Vol. 1. Cambridge: Harvard University Press, 1964.

———. "Greek Philosophy in Philo and the Church Fathers." In *The Crucible of Christianity,* edited by Arnold Toynbee. New York: World Publishing Co.; London: Thames and Hudson, 1969.

———. "Philo Judaeus." In *Studies in the History of Philosophy and Religion.* Vol. 1. Cambridge: Harvard University Press, 1973.

Zum Brunn, Émilie, and Alain de Libera. *Maître Eckhart: Métaphysique du verbe et théologie négative.* Paris: Beauchesne, 1984.

Index of Names

Index of Topics

The Immanence of the Infinite: Hans Blumenberg and the Threshold to Modernity was designed and composed in Monotype Bulmer by Kachergis Book Design, Pittsboro, North Carolina; printed on 55-pound Sebago 2000 Antique and bound by The Maple-Vail Book Manufacturing Group of York, Pennsylvania.

www.ingramcontent.com/pod-product-compliance
Lightning Source LLC
LaVergne TN
LVHW040151080826
844660LV00014B/925/J